The
Collapse
of Canada?

The Collapse of Canada?

R. Kent Weaver, *editor*

KEITH G. BANTING
STÉPHANE DION
ANDREW STARK

The Brookings Institution
Washington, D.C.

Copyright © 1992 by
THE BROOKINGS INSTITUTION
1775 Massachusetts Avenue, N.W., Washington, D.C. 20036

Library of Congress Cataloging-in-Publication data:

The Collapse of Canada? / R. Kent Weaver, editor.
    p.   cm.
    Includes bibliographical references and index.
    ISBN 0-8157-9254-9 (alk. paper) — ISBN 0-8157-9253-0
(alk. paper : pbk.)
        1. Federal government—Canada. 2. Canada—
Constitutional history.
3. Canada—Politics and government—1945–   I. Weaver, R.
Kent. 1953–
JL27.C58   1992
321.02'0971—dc20   91-48027
                                                        CIP

9 8 7 6 5 4 3 2 1

The paper used in this publication meets the minimum
requirements of the American National Standard for
Information Sciences—Permanence of Paper for Printed
Library Materials, ANSI Z39.48-1984.

Foreword

THIS PROMISES to be a critical year in Canadian history. A series of constitutional crises, centering largely on the status of the province of Quebec, have preoccupied the country for more than a decade. One package of constitutional reforms—the Meech Lake Accord—failed to be ratified in 1990. The current round of negotiations will come to a climax in 1992. The federal government will issue new proposals for constitutional change this spring, and Quebec legislation calls for a provincial referendum on sovereignty later in the year.

It is not clear whether a compromise can be struck between the agenda of the federal government and the conflicting goals of the provinces. Moreover, even if a seemingly clear choice is made between constitutional agreement or independence for Quebec, there are many difficult issues that still must be resolved.

The reasons for Canada's prolonged constitutional conflict are poorly understood outside that country. The authors of this book attempt to remedy that lack of understanding by explaining the origins and evolution of the Canadian constitutional crisis, its current manifestations in Quebec nationalism and ideological opposition to that nationalism in English Canada, and the implications of continued constitutional discontent and of the possible breakup of Canada.

The editor of this volume, R. Kent Weaver, is a senior fellow in the Brookings Governmental Studies program. The other contributors are Keith G. Banting, professor of political studies and public administration and associate dean of the School of Graduate Studies at Queen's University in Kingston, Ontario; Stéphane Dion, associate professor of political science at the University of Montreal; and Andrew Stark, formerly a policy adviser in the Prime Minister's Office in Ottawa and now a fellow in ethics and the professions at Harvard University. Banting, Dion, and Stark were all guest scholars at Brookings during the 1990–91 academic year, and this volume grew out of a seminar they held for the Brookings staff in May 1991.

vii

The editor wishes to thank Georges Dubé and Kathleen Weldon for research assistance; Lisa D. Pace, Susan J. Thompson, and Antoinette T. Williams for word processing assistance; and Susan A. Stewart for her assistance in managing the project. Nancy D. Davidson and Barbara de Boinville edited the manuscript; Roshna M. Kapadia and Todd L. Quinn verified the factual content; Susan L. Woollen prepared the manuscript for typesetting; and Max Franke prepared the index.

The interpretations and conclusions presented here are solely those of the authors and should not be ascribed to the persons whose assistance is acknowledged above or to the trustees, officers, or other staff members of the Brookings Institution.

BRUCE K. MACLAURY
President

March 1992
Washington, D.C.

Contents

**If Quebec Separates: Restructuring
Northern North America**   **159**

Tables

The
Collapse
of Canada?

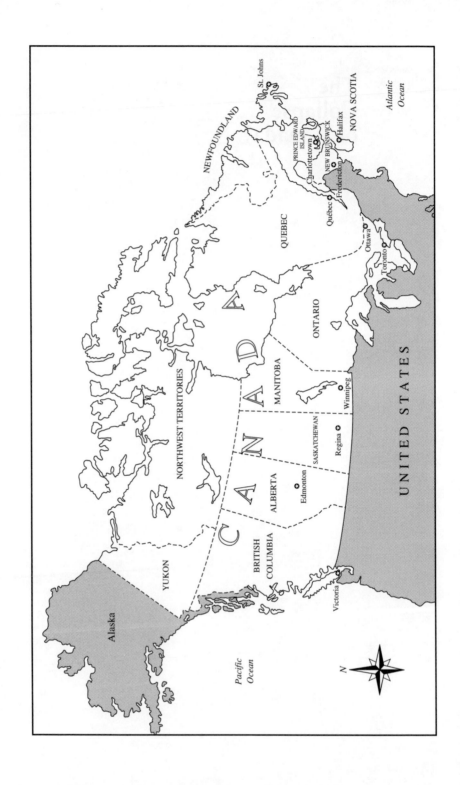

R. KENT WEAVER

Constitutional Conflict in Canada

THERE IS NO one-way mirror along the Canadian-U.S. border; it just seems that way. Canadians—or at least those whose first language is English—are inundated with information about the United States. In addition to considerable coverage of the United States in Canadian broadcast and print media, American publications such as *Time* and the *Wall Street Journal* are widely available in Canada, and most Canadians can watch U.S. news programs on cable television. U.S. media coverage of Canada, on the other hand, usually consists primarily of comparisons of the Canadian and U.S. health care systems. Coverage of other events in Canada is almost nonexistent except during elections and at times of national crisis. Although Americans have very favorable impressions of Canada,[1] they remain remarkably ignorant of some basic facts of Canadian political life. In a 1991 poll, for example, only 13 percent of American adults surveyed knew that the prime minister of Canada was Brian Mulroney.[2] The percentage of Canadian *second graders* in an earlier survey who could correctly identify the president of the United States was twice as high.[3]

Despite their limited access to information about Canada, many Ameri-

1. Public opinion surveys in the United States in 1976, 1979, and 1989 consistently found that more than 90 percent of those surveyed had favorable attitudes toward Canada—by far the highest of any country surveyed. See "Americans Rate Foreign Nations," *Gallup Opinion Index*, no. 169 (August 1979), pp. 35–36; and "Major Shifts Found in Americans' Perceptions of Foreign Lands," *Gallup Report*, no. 284 (May 1989), pp. 2–3.

2. George Gallup, Jr., and Frank Newport, "Free Trade Arguments Aside, Americans Know Little about Canada and Mexico," *Gallup Poll Monthly*, no. 307 (April 1991), p. 29. In the same poll, only 16 percent of Americans surveyed could correctly identify Canada's capital city (Ottawa), and only 8 percent knew that Canada is the leading trading partner of the United States.

3. Donald Higgins, "The Political Americanization of Canadian Children," in Jon H. Pammett and Michael S. Whittington, eds., *Foundations of Political Culture: Political Socialization in Canada* (Toronto: Macmillan, 1976), p. 254.

cans sense that something very important, and very troubling, is going on in their northern neighbor. In the spring and early summer of 1990, for example, U.S. media coverage of Canada suddenly became much more frequent and more alarming. It suggested that Canada might be in danger of breaking up; in particular, the overwhelmingly French-speaking (or francophone) province of Quebec might separate from Canada. After an eighteen-month lull, media coverage is increasing once again as Canada approaches another crisis point. In 1992, federal constitutional proposals are to be presented, and a referendum is scheduled in Quebec on sovereignty for the province.

An American attempting to follow Canada's constitutional crisis in the U.S. media over the past five years is likely to have picked up the following basic story line. In 1987, Prime Minister Brian Mulroney and the leaders (premiers) of Canada's ten provinces negotiated a package of revisions to Canada's constitution, called the Meech Lake Accord after the prime ministerial retreat in Quebec where it was negotiated. The package included a clause that would recognize in the constitution Quebec's status as a "distinct society" within Canada. Other clauses would have given Quebec an increased role in regulating immigration to the province, allowed the provinces (including Quebec) to nominate justices of the Supreme Court of Canada and members of the Senate, limited the spending powers of the federal government in areas that constitutionally are under provincial jurisdiction, and given Quebec (and all other provinces) a veto power over future amendments to the constitution in some areas.[4] The accord faced a three-year deadline for ratification by the federal Parliament and the legislatures of the ten provinces.

After the accord was negotiated in 1987, however, provincial elections brought new governments to power in several provinces. By 1990, the legislatures in two of those provinces (Manitoba and New Brunswick) refused to give their assent, while in a third (Newfoundland), the legislature revoked the approval that had previously been given. A frantic last round of negotiations secured the agreement of the premiers of New Brunswick and Manitoba, but failed to produce a promise by the premier of Newfoundland to support the existing accord.

On June 22, 1990, the accord received a dual coup de grace. A native member of the Manitoba provincial legislature named Elijah Harper, angered because the Meech Lake Accord did not address the concerns of

4. For the text of the Meech Lake Accord, see Michael D. Behiels, ed., *The Meech Lake Primer: Conflicting Views of the 1987 Constitutional Accord* (University of Ottawa Press, 1989), pp. 539–46.

native groups, refused to agree to a series of procedural motions requiring unanimous consent. In the absence of that consent, the measure could not be adopted by the legislature before the June 23 deadline. In Newfoundland, the provincial premier, denouncing pressure by Ottawa, refused to allow the provincial legislature to vote on the accord.[5] The long debate over the accord and its ultimate rejection boosted separatist sentiment within Quebec, raising once again the specter of a breakup of Canada, which had seemed to fade after Quebecers rejected separation in a 1980 referendum.

A few days after the failure of the Meech Lake Accord, the U.S. media virtually ceased giving any attention to the story of Canada's constitutional crisis, except for a brief mention when the Canadian government offered new constitutional proposals in September 1991. The metaphorical one-way mirror was once again in place.

The limited information available to Americans generally left a number of important questions unanswered. Why, for example, was a package of revisions to Canada's constitution needed in the first place? Why did debates over constitutional reform take the form of negotiations between the "first ministers" (the federal prime minister and the provincial premiers) rather than, as in the United States, very separate processes of congressional debate and ratification followed by consideration of the proposals by state legislatures? Why all the talk of separation, instead of simply trying again with new negotiations? And what were the implications if Quebec did separate—for Quebecers, for Canadians outside Quebec, and for the United States?

This limited information may also have conveyed some misleading impressions about Canada's constitutional crisis. First, episodic coverage in the U.S. media suggests that the conflict is itself episodic. It is not. In fact, these periodic crises reflect chronic discontent with Canadian governing institutions. The periods of relative quiet that follow occasional crises result more from stalemate or leaders' exhaustion than from a resolution of problems that is accepted as reasonable by all parties. The crisis that arose over ratification of the Meech Lake Accord is just the latest manifestation of this chronic discontent. But the roots of one crisis are always to be found in discontent with the disposition of past crises.

---

5. A chronology of the last day's events appears in "Countdown to Failure," *Maclean's*, July 2, 1990, p. 24. A more extensive chronology can be found in Darrel R. Reid, "Chronology of Events July 1989–June 1990," in Ronald L. Watts and Douglas M. Brown, eds., *Canada: The State of the Federation 1990* (Kingston: Queen's University, Institute of Intergovernmental Relations, 1990), pp. 233–68.

Indeed, the current constitutional crisis in Canada is so deeply rooted in past events that it is hard to find a reasonable cutoff point in providing historical background for the story.

Second, the limited coverage in the U.S. media might leave the impression that institutional "solutions" are possible that might put an end to Canada's recurrent crises. They are not. Even if the Meech Lake Accord had been ratified, further constitutional negotiations would have been necessary. In part, they would have been required to address the concerns of groups that felt excluded from the Meech Lake process. But there is little doubt that Quebec, too, would eventually have demanded renegotiation. The constitutional proposals put forward by Quebec Premier Robert Bourassa in 1986, which with some modifications were incorporated in the Meech Lake Accord, reflected a low ebb in nationalist sentiment in the province at that time. There is little doubt that as nationalist sentiment increased again, any provincial government, be it Bourassa's Liberals or the pro-separation Parti Québécois, would eventually have demanded different terms. Rather than permanent solutions, the most that could have been hoped for was a temporary accommodation and a temporary respite from constitutional negotiations.

The third misunderstanding that might arise is that Canada's constitutional crisis is strictly a conflict between English-speaking and French-speaking regions or groups. It is not. The lines of conflict are both deep and complex. They pit not only anglophones against francophones, but the federal government against the provinces, more populous provinces against less populous ones, and the more industrialized provinces of central Canada (Quebec and Ontario) against the less industrialized regions on Canada's western and eastern peripheries.

To help understand Canada's constitutional crisis, then, it is necessary to get a deeper understanding of its roots in Canadian society and politics. This volume attempts to lay that essential groundwork, with a particular focus on educating American readers who may know little about the history of constitutional conflict in Canada.

Each chapter is intended to build on those that precede it. My opening chapter begins with some very general questions: What general options are available for regulating conflict, and what are the risks and opportunities associated with each option? What conditions are needed if specific types of political institutions are to succeed in resolving conflicts peacefully? I then examine the basic divisions within Canadian society and the institutions used to manage political conflict in Canada in light of these questions. I focus on two chronic divisions in Canadian society—between francophones and anglophones, and between industrialized central Canada and regions at the periphery—and the institutional arrangements that are used to regulate them. I argue that the operation of Canadian institutions has exacerbated these tensions in some critical ways. I also show how differing interests among the participants in constitutional negotiations and a constitutional amendment process that demands unanimity in practice even when it does not do so in theory have both kept constitutional negotiations on the agenda and virtually ensured that they will fail to reach an agreement.

Stéphane Dion's chapter focuses on the phenomenon of Quebec nationalism and the reasons it has taken a more strongly separatist tone in recent years. The chapter shows that far from being a stable and monolithic force, support for an independent Quebec has many shadings and has fluctuated considerably over time. Dion argues that these fluctuations, and the unprecedented support for separation since the collapse of the Meech Lake Accord, can be best explained by looking at the interaction of three factors: a permanent sense of linguistic insecurity and fear of being anglicized, a growing but fragile sense of self-confidence that Quebec has the economic and governmental institutions needed to survive on its own, and a short-term, catalytic sense of rejection by the rest of Canada in the wake of the collapse of the Meech Lake agreement. Only if these feelings are all at high levels when Quebecers are faced with the choice of separation is secession likely. Although Dion feels that this conjunction will not occur with sufficient strength to lead to Quebec's separation, he acknowledges that it is certainly not implausible, in either the short term or the long term.

Andrew Stark's chapter examines conflicts within English Canada and the effects that these conflicts have had on reaching an agreement among the federal government, the anglophone provinces, and Quebec. His focus is on the politics of ideas. The notion of special status and increased powers for Quebec, he claims, runs counter to four important ideological currents in English Canada. Pierre Trudeau's belief in a bilingual Canada with a strong federal state has many followers in English Canada, who reject special status and increased powers for Quebec. The other three ideological currents are social democratic-oriented Canadian nationalism, a western-based "Reform" movement, and an evolving ideology associated with the multicultural, linguistic-minority, aboriginal, and gender groups recognized in Canada's new Charter of Rights and Freedoms.

To the extent that English Canadians remain committed to these four
ideologies or versions of them, Stark suggests, Quebec's separation is
likely in the long run if not in the short run.

Keith Banting's chapter on the future of "northern North America"
focuses on what would happen if Quebec does decide to separate. He
argues that although Quebec would begin its existence as an independent
state with many advantages—especially the act of national self-affirma-
tion—it would also face many problems. Working out the details of
coexistence and cooperation with a resentful English Canada would be
time-consuming and potentially disruptive to the economic climate of
both successor states. Even the issues of borders and passive acceptance
of an independent Quebec by ethnic minorities (both native peoples and
anglophones) cannot be taken for granted. Independence for Quebec
would be even more disruptive for the rest of Canada. Most obviously,
the country would be split into two noncontiguous sections. Federal
institutions would need to be restructured, the legitimacy of current federal leaders would be called into question (both the federal prime minister
and the leader of the official opposition are currently from Quebec), and
richer regions might be less willing to continue existing subsidies to poorer
regions of Canada. The United States would also be faced with some
difficult choices, notably whether to remain silent during the debate in
Quebec over separation, what terms to impose to include Quebec in the
free trade agreement, and—under pessimistic scenarios—how to deal
with applications from some provinces for statehood if Quebec independence led to a collapse of Canada.

Although prognostication is always a temptation for political scientists,
we have tried to avoid making detailed predictions about Canada's political future here. The current situation is too volatile to make prediction
worthwhile. Thus our somewhat apocalyptic title, *The Collapse of Canada?*, is deliberately phrased as a question rather than as a prediction. We
do believe that Quebec separation is a very real possibility, despite the
fact that, as Dion and Banting note, separation poses very real risks for
both Quebec and English Canada. The only prediction that we are prepared to make is that regardless of whether Quebecers choose to establish
a separate sovereign state, Canada's constitutional crisis will continue in
ebbs and flows for the forseeable future.

R. KENT WEAVER

Political Institutions and Canada's Constitutional Crisis

THE CLOSELY LINKED issues of constitutional reform and the status of Quebec within Canada have been high on the Canadian political agenda for almost thirty years. At times these issues have faded into the background as other topics—free trade, energy, unemployment, or inflation, for example—have come to the fore. But even when Quebec and the constitution have been off the front pages of newspapers and the nightly television news, there was little doubt that they would eventually return to the top of the agenda. When these issues have returned, they have often taken the form of crises that appeared to threaten the continued existence of Canada or its governing institutions. And there is little doubt that the prolonged conflict has cost Canada dearly. As Canadian political scientist Peter Russell has argued, "This inward navel-gazing has drained the creative energy of our leaders. It has frustrated, demoralized, and yes, even bored, our people. It has undermined Canada's ability to deal with pressing practical problems within and to respond effectively to global opportunities without."[1]

Canada's constitutional debate has involved both a discussion of which institutions should be used to manage conflict and govern policymaking in Canada and fundamental disagreements about the nature of the Canadian political community. Given its heavy symbolic content, constitutional discourse has been replete with themes of honor, pride, and recognition—and also fear, distrust, betrayal, and the casting of blame.[2] In practice,

The author would like to thank Keith G. Banting, John C. Courtney, Stéphane Dion, Kathryn Harrison, Richard Johnston, Jonathan Lemco, Leslie A. Pal, Peter H. Russell, Richard Simeon, Andrew Stark, and Joseph White for helpful comments on earlier versions of this chapter, but reluctantly absolves the aforementioned of responsibility for any remaining errors of fact or interpretation.

1. Peter H. Russell, "Can the Canadians Be a Sovereign People?" *Canadian Journal of Political Science*, vol. 24 (December 1991), forthcoming.

2. See in particular Alan C. Cairns, "Ritual, Taboo, and Bias in Constitutional Controversies in Canada, or Constitutional Talk Canadian Style," and "Passing Judgement

the symbolic and institutional elements of Canada's constitutional crisis have been intertwined. Because levels of trust are low, more groups seek to become involved in the constitutional reform process; they attempt to entrench in the constitution guarantees that might otherwise be granted informally or through regular legislation; and they try to use veto points in the process to ensure that institutional reforms do not work against them in the future. As more politics becomes "constitutionalized," the constitutional reform agenda becomes hugely overburdened, making disputes all the more difficult to resolve.

This chapter offers an interpretation of the role of political institutions in Canada's constitutional crisis, focusing on three issues. First, institutions have been widely blamed, at least in part, for exacerbating conflict and group fears. To what extent are the existence and character of Canada's constitutional discontents due to failings of existing institutions? Second, institutional procedures affect the ways the crisis is resolved. Have Canadian political institutions produced constitutional stalemate, and are there any ways around this? Third, institutional reforms are looked to for solutions. To what extent are "institutional fixes" possible, and what might they look like?

I begin by laying out a simple framework to analyze institutional options for managing conflict. In the second section of the chapter I provide a brief overview of two critical centrifugal forces in Canadian politics: the division between francophones and anglophones and the conflict between central Canada and the eastern and western peripheries of the country.[3] I then discuss how Canadian political institutions have in fact managed these conflicts, including the ways they have shaped the incentives and strategies of politicians. Finally, I give a brief overview of recent constitutional crises and negotiations in Canada—including the negotiation of the Meech Lake Accord, its subsequent collapse, and the federal government's September 1991 proposals for constitutional reform—and suggest some lessons for current reform efforts.

My argument is not that Canadian institutions alone explain why Canada faces a constitutional crisis. Social divisions in Canada run very deep, and the linguistic divide between English- and French-speaking Ca-

---

on Meech Lake," in *Disruptions: Constitutional Struggles, from the Charter to Meech Lake,* ed. Douglas E. Williams (Toronto: McClelland and Stewart, 1991), pp. 199–222, 223–63.

3. Donald V. Smiley referred to these cleavages, together with the relationship with the United States, as the "three axes of Canadian federalism." See Smiley, *Canada in Question: Federalism in the Eighties* (Toronto: McGraw-Hill Ryerson, 1980), chap. 8.

nadians poses particularly intractable problems of conflict management. Considering its complex and intense social divisions, Canada has had an extraordinarily high level of social peace since the British North America Act of 1867 laid the foundations for the modern Canadian state. But Canadian political institutions have shaped, and in many ways reinforced, social divisions.[4] They have also critically shaped the form the constitutional crisis has taken, the mechanisms used to try to resolve it, and the potential solutions prescribed for it. In particular, Canada's political institutions have both exacerbated alienation in the western region of the country and contributed to repeated stalemate in constitutional reform.

Political Institutions and the Management of Social Conflict

Managing societal conflicts is one of the most important and difficult tasks for any government. This task becomes even more difficult when societies are divided by cleavages: deep, long-standing divisions based on such factors as race, religion, region, language, and class. These divisions are generally marked by distinct group values, identities, and institutions. Successful conflict management in a democratic society does not mean that there is no conflict, but rather that conflict is resolved in a way that all parties accept as legitimate, even if the outcome is not particularly to their liking. The most obvious indicator of successful cleavage management is the absence of symptoms of deep alienation from the system— political violence (such as riots, assassinations, and bombings) and political parties or movements that seek drastic changes in the countries' institutions or boundaries.[5] Canada has largely avoided political violence, but peaceful challenges to its boundaries and institutions have been endemic in recent years.

Managing conflict in deeply divided societies while maintaining democratic decisionmaking requires that political institutions do at least four things that are partially in conflict with one another. First, institutions must provide mechanisms to allow the interests of a variety of groups to be represented; although the level of representation afforded to each group may not be consistent over time (for example, because of party

4. See Alan C. Cairns, "The Governments and Societies of Canadian Federalism," *Canadian Journal of Political Science*, vol. 10 (December 1977), pp. 695–725.

5. See Richard Gunther and Anthony Mughan, "Political Institutions and Cleavage Management," in R. Kent Weaver and Bert A. Rockman, eds., *Do Institutions Matter? Government Capabilities in the United States and Abroad* (Brookings, forthcoming).

alternation in power), groups must not feel that they are permanently excluded from power and must believe that government is at least intermittently responsive to their interests. Second, institutions must protect the rights of minorities against discrimination and oppression by majorities.[6] Third, institutions must foster a political resolution of problems rather than stalemate. Finally, they must give leaders of all groups incentives to affirm the legitimacy of the institutions and to act in ways that sustain them. Obviously, there are some trade-offs between these tasks: a "unit-veto" system, in which unanimity is necessary for any action, is clearly the strongest protection for minority rights, but it is also a recipe for stalemate.

These four tasks can be performed through a variety of mechanisms, however, and the mechanisms chosen may shape as well as reflect divisions within the society.[7] Broadly speaking, one may think of conflict management as taking place either through simple majority rule or through a variety of mechanisms that attempt to limit or qualify majority rule. Each mechanism offers distinctive opportunities (potential positive effects) for managing conflict, as well as distinctive risks (potential negative effects) and limitations (areas in which opportunities are unlikely to be realized).[8]

Majoritarian Mechanisms

Majoritarian mechanisms offer relatively unrestricted power for political majorities; indeed, they sometimes "manufacture" majorities from

6. This standard is associated in particular with the work of Arend Lijphart. See, for example, *Democracies: Patterns of Majoritarian and Consensus Government in Twenty-One Countries* (Yale University Press, 1984).

7. See Roger Gibbins, *Regionalism: Territorial Politics in Canada and the United States* (Toronto: Butterworths, 1982), p. 5.

8. I refer to institutional effects as opportunities, risks, and limitations instead of "advantages" and "disadvantages" (which imply uniformity at least of direction if not strength) because the direction and strength of effects associated with any particular mechanism depend on the nature of the cleavages being managed and a variety of other factors. For a discussion of this framework and an application to the United States, see Arend Lijphart, Ronald Rogowski, and Kent Weaver, "Separation of Powers and Cleavage Management," and R. Kent Weaver and Bert A. Rockman, "Assessing the Affects of Institutions," in Weaver and Rockman, eds., *Do Institutions Matter?* The five institutional options outlined here are not intended to exhaust all mechanisms for ameliorating conflict, but rather to categorize major options for organizing decisionmaking. Intergroup conflict can be ameliorated in other ways as well, such as by transferring resources to aggrieved groups through grants from central authorities, purely symbolic moves (appointing members of minority groups to prestigious and highly visible ceremonial posts with no real decisionmaking authority), and cooptation of minority elites.

mere plurality preferences. The classic institutional expression of majoritarianism is the British Westminster model, which is used in Canada at both the federal and provincial levels of government. Single-member districts with plurality electoral rules reward only the one party or candidate that wins the most votes, regardless of whether that party or candidate wins a majority. This system tends to produce two dominant parties: voters perceive that votes for smaller parties are likely to be wasted, since those parties' candidates are not likely to win. (This differs from proportional representation systems, where parties are usually rewarded seats roughly coincident with their share of the total vote in a region.) Limiting the number of competing parties to two tends to produce single-party majority governments. Legislative majorities are relatively unrestricted either by an independent executive (the prime minister and the cabinet are chosen from the party or parties able to command a parliamentary majority), by independent courts, or by explicit constitutional limitations or prohibitions on what actions the parliament can take. In the absence of a written constitution, simple parliamentary majorities can in theory also amend the "rules for making rules."

The opportunities associated with majoritarian mechanisms are relatively clear. Most obviously, they are conducive to avoiding stalemate. In addition, they may give politicians incentives to make appeals to voters across cleavage lines in order to build a majority or plurality of support. The risks of majoritarianism are equally clear: minorities may be severely underrepresented, it is relatively easy for majorities to oppress minorities, and the very visibility of the divide between those in the government and those outside it may pose strong incentives for political elites on the outside to develop political strategies based on attacking the institutional framework itself. In Canada, for example, Quebecers and "outer Canadians" have feared being systematically overruled by English Canada and central Canada, respectively. Risks associated with majoritarianism may be limited by noninstitutional concerns, such as broadly held loyalty to institutions, conventions that limit government interference with individual rights, or informal nonmajoritarian practices to ensure a broadening of representation.

Consociational Mechanisms

Consociational mechanisms involve broad consultation and bargaining among elites representing the most important groups in a society, with groups choosing their own representatives.[9] Bargaining is often quite centralized—for example, in a cabinet—but may occur in other arenas as well. A number of specific institutional mechanisms can be used to facilitate consociational bargaining: proportional representation increases the probability that minority groups will be represented, while oversized coalitions in parliamentary systems increase the number of groups likely to be consulted.

Consociational mechanisms offer opportunities to attain each of the conflict management tasks outlined earlier: they may allow broad group representation and give minorities an effective voice to resist oppression (especially if a rule of consensus is followed in decisionmaking), they provide strong incentives for elites to collaborate in supporting the institutional status quo, and, if all groups can reach an agreement in the bargaining process, formal adoption of policy changes can occur swiftly. Consociationalism also carries some important limitations and risks, however. The most obvious are political stalemate and the potential for blackmail. If all parties must agree to a settlement, a single intransigent party can block agreement or demand extremely favorable terms. Because consociational mechanisms tend to be closed to all but officially recognized participants, they may also lead to the exclusion of unorganized or diffuse interests (such as women, consumers, or environmentalists), those with few resources (the poor and aboriginal peoples), or those whom the "gatekeepers" in government and organized interests simply find it convenient to exclude.

For consociationalism to work effectively, moreover, requires a set of conditions that frequently cannot be met. All of the relevant elites must be committed to preserving the system rather than making radical changes

9. The classic analysis of consociationalism is Arend Lijphart's discussions in *The Politics of Accommodation: Pluralism and Democracy in the Netherlands* (University of California Press, 1968), and *Democracy in Plural Societies: A Comparative Exploration* (Yale University Press, 1977). For an application of the consociational model to Canada, see Kenneth McRae, ed., *Consociational Democracy: Political Accommodation in Segmented Societies* (Toronto: McClelland and Stewart, 1974); and Garth Stevenson, "The Decline of Consociational Democracy in Canada," paper prepared for the 1991 annual meeting of the American Political Science Association. The analysis of consociationalism employed here is somewhat different from Lijphart's in focusing on mechanisms that facilitate centralized elite bargaining while excluding multiple veto points and constitutional limitations on majority action; the latter are discussed separately below as "limited-government" mechanisms. Similarly, the focus is on decisionmaking processes rather than on outcomes; while Lijphart associates group autonomy and separation with consociationalism, that is merely one possible outcome of consociational bargaining as the term is used here.

in it. Elites must also be given substantial autonomy by their groups to strike bargains; if they are always "watching their backs" to ensure that they are not attacked by more radical elements within their constituencies as sellouts, they may feel a need to be intransigent in their demands, increasing the likelihood of stalemate. Consociationalism also becomes more difficult as more groups demand representation and the potential for group vetoes becomes more severe.

Limited-Government Mechanisms

Whereas consociational mechanisms manage conflict by centralizing decisionmaking, limited-government mechanisms manage conflict by complicating the sequence of decisionmaking or by barring some issues from the agenda altogether. These mechanisms can be of two types. One makes government decisions more difficult through procedural obstacles (such as requirements for supermajorities or concurrent majorities in the legislature) or through multiple veto points (such as bicameral legislatures, separation of legislative and executive power, and ratification by subnational governments). These majority-limiting mechanisms may be applied to all legislation or merely a subset of issues especially sensitive to the linguistic, cultural, or religious concerns of various groups.[10] A second type of mechanism limits government options by preventing them entirely through constitutional prohibitions (for example, forbidding restrictions on freedom of the press) or by constitutionally requiring specific actions (for example, government support for separate schools for specific religious groups).[11]

The opportunities provided by such mechanisms are again fairly obvious. Multiple veto points may prevent political majorities from using government to oppress minority groups and may give minorities leverage both to protect existing rights and privileges and to win enactment of favorable new policies in exchange for acquiescing in legislation sought by the majority. But minorities can take advantage of these opportunities only if they hold veto power at one or more of the key veto points.

10. Limited-government mechanisms, by placing multiple veto points in the way of majority action, may promote consociational bargaining between cleavage segments but do not necessarily do so. Consociational mechanisms rely on centralization of decisionmaking, while limited-government mechanisms rely on sequential decisionmaking or agenda limitation.

11. Of course, these constitutional mandates are themselves not exempt from change, but usually they are subject to supermajority or multiple veto point requirements.

Bicameral legislatures did not, for example, prevent passage of Jim Crow laws in southern state legislatures in the United States because blacks were excluded from power at all stages of the political process. Limited-government mechanisms are also generally ineffective at redressing current grievances as opposed to preventing future ones, since they tend to freeze the status quo in place. Indeed, these mechanisms may lead to a government that is unable to respond to pressing national problems because of minority vetoes.[12]

Devolutionary Mechanisms

Devolutionary mechanisms, in contrast to consociational and limited-government mechanisms, give decisionmaking autonomy to groups or territorial units, thus making centralized bargaining less necessary. Usually this devolution of authority takes place along geographic lines, through federal arrangements, but it may also occur with interspersed groups—for example, through separate school systems for different religious denominations.

Devolutionary mechanisms create opportunities to get items off the central agenda and defuse potential intergroup conflicts. But they also have distinctive limitations. There are some policy fields that cannot be as easily delegated to distinct groups as denominational schools, especially where "spillover" effects from one group's actions or from one policy sector to another are inevitable. Regulation of air and water pollution and the formulation of foreign policy are obvious examples. The use of devolutionary mechanisms is also likely to lead to wrangling about which policy areas should be under national or provincial jurisdiction; more seriously, it may provide incentives for politicians at either level to build support by taking intransigent or even antisystem stances in opposition to the other level of government. Even more seriously, federalism poses the risk that regional majorities may use their authority to trample on the rights of minorities in their own regions.[13] Federalism may also reinforce

12. These minority vetoes may be held by "minorities of the majority"—intransigent opponents of any concession to minority groups. Conservative southern legislators in Congress in the 1950s and early 1960s are an example.

13. See Garth Stevenson's argument that with respect to "Chinese in British Columbia, Hutterites in Alberta, or Jehovah's Witnesses in Quebec, . . . provincial governments were more responsive to the hostile sentiments directed against these minorities than was the more remote central government." Stevenson, *Unfulfilled Union: Canadian Federalism and National Unity*, 3d ed. (Toronto: Gage, 1989), p. 17.

subnational identities relative to national ones. Devolutionary mechanisms are likely to work best, then, when distinct groups are geographically separated, when the policy areas that concern and divide them can be easily compartmentalized, and when there is a consensus among groups on those jurisdictional boundaries.

Arbitral Mechanisms

Arbitral mechanisms place decisionmaking authority in the hands of officials who are not directly accountable to voters or who are only weakly accountable and thus need not be concerned about maintaining the political support of majorities. While a purely arbitral system would not be a democratic one, most democratic systems do have significant arbitral admixtures—judges appointed for life or for very long terms, independent regulatory commissions, autonomous central banks—and these entities are often used to make politically unpopular decisions. In fact, the Canadian province of Newfoundland (at that time an autonomous British dominion) was governed by an appointed commission from 1934 to 1949 after becoming bankrupt during the Great Depression.[14]

Arbitral institutions offer an opportunity to resist decisions demanded by political majorities that would oppress minority rights, especially if those institutions enjoy widespread legitimacy. But they also have significant risks and limitations. Making decisionmakers less dependent on responsiveness to political majorities does not, of course, guarantee that they will protect minorities or represent their interests, especially if they are appointed by or from the majority. Moreover, unchecked power for arbitral institutions carries with it a risk of tyranny. And arbitral officials can succeed in managing conflict only so long as they enjoy legitimacy. As will be shown in the case of Canada, when social divisions are strong, the procedures used to appoint arbiters are themselves likely to be criticized as insufficiently responsive to the concerns of minority groups.

Centrifugal Forces in Canadian Society

The likelihood that any of the institutional mechanisms outlined above will—alone or in combination with others—succeed in managing Canadian societal divisions involves two related considerations. First, does

14. See S. J. R. Noel, *Politics in Newfoundland* (University of Toronto Press, 1971), chaps. 11–16.

Canada have the social and political conditions that will allow a given type of mechanism to work well—or to work at all? In the case of consociational mechanisms, for example, are elites committed to the system, is there a high degree of trust among them, and do they have enough autonomy to negotiate agreements free from mass interference? If these conditions change, mechanisms that worked well at one time may lead to discontent or disaster in another.

Equally important are the distinctive risks, limitations, and opportunities that each type of mechanism poses for conflict management in Canada. (Which of these effects is dominant, of course, depends on social and political context.) Canada, like most other countries, uses several types of mechanisms to compensate for any weaknesses that might arise with a single mode of conflict management. There is an obvious symbiosis between some of these mechanisms; for example, constitutional rights (a limited-government mechanism) may mean little without the arbitral mechanism of an independent judiciary. But the use of multiple mechanisms may also lead to institutional stalemate and give elites from some institutions incentives to challenge the legitimacy of decisions made by other institutions.

This section looks at the social and political challenges to conflict management in Canada; the next section looks at the actual record of Canadian institutions in managing conflict. I begin by briefly outlining how Canada's geography and history created important centrifugal forces in Canadian society. The evolution of the two most important of these forces—cleavages between francophones and anglophones, and between the central region of the country and its peripheries—has weakened the mechanisms traditionally used to manage conflict in Canada, either by undermining the social conditions needed for them to function or by giving those mechanisms powerful opponents.

The Shaping Roles of Geography and History

Canada is an immense country—the second largest territory in the world. But most of the huge land mass is inhospitable to dense human settlement: the climate is too cold, the growing season too short, the soil too barren, and the obstacles to reaching foreign markets too great. Most of Canada's 26.5 million people live along its ocean coastlines and in a narrow belt of land along its southern border with the United States. Canada is divided into ten provinces and two territories, but more than

60 percent of its population lives in just two of these provinces, Ontario and Quebec.

Most countries have been shaped in important ways by their geography; Canada has been shaped by an open defiance of geography.[15] Although the Great Lakes–St. Lawrence system and Hudson Bay facilitated trade, settlement, and communications in the interior of the continent, neither was an optimal basis for an independent "dominion of the North." Hudson Bay, opening into the Arctic Ocean, is closed to ships by ice for most of the year; moreover, it is cut off from its potential agricultural hinterland by unnavigable rivers and the permafrost and poor soil of the Canadian shield, which stretches south all the way to Lakes Superior and Huron. The agricultural regions of the Prairie provinces are separated from southern Ontario by a thousand desolate miles north of those lakes.

The St. Lawrence–Great Lakes system had its disadvantages too. Its rapids and the great falls at Niagara were both surmountable (at great cost) by canals—at least in the warm months. Not easily surmountable, however, was the fact that after 1776 the Great Lakes border was shared with the United States, which not only was oriented toward a different (and rival) trading system, but also was seen as hostile to British and Canadian interests and covetous of Canadian territory. Thus this spectacular passageway to the interior of the continent was both militarily vulnerable and lacking the richer southern part of its hinterland.

Canada's history also planted seeds of disunity. British and French colonial forces engaged in prolonged jostling for control of the area that was to become central and eastern Canada. The British gradually won out, first in Acadia (now the Maritime provinces),[16] culminating in expulsion of French settlers by the British in 1755. The more important changes, however, came in 1759 at Quebec City, when British forces under Wolfe defeated Montcalm's French forces, and the Treaty of Paris in 1763,

15. The classic expressions of the role of geography in Canadian development, and in particular the role of the St. Lawrence and Hudson Bay, are the works of Harold Adams Innis and Donald Grant Creighton. See especially Innis, *The Fur Trade in Canada: An Introduction to Canadian Economic History*, rev. ed. (University of Toronto Press, 1956); and Creighton, *The Empire of the St. Lawrence* (Toronto: Macmillan, 1956). Innis and Creighton emphasize the advantages of these waterways for creation of a single trading system in Canada rather than their shortcomings.

16. The term "Maritime provinces" is generally limited in Canadian usage to the three old provinces of Nova Scotia, New Brunswick, and Prince Edward Island, while the term "Atlantic region" includes Newfoundland, which did not join Canada until 1949. The term "Prairie provinces" includes Alberta, Saskatchewan, and Manitoba, while the term "Western region" also includes British Columbia.

which legitimized the British conquest. Henceforth, North America east of the Mississippi would be under a British flag,[17] but Quebec retained a strongly entrenched population that was French-speaking, passionately Catholic, and utterly determined to avoid assimilation with its English-speaking Protestant conquerors.

Thus by the "confederation" agreement of 1867, when Quebec and Ontario (at that time a single province)[18] joined with Nova Scotia and New Brunswick to form a federation under the British crown,[19] geography and history had already sown the seeds for the two most important divisions threatening Canada today: differences in language, culture, and religion between francophones and anglophones, and geographic isolation and differing economic interests of the West, central Canada, and the Atlantic region.[20]

Linguistic and Cultural Conflict

The conflict between the interests of Canada's two official language groups—anglophones and francophones—is the most obvious and visible of Canada's cleavages. Because it is also the subject of Stéphane Dion's chapter, I will attempt here simply to provide some historical context and outline briefly how its evolution has affected the likelihood that it could be managed by specific types of mechanisms.

Conflict between Canada's two dominant European linguistic and cultural groups critically affected the very shape of Canadian confederation: a highly centralized unitary government was favored by many of the anglophone ministers from "Canada West" (today Ontario) and the Maritime provinces, but opposed by francophones from Quebec, who saw that it would make them subject to the will of a Protestant, anglophone

17. France gained the islands of St. Pierre and Miquelon in the Gulf of St. Lawrence and limited fishing rights off Newfoundland.

18. See J. M. S. Careless, *The Union of the Canadas: The Growth of Canadian Institutions, 1841–1857* (Toronto: McClelland and Stewart, 1967); and Stevenson, *Unfulfilled Union*, chap. 2.

19. Other provinces joined later: Manitoba became a province in 1870, British Columbia in 1871, Prince Edward Island in 1873, Saskatchewan and Alberta in 1905, and Newfoundland in 1949.

20. I do not mean to suggest that there are no other politically important divisions in Canadian society. Clearly there are such divisions, for example, along class lines. But these generally do not threaten the survival of Canada as a single state.

majority.²¹ Anglophones, in turn, saw the eventual assimilation of franco-phones into their culture as a desirable and almost inevitable outcome—and had already shown themselves quite willing to use institutional mechanisms to hasten the inevitable. In 1841, the colonies of Upper and Lower Canada (now Ontario and Quebec, respectively) were united in a single province of Canada, ensuring an anglophone majority in the common legislature. But instead of promoting assimilation, this arrangement led to incipient federalism and consociationalism, as well as government paralysis and policymaking stalemate. The shortcomings of the Upper Canada–Lower Canada union were among the leading causes of the broader confederation in 1867.²² Under confederation, Quebec became part of a still broader union, but was assured governmental autonomy as a separate province, notably in the area of education, to resist assimilationist pressures from Canada's anglophone, Protestant majority.

Events outside Quebec in the decades immediately after 1867 raised Quebecers' consciousness of the existence of French-Canadian communities in other provinces and concern for their rights, but they also raised serious doubts about whether viable French-Catholic communities could be built and maintained in provinces where francophones were a minority.²³ Guarantees made to francophones outside Quebec concerning education and the functioning of provincial governments were eroded by the provinces in this period. The failure of the federal government to use its authority under the British North America Act to enact remedial legislation to protect francophone rights suggested that devolutionary mechanisms posed real risks for francophone minorities and that attempts to protect minorities by constitutional limited-government guarantees and prohibitions were likely to be of little help against determined anglophone majorities.²⁴ The federal government's forceful response to an uprising

21. There was also opposition to a unitary system in the Maritime provinces. See Peter B. Waite, *The Life and Times of Confederation, 1864–1867* (University of Toronto Press, 1962).

22. On this period, see Gerald M. Craig, ed., *Lord Durham's Report: An Abridgement of Report on the Affairs of British North America* (Toronto: McClelland and Stewart, 1963); Careless, *Union of the Canadas*; and William Ormsby, "The Province of Canada: The Emergence of Consociational Politics," in McRae, ed., *Consociational Democracy*, pp. 269–74.

23. On this period, see A. I. Silver, *The French-Canadian Idea of Confederation, 1864–1900* (University of Toronto Press, 1982).

24. Erosion of these guarantees was most contentious in the Prairie region of Canada (roughly the current provinces of Manitoba, Saskatchewan, and Alberta). Manitoba had a francophone majority among its small European population when it became a province in 1870, and official-language status for French and separate confessional schools were

by Métis (mixed white and native peoples) on the prairies led by the francophone Louis Riel and its subsequent hanging of Riel in 1885 also caused hopes for a Catholic, French-Canadian society to become more clearly focused on Quebec.

Relations with Britain and the place of Canada within the British Empire (later Commonwealth) were also an enduring source of division between francophones and anglophones through much of Canadian history. Political crises erupted during World Wars I and II centering on the extent to which Canada should follow Britain's lead into these conflicts and whether Canada should impose conscription in order to raise manpower for fighting overseas. During both wars, elections to authorize conscription (a general election in the first case, a referendum in the second) found Quebecers voting overwhelmingly against conscription and voters in the anglophone provinces voting in favor.

For most of the period up to 1960, however, a relatively stable, if sometimes tense, pattern of conflict management emerged, based largely on a system of consociational bargaining between anglophone and francophone elites within the federal cabinet, accompanied by devolutionary mechanisms that gave Quebec substantial autonomy in social, cultural, and educational policy. The Quebec provincial government in turn allowed the anglophone minority in the province substantial control over their own affairs.

---

guaranteed in the Manitoba Act. The Manitoba legislature passed legislation contrary to these guarantees as anglophone settlers became a majority in the province and simply ignored court judgments that legislation needed to be passed in both official languages. After the federal election of 1896, the new federal Liberal government of Sir Wilfrid Laurier—a francophone, Catholic Quebecer—chose to negotiate a compromise with the Manitoba government rather than pass remedial legislation out of fear that a backlash among anglophones would create irresistible pressures for an end to separate confessional schools in other provinces. See Janice Staples, "Consociationalism at the Provincial Level: The Erosion of Dualism in Manitoba, 1870–1890," in McRae, ed., Consociational Democracy, pp. 288–99; H. Blair Neatby, Laurier and a Liberal Quebec: A Study in Political Management (Toronto: McClelland and Stewart, 1973), chaps. 5–6; and Ian Greene, The Charter of Rights (Toronto: James Lorimer, 1989), pp. 194–202. On disputes regarding confessional schools in other provinces, see Keith A. McLeod, "Politics, Schools and the French Language," in Norman Ward and Duff Spafford, eds., Politics in Saskatchewan (Don Mills, Ont.: Longmans Canada, 1968), pp. 124–50; Peter M. Toner, "New Brunswick Schools and the Rise of Provincial Rights," in Bruce W. Hodgins, Don Wright, and W. H. Heick, eds., Federalism in Canada and Australia: The Early Years (Waterloo: Wilfrid Laurier University Press, 1978), pp. 125–35; and Robert C. Vipond, "Constitutional Politics and the Legacy of the Provincial Rights Movement in Canada," Canadian Journal of Political Science, vol. 18 (June 1985), pp. 278–81.

In Ottawa, the principal agent of accommodation was the federal Liberal party.[25] The Liberal party was overwhelmingly dominant in federal elections from 1896 until 1957, forming the government for all but about fifteen years of this period. The Liberals, in turn, were dependent for this success on their electoral dominance in Quebec, which they helped to maintain through an informal process of alternating francophone Quebecers and anglophones from other provinces as party leaders.[26] Quebec Liberals used their strong voice in the governing party caucus, and especially in the cabinet, to act as a conservative force resisting expansion of the welfare state.[27]

Quebec nationalism in this period was exemplified by the long premiership of Maurice Duplessis (1936–40, 1944–59). The nationalism of Duplessis's Union Nationale party was primarily a conservative phenomenon, resisting the encroachment of secularism, federal government programs, and a modern welfare state that were seen as threatening Quebec's status as the bastion of French and Catholic culture in North America. But at the same time the Duplessis government cooperated with American and English-Canadian firms that dominated the Quebec economy, and it did nothing to undermine the status of English as the primary language of big business in Quebec, the largely English face of Montreal (Quebec's largest, and majority francophone, city), or the near exclusion of francophones from the province's managerial classes.[28] Nor did it interfere with the province's largely autonomous anglophone social institutions (notably schools, universities, and hospitals).

25. Canada differs from the classical consociational model outlined by Lijphart in the use of "catch-all" brokerage parties rather than separate parties for each cleavage segment as the main instrument for elite bargaining. See Brian Barry, "The Consociational Model and its Dangers," *European Journal of Political Research*, vol. 3 (1975), pp. 393–412.

26. This procedure continues today. Federal Liberal leaders in the twentieth century are Wilfrid Laurier (1887–1919), W. L. Mackenzie King (1919–48), Louis St. Laurent (1948–58), Lester Pearson (1958–68), Pierre Trudeau (1968-84), John Turner (1984–90), and Jean Chrétien (1990–present). See John C. Courtney, *The Selection of National Party Leaders in Canada* (Toronto: Macmillan, 1973), p. 140.

27. See R. Kent Weaver, "The State and the Welfare State in the United States and Canada," paper prepared for a conference on the New Institutionalism, Boulder, Colorado, January 1990.

28. See Marc V. Levine, *The Reconquest of Montreal: Language Policy and Social Change in a Bilingual City* (Temple University Press, 1990), chap. 2; and Herbert F. Quinn, *The Union Nationale: Quebec Nationalism from Duplessis to Lévesque*, 2d ed. (University of Toronto Press, 1979), chap. 5.

This pattern of accommodation, with the British retaining control of the economy and francophones within Quebec retaining autonomy over their own cultural institutions, worked well so long as Quebec society remained largely rural and its elites conservative. It became increasingly untenable, however, as demographic and cultural changes profoundly altered the challenges facing and the goals held by the francophone community. First, francophones in Quebec became increasingly urban in the period after World War I, which led them into contact and competition with anglophone employers, where they tended to be excluded from managerial positions and found that the language of work was usually English.[29]

In addition, there was a new wave of immigrants after World War II, largely into Montreal, whose native language was neither French nor English. Those new immigrants (called allophones) overwhelming sent their children into English schools and assimilated into the English-speaking community.[30] Francophones' already precarious position in Montreal seemed further threatened. Moreover, their own birthrate—which had traditionally been one of the highest in the world, allowing them to avoid being swamped as anglophones were bolstered by wave after wave of European immigration—declined precipitously after 1960. This decline called into question both the ability of francophones to remain dominant in their home province and lowered the overall weight of Quebec within Canada.[31]

By the late 1960s, the question of how to ensure that immigrants assimilated into the francophone rather than anglophone communities in

29. See Everett C. Hughes, *French Canada in Transition* (University of Chicago Press, 1943). Urbanization also contributed to secularization, with the Catholic clergy in Quebec declining in both numbers and influence over their congregations. On secularization in Quebec, see Kenneth McRoberts, *Quebec: Social Change and Political Crisis*, 3d ed. (Toronto: McClelland and Stewart, 1988), pp. 57–59; and Fernand Ouellet, "The Quiet Revolution: A Turning Point," in Thomas S. Axworthy and Pierre Elliott Trudeau, eds., *Towards A Just Society: The Trudeau Years*, trans. Patricia Claxton (Viking, 1990), pp. 313–41.

30. By 1970, "[a] reasonable projection was that immigrant Anglicization would place a majority of Montreal's first-graders in English-language schools by the early 1980s." Levine, *Reconquest of Montreal*, p. 61. See more broadly pp. 55–65.

31. See Roger Gibbins, *Conflict and Unity: An Introduction to Canadian Political Life*, 2d ed. (Scarborough, Ont.: Nelson Canada, 1990), pp. 45–54, for an excellent review of demolinguistic trends in Canada. For a pessimistic view of the impact of demographic trends on the prospects of the francophone community in Quebec, see the brief of the Mouvement National des Québécois to the Bélanger-Campeau Commission, excerpted in Richard Fidler, trans. and commentary, *Canada Adieu? Quebec Debates Its Future* (Lantzville, B.C.: Oolichan Books, 1991), pp. 229–34.

Montreal had become an important issue in Quebec, with nationalists demanding that immigrants' children be compelled to attend French schools. Meanwhile, francophones outside Quebec and the francophone areas of New Brunswick continued to assimilate into the anglophone community at a rapid rate.[32] Although a relatively small percentage of the population, they remained important in absolute size.[33]

Political change began to reflect these demographic shifts with the election of a Liberal provincial government in Quebec headed by Premier Jean Lesage in 1960.[34] The ensuing changes in Quebec, known as the "Quiet Revolution," encompassed a variety of social and governmental shifts, all having their roots in a more assertive and secular nationalism.[35] The Quebec government under Lesage took control of the province's educational and social welfare institutions away from the church, embraced industrialization, and saw the provincial government, rather than the English-speaking business class, as a primary engine of development. To fulfill this enlarged role, the provincial government sought to increase its powers, either through a general devolution of powers to the provinces or through the granting of "special status" to Quebec, just at the time that a new federal Liberal government headed by Prime Minister Lester Pearson was attempting a series of new initiatives in areas under provincial jurisdiction, for example, pensions and health care. There were repeated clashes between the Quebec government and Ottawa over how these initiatives were to be managed—and in particular whether and on what terms Quebec could opt out to manage its own programs. Conflict also increased over efforts by successive Quebec governments to increase control over the languages of education and work within the province.[36]

For many Quebecers, however, increased powers of the provincial government and protections for the French language within Quebec were not adequate to preserve and enhance Quebec's distinct character. Only

---

32. See Karen Taylor-Browne, "The Francophone Minority," in Roger Gibbins and others, eds., *Meech Lake and Canada: Perspectives from the West* (Edmonton: Academic Printing and Publishing, 1988), pp. 185–200.

33. See Gibbins, *Conflict and Unity*, p. 54.

34. The parties using the Liberal label at the federal and provincial levels in Quebec have been organizationally distinct since 1964. See David M. Rayside, "Federalism and the Party System: Provincial and Federal Liberals in the Province of Quebec," *Canadian Journal of Political Science*, vol. 11 (September 1978), pp. 499–528.

35. On the Quiet Revolution, see McRoberts, *Quebec.*

36. These conflicts are traced in more detail in Stéphane Dion's chapter. See also Levine, *Reconquest of Montreal*; and Graham Fraser, *P.Q.: René Lévesque and the Parti Québécois in Power* (Toronto: Macmillan, 1984).

a much more drastic change in political status would suffice. One sign of tensions—although a tiny force in numbers—was the Quebec Liberation Front (FLQ), which carried out a series of bombings in the province during the late 1960s to press its campaign for an independent Quebec. This campaign culminated in the "October crisis" of 1970, when the FLQ kidnapped Quebec's labor minister and a British diplomat. These actions prompted the federal prime minister, Pierre Trudeau, to invoke the War Measures Act, sending federal troops into Quebec and suspending civil liberties.[37]

The October crisis proved to be the end of violent expressions of separatist sentiment in Quebec. But separatist political parties, a marginal electoral force in the province through most of the 1960s, acquired a mainstream political vehicle in 1968, when René Lévesque, who had been a leading minister in the Lesage government, founded the Parti Québécois (PQ). The PQ proposed a program of "sovereignty-association"—political independence for Quebec combined with close economic links between Quebec and English Canada. By 1970, the party had become the leading opposition party in provincial elections. In 1976 the Parti Québécois won a majority of seats in the provincial legislature, the National Assembly, and formed the government of Quebec through 1985.[38]

This more assertive Quebec nationalism was met by an equally assertive federal response from Ottawa beginning in the late 1960s. In 1968 Pierre Trudeau became prime minister of Canada. Trudeau, a bilingual Quebecer who was deeply suspicious of Quebec nationalism, posited an alternative vision of Canada—a country in which Canadians of either language group could feel at home in any part of the country.[39] This view was backed up with a variety of policy initiatives, including guarantees that Canadians could receive services from the federal government in English or French anywhere in Canada, bilingual packaging requirements, and efforts to

37. Quebec's labor minister, Pierre Laporte, was murdered by the FLQ after the federal government invoked the War Measures Act; British diplomat James Cross was later released. On the October crisis, see Denis Smith, *Bleeding Hearts . . . Bleeding Country* (Edmonton: M. G. Hurtig, 1971); and John Saywell, *Quebec 70: A Documentary Narrative* (University of Toronto Press, 1971).

38. The Parti Québécois does not participate in federal elections. After the failure of the Meech Lake Accord, a breakaway party of former Conservative and Liberal federal members of Parliament called the Bloc Québécois was formed to compete federally. See Stéphane Dion's chapter for details.

39. For details, see Andrew Stark's chapter in this volume and Stephen Clarkson and Christina McCall, *Trudeau and Our Times*, vol. 1: *The Magnificent Obsession* (Toronto: McClelland and Stewart, 1990).

employ more francophones at upper levels of the federal public service. The Trudeau government also attempted to undercut French-English divisions by pressing for a Charter of Rights and Freedoms that would create a stronger pan-Canadian identity, supporting groups representing the broader "multicultural" (that is, non-British or French in origin) heritage in Canadian society, and refusing to grant Quebec "special status" distinct from other provinces in the constitution and in government programs.

The stage was thus set in Quebec for repeated clashes between forces favoring and opposing some sort of accommodation within a federal structure. The first critical round was won by pro-federalist forces in a Quebec provincial referendum on May 20, 1980. The referendum question called for giving the provincial government a mandate to negotiate sovereignty-association with the federal government, rather than for actually deciding on sovereignty, and promised a second referendum before sovereignty would occur. Despite this wording, which was intended to draw support as broadly as possible, Quebec's voters voted "no" by a three-to-two margin, with francophones rejecting the initiative by a very slim majority.[40] As separatist sentiment in Quebec declined in the aftermath of the referendum, even the Parti Québécois began to take a softer line toward sovereignty under both Lévesque and his successor as PQ leader and premier, Pierre-Marc Johnson. The return of the Liberal party to power in Quebec in 1985 and the negotiation of the Meech Lake Accord in 1987, which granted Quebec (and the other provinces) several constitutional concessions, appeared to solidify a federalist choice—until the accord was rejected in June 1990. After that event, as Dion shows in his chapter, separatist sentiment in Quebec soared to unprecedented levels.

In concluding this brief review of the evolution of Canada's linguistic and cultural cleavage, it is critical to underline how the changing nature of that cleavage has affected the conditions that facilitate each of the conflict management strategies outlined earlier. Despite the formally majoritarian nature of Canada's parliamentary system, both anglophone and francophone elites in Ottawa sought to prevent the emergence and resolution of policy conflict along linguistic lines. Francophone elites feared oppression of the francophone minority. Anglophone elites feared that making the linguistic division more visible, salient, and alienating could threaten national unity. The latter outcome is most evident in the conflicts over conscription during World Wars I and II.

<hr />

40. On the referendum campaign, see Clarkson and McCall, *Trudeau and Our Times*, vol. 1, chaps. 10, 11.

Social change has also undermined the various nonmajoritarian strategies for managing Canada's linguistic-cultural cleavage, however. Consociationalism, for example, requires that members of each "cleavage segment" be relatively unified in their views and give their leaders wide discretion to bargain in their interests and that leaders of all groups be committed to maintaining at least the broad outlines of the current system. Consociational bargaining clearly has been an important mechanism for managing Canada's cultural-linguistic cleavage in the past, with the federal cabinet serving as the primary vehicle through the onset of the "Quiet Revolution" in Quebec and direct bargaining between the Ottawa and Quebec City governments increasingly displacing it in the years since. But none of the conditions needed to make consociationalism work well currently exist in Canada.[41] Quebecers are deeply split, and not wholly consistent, in their attitudes toward Canada and sovereignty. Certainly their electoral mandate was split through most of the period from 1960 to 1984, as they repeatedly elected committed federalists to the federal House of Commons and provincial governments that challenged Ottawa. In this situation, it could not be clear in consociational bargaining who spoke for Quebecers, as federal and provincial politicians with very different viewpoints claimed and competed to do so. Moreover, as Dion shows, public opinion in Quebec is quite volatile over time. Thus provincial elites have had limited room to bargain and have always had to be careful not to be blindsided by an upswing in nationalist sentiment. Finally, one segment of Quebec's leadership—the Parti Québécois—is committed to altering the rules of the game through attaining political sovereignty for Quebec rather than maintaining the current bargaining game.

Social and political developments in Quebec and Canada also weakened the prospects that other nonmajoritarian mechanisms could manage this linguistic and cultural conflict. Many Quebec francophones, and a succession of Quebec provincial governments, have favored increased devolution of powers to the province as a way to preserve and promote Quebec's identity. But there is great disagreement about the form and scope of this devolution. For the Parti Québécois, no devolutionary strategy short of political sovereignty would be adequate to meet these objectives, and even the "federalist" Quebec Liberal party has proposed a major transfer of powers to Quebec.[42] However, governments in many

41. For an excellent analysis of the cultural-linguistic cleavage in Canada in terms of consociationalism, see Stevenson, "The Decline of Consociational Democracy in Canada."

42. See Québec Liberal Party [Allaire Commission], A Québec Free to Choose: Report of the Constitutional Committee (January 28, 1991).

of the anglophone provinces have been adamantly opposed to an asymmetrical devolution that gives powers to Quebec but not to them. Moreover, they are far from united in favoring a weakening of Ottawa. Finally, the existence of a sizable non-French-speaking minority in Quebec and significant francophone minorities in several other provinces increases the risk that if devolutionary mechanisms are used to regulate conflict, provincial governments will take actions perceived by minority language groups as oppressive. Thus language minorities have generally been suspicious of increased devolution of authority.

Groups representing minority language speakers in each region tend to favor limited-government guarantees of minority rights and prohibitions on discriminatory actions by provincial governments (for example, in schooling), with enforcement by an arbitral institution, the courts. But these limitations are perceived in Quebec as a threat to the survival of Quebec's distinctive francophone character within overwhelmingly English-speaking North America. And the use of arbitral institutions—notably courts—depends upon the acceptance by all participants of the neutrality of the arbiters and the legitimacy of their decisions. But Quebec governments have increasingly questioned the neutrality and legitimacy of a judiciary appointed by Ottawa and focused on enforcing individually oriented language rights.

Conflict between Center and Periphery

The conflict between central Canada (Ontario and Quebec) and the Atlantic and western peripheries of the country is not as old as the conflict between anglophone and francophone Canada,[43] but it does date back at least as far as the debates over confederation in the 1860s.[44] Westerners, it should be noted, were not part of these negotiations at all. The vast prairie region and the area around Hudson Bay were under the control of the Hudson's Bay Company until it was purchased by the Canadian government in 1869, and it had a minuscule European settler popula-

43. For an excellent introduction to regional politics outside of Quebec, see Gibbins, *Conflict and Unity*, chap. 4.
44. See the chapters on the Maritime provinces in Waite, *Life and Times of Confederation*. See also James Hiller, "Confederation Defeated: The Newfoundland Election of 1869," in James Hiller and Peter Neary, eds., *Newfoundland in the Nineteenth and Twentieth Centuries: Essays in Interpretation* (University of Toronto Press, 1980), pp. 67–94.

tion.[45] British Columbia, Britain's west coast colony, did not join Canada until 1871, on the promise that a railway would be built to join it with central Canada. More than one hundred years after confederation, a basic population imbalance remains between central Canada and the eastern and western peripheries. Quebec and Ontario host the the majority of Canada's population (26 and 36 percent, respectively), while the four western provinces together are home to 29 percent of Canada's population and the four Atlantic provinces to only 9 percent.

Perceptions of political impotence on the peripheries have been exacerbated by perceptions of economic injustice. Canada's first prime minister, Sir John A. MacDonald, promoted the creation of a western agricultural hinterland through a tripartite national policy of railway construction to provide access to the West, high tariffs to promote domestic industry, and immigration to populate the West. Politicians and business people on the peripheries have long complained that federal policies have continued to favor industrial development in Ontario and Quebec and perpetuate the role of the peripheries as producers of primary products (wheat from the prairies, lumber in British Columbia and the Atlantic region, mineral and energy resources in the West and North, and fish from the Atlantic provinces.)[46] While selling their primary goods into world markets where they could not control prices, Canadian tariff policies forced them to pay above–world market prices for manufactured goods. Westerners in particular believe their continued dependence on primary production has resulted not just from distance from major markets, but also from transportation policies that discouraged economic diversification in those regions, federal procurement policies that favored central Canadian producers,[47] resource policies that treated the peripheral provinces as continued colonies,[48] and a highly centralized banking system centered in Toronto and Montreal. In recent years, struggles over energy policy between

45. See Donald Swainson, "Canada Annexes the West: Colonial Status Confirmed," in Hodgins and others, eds., Federalism in Canada and Australia, pp. 137–57.

46. Scholars are divided on whether economic underdevelopment in the peripheries resorts primarily from market forces or discriminatory federal policies. Compare, for example, David Jay Bercuson, ed., Canada and the Burden of Unity (Toronto: Macmillan, 1977); and Kenneth H. Norrie, "Some Comments on Prairie Economic Alienation," in J. Peter Meekison, ed., Canadian Federalism: Myth or Reality, 3d ed. (Toronto: Methuen, 1977), pp. 325–40.

47. See David Kilgour, Inside Outer Canada (Edmonton: Lone Pine, 1990), chap. 7.

48. Particularly galling to westerners was the fact that when the three Prairie provinces attained provincial status, they were not given the same control over lands and natural resources as other provinces. This was changed in 1930.

the oil- and natural gas-producing province of Alberta and the federal government have been the most dramatic manifestation of periphery-center tensions.

Beyond shared grievances with central Canada, however, there is little in the way of a common culture or collective interest that unites "outer Canada" and distinguishes it from the rest of the country; in this respect, the center-periphery cleavage is very different from that between Quebec and the rest of Canada. Even if the Atlantic and western regions are viewed separately, there are only a limited number of issues on which there is strong agreement across the Atlantic provinces (notably support for federal regional development assistance and transfers to poorer provinces to support social services) and in western Canada (notably increased provincial control over natural resources). These patterns largely reflect variations in resource endowments. The four Atlantic provinces, with their heavy dependence on fisheries and other troubled industries (such as an uncompetitive coal industry in the Cape Breton Island region of Nova Scotia), show up at the bottom of Canadian personal income statistics and the top of unemployment statistics.[49] The situation in the West is much more mixed, however. Personal income levels in oil- and natural gas-rich Alberta and in British Columbia are among the highest in Canada.

The Atlantic region and the West have also differed in their political responses to economic grievances. Protest in the Atlantic region has generally been channeled through the established Conservative and Liberal parties. In the West, and in particular in the three Prairie provinces of Alberta, Saskatchewan, and Manitoba, regional protest has often taken the form of separate, regionally based political parties at the federal or provincial levels or support for a national party out of power in Ottawa. Thus westerners have more often felt excluded from power in Ottawa (an effect exacerbated by Canada's electoral system, as will be discussed below) than Atlantic Canadians, and pressure from "outer Canada" for institutional reform has come primarily from the West.

Finding an acceptable formula to respond to "outer Canadian" concerns has proven nearly as difficult as responding to Quebec, however.

---

49. Ottawa uses a variety of mechanisms to transfer income to poorer provinces. Equalization grants, for example, are intended to allow provinces with lower tax bases to provide a level of basic services that are roughly comparable to those in better-off provinces without above-average taxes. A variety of regional development schemes have also been used by Ottawa to foster regional development in the Atlantic region and the West. And numerous federal income transfer programs—notably unemployment assistance and the guaranteed income supplement for pensioners—also aid poorer provinces.

These interests have increasingly been perceived and articulated along provincial rather than regional lines, and there have been intermittent devolutionary pressures from the West. (This has been especially true during booms, when resource prices are high and conflict between the provinces and Ottawa over taxation and management of resources has been intense; during times of "bust" there has been a greater concern with extracting resources from Ottawa.) But devolution has been a less much less consistent theme in demands from the periphery than has been the case in Quebec. Although devolutionary mechanisms have a natural outlet in the provinces, provincial governments in "outer Canada" have generally feared crippling of Ottawa's power to manage the national economy and (especially in the Atlantic region) have seen a strong central government as necessary to facilitate transfer payments to poorer provinces.

The major theme of demands from the periphery has been that federal institutions must be reformed to give the less populous provinces a stronger voice ("the West wants in" is a common slogan). Such institutions can take several forms, but each has shortcomings as a vehicle for increasing representation of the peripheries in Ottawa.

Consociational mechanisms have a natural set of participants in the provincial premiers, but the fact that the West and the Atlantic region each consist of four separate provinces, quite often with very distinct interests and viewpoints, immensely complicates the process of consociational elite bargaining by multiplying both participants and interests that need to be accommodated. Limited-government mechanisms that rely on multiple veto points are likely to be helpful in addressing the concerns of outer Canada only if those interests are essentially negative ones—to prevent "oppressive" acts. The same is true of the arbitral institution of the courts: neither ensures that peripheral interests will be included in policymaking on a consistent basis.

Other Centrifugal Forces

Several other important forces in addition to the two critical centrifugal forces of language and region have complicated conflict management in Canada in recent years. Three of these forces deserve brief mention.

The continental tug. Since before confederation, Canadians have had to deal with the United States as a neighbor and a rival for economic and political dominance of North America. Immigration of Loyalists from the former colonies to the south was an important source of population growth in the northern colonies after 1783 and not surprisingly gave those colonies a strongly pro–British Empire, anti-American, and anti-republican cast.[50] The fear of invasion from the United States after the American Civil War led the British imperial government to encourage confederation in 1867 as a way to strengthen its North American colonies.

After confederation, conflict over relations with the United States centered on the degree to which tariffs should be used to protect Canadian manufacturers, or at least to compel American firms to build branch plants in Canada to serve the Canadian market. From confederation through the early twentieth century, the Liberals were generally the party of trade liberalization, and a few elections—notably those of 1891 and 1911—centered on the trade issue. The issue was not an electoral winner for the Liberals,[51] and it largely disappeared as a major election issue for more than seventy years after the "reciprocity" election of 1911.

Canada's economic and national security relationships with its southern neighbor grew much closer in the twentieth century, as a succession of Canadian governments saw greater North American integration as essential for national security and economic growth.[52] The United States, rather than Britain, became the prime source of external capital for Canadian government and industry.[53] Canada became the United States' biggest trading partner. National security linkages, forged especially during World War II, grew much stronger as well. In cultural sectors, too, the American influence on Canada—especially English Canada—increased.

The growing American role was a source of alarm to many Canadians.[54] Only rarely has it been an important election issue in recent years,

50. On the Loyalist migration and its effects, see Ramsay Cook, *Canada: A Modern Study* (Toronto: Clarke Irwin, 1964), pp. 13–18.

51. It is not, however, clear, that the Liberals' support for free trade was the cause of their defeat. In each case, there were other factors that contributed to their loss. See Richard Johnston and Michael B. Percy, "Reciprocity, Imperial Sentiment, and Party Politics in the 1911 Elections," *Canadian Journal of Political Science*, vol. 13 (December 1980), pp. 711–29.

52. On the sources of these changes, see especially J. L. Granatstein, *How Britain's Weakness Forced Canada into the Arms of the United States* (University of Toronto Press, 1989).

53. The classic study is A. E. Safarian, *Foreign Ownership of Canadian Industry*, 2d ed. (University of Toronto Press, 1973). For critiques of American investment from the left, see Kari Levitt, *Silent Surrender: The American Economic Empire in Canada* (New York: Liveright, 1971); and Glen Williams, *Not for Export: Toward a Political Economy of Canada's Arrested Industrialization* (Toronto: McClelland and Stewart, 1983).

54. As Andrew Stark notes in his chapter, this concern was especially intense in the social-democratic New Democratic Party (NDP), Canada's third largest national political party. However, the party is by no means united in its views on relations with the United States, and in particular American labor unions. Disagreements over these issues were an

however. The notable exception was 1988, when Prime Minister Brian Mulroney's Conservative government fought an election campaign dominated by the issue of whether to ratify the free trade agreement that his government had negotiated with the United States.[55] The changing nature of the U.S.-Canada relationship has nonetheless affected the prospects for conflict management in Canada in important ways. The decline of a perceived American threat weakened the incentives for elite accommodation that were such a strong incentive for the fathers of confederation in the 1860s.[56] Thus a critical underpinning of consociational cleavage management has been undermined. Even more important, the apparent assurance of access to U.S. markets offered by the free trade agreement may undermine Quebecers' perceptions that staying within Canada is economically necessary.

New voices. Canadian politics has in recent years been profoundly democratized and become more oriented toward individual rights and a greater variety of group rights. Native peoples, women, the disabled, and ethnic minorities are among the groups that have demanded not only that their concerns be addressed but that they be included in the decisionmaking process. The sources of this change are several. To a significant degree, as Andrew Stark argues in his chapter, this opening up of bargaining has been legitimized by the 1982 Charter of Rights and Freedoms and fostered by government funding of multicultural groups.[57] The American "rights revolution" has also had an impact. Group grievances have also been given added symbolic weight by catalytic events: in the case of native peoples, long-standing resentments over land issues and self-government were given

---

important component of a serious split in the party in the late 1960s and early 1970s. See Desmond Morton, *NDP: Social Democracy in Canada*, 2d ed. (Toronto: Samuel Stevens Hakkert, 1977). Conflict over relations with the United States also resonated within the Liberal and Conservative parties. See Peter C. Newman's portrait of Walter Gordon in *The Distemper of Our Times: Canadian Politics in Transition, 1963–1968* (Toronto: McClelland and Stewart, 1968), chap. 16; and George Grant, *Lament for a Nation: The Defeat of Canadian Nationalism* (Toronto: McClelland and Stewart, 1965).

55. See G. Bruce Doern and Brian W. Tomlin, *Faith and Fear: The Free Trade Story* (Don Mills, Ont.: Stoddart, 1991); Alan Frizzell, Jon H. Pammett, and Anthony Westell, *The Canadian General Election of 1988* (Ottawa: Carleton University Press, 1989); and Robert M. Campbell and Leslie A. Pal, *The Real Worlds of Canadian Politics: Cases in Process and Policy*, 2d ed. (Peterborough, Ont.: Broadview Press, 1991), pp. 187–266.

56. The role of the American threat as an incentive for elite accommodation is mentioned by Stevenson in "The Decline of Consociational Democracy in Canada," p. 6; and Gibbins, *Regionalism*, pp. 24–25.

57. See Alan C. Cairns, "Constitutional Minoritarianism in Canada," in Ronald L. Watts and Douglas M. Brown, eds., *Canada: The State of the Federation 1990* (Kingston: Queen's University, Institute of Intergovernmental Relations, 1990), pp. 71–96.

focus by the six-month-long, occasionally violent uprising by Mohawk warriors in southern Quebec in 1990, by the opposition of Ojibway chief Elijah Harper to the Meech Lake Accord in the Manitoba legislature (which delivered the coup de grace to the accord), and by the efforts of Cree in northern Quebec to block Hydro-Quebec's huge Great Whale power project, which would flood thousands of acres of their land.[58]

Whatever its implications for governmental responsiveness, this democratization has complicated cleavage management. The implications are particularly severe for consociational bargaining, which works best when the number of bargainers can be limited, knotty issues are excluded from the agenda, and the ability of bargainers to make binding commitments is unquestioned. This has become more difficult in Canada in recent years. More voices have clamored to be heard, they have challenged the legitimacy of closed bargaining, and they have persistently raised issues that not only were difficult to resolve but also inflamed tensions between existing elites.[59]

Big deficits. Although money cannot buy happiness, it can help to assuage conflict between competing levels of government. Money, in the form of grants and tax concessions, can be used by the federal government to buy the support or acquiescence of provincial governments for federal government programs or proposals for institutional reform. A flush federal treasury strengthens Ottawa's bargaining hand. In recent years, Ottawa's hand has been very weak indeed, as it has consistently rolled up deficits that are among the highest in the OECD countries. Thus Ottawa has been forced to undertake major revenue-raising initiatives—increased energy taxation under Trudeau and the goods and services (value-added) tax under Mulroney—while cutting back on transfers to the provinces.

Canadian Institutions and Conflict Management

Changing social conditions in Canada have undermined the ability of both majoritarian and majority-limiting mechanisms to manage conflict. This is especially true of language conflict. Institutions also matter, how-

---

58. On aboriginal concerns generally, see David C. Hawkes and Marina Devine, "Meech Lake and Elijah Harper: Native-State Relations in the 1990s," in Frances Abele, ed., *How Ottawa Spends, 1991–92: The Politics of Fragmentation* (Ottawa: Carleton University Press, 1991), pp. 33–62. On the Mohawk uprising, see Campbell and Pal, *Real Worlds of Canadian Politics*, 2d ed., pp. 267–345.

59. In the case of the Great Whale project, for example, the Cree have used the courts to force the federal government to intervene in their dispute with Quebec, which Ottawa would have preferred not to do.

ever: both majoritarian and nonmajoritarian institutional arrangements may interact with societal divisions in ways that reinforce social divisions and inhibit successful cleavage management. My concern in this section is both to provide an overview of Canadian political institutions and to show that they have posed a number of important limitations and risks for management of the critical divisions in Canadian society, especially conflict between Canada's center and periphery.

Canadian political institutions are a complex mixture of largely British arrangements that encourage majority rule and homegrown or American-inspired arrangements that limit it in various ways. Most of the formal institutional features of the Canadian federal government are clearly majoritarian in nature: the fusion of executive and legislative powers, single-member electoral districts, and a weak second chamber in the federal legislature. Canada's recurrent constitutional crises do not spring simply from a clash between a majoritarian institutional heritage and a complex, divided society, however. Some Canadian institutions are clearly nonmajoritarian: the provinces have extensive power, judicial review and the 1982 Charter of Rights serve as a growing arbitral check on legislative majorities, and Canada's constitution is formally one of the most difficult to amend of any Western democracy. Equally important, there are many informal mechanisms that are nonmajoritarian, most notably the extensive consociational-style bargaining among provincial representatives known as "executive federalism."

Electoral Rules and the Party System

Electoral rules exercise a critical influence both on whose views are represented and on the types of governments that are likely to be formed. Canada's use of single-member districts with plurality electoral rules for choosing members of the House of Commons tends, as in the United States, to produce a two-party system—at least in any given region.

These electoral rules have also exacerbated the effects of regional cleavages, however.[60] Until the 1984 federal election, the Progressive Conserva-

---

60. The classic statement of this argument is Alan C. Cairns, "The Electoral System and the Party System in Canada, 1921–1965," *Canadian Journal of Political Science*, vol. 1 (March 1968), pp. 55–80. For important qualifications of Cairns's argument, see Richard Johnston and Janet Ballantyne, "Geography and the Electoral System," *Canadian Journal of Political Science*, vol. 10 (December 1977), pp. 857–66; and Nelson Wiseman, "Cairns Revisited: The Electoral and Party System in Canada," in Paul W. Fox and Graham White, eds., *Politics: Canada*, 7th ed. (Toronto: McGraw-Hill Ryerson, 1991), pp. 265–74. For a counterargument stressing the incentives that a first-past-the-post system gives parties to accommodate regional demands, see John C. Courtney, "Reflections on Reforming the

tive party had been weak in Quebec throughout most of the twentieth century. Because the Conservative vote in Quebec was both small and spread fairly broadly across electoral districts in the province, the party's yield in seats has been far less than its share of the votes in the province. The same has been true for the Liberals in Western Canada since the 1950s.

The combination of plurality legislative elections and reliance on single-party cabinets (to be discussed further below) in turn has meant that one or more regions have been severely underrepresented in most recent Canadian governments (see table 1). During the long period of Liberal dominance under Prime Ministers Pearson and Trudeau from 1963 to 1984, MPs from Ontario and Quebec never constituted less than three-quarters of the government caucus. Westerners were consistently, and dramatically, underrepresented in these Liberal governments. This situation was reversed in the brief Progressive Conservative minority government of Joe Clark in 1979–80, which was dominated almost equally by westerners and Ontarians, while Quebecers were dramatically underrepresented in the government caucus. Because the Liberals were so rarely out of power in this twenty-year period, the Canadian electoral system significantly exacerbated western alienation from federal institutions. As a result of the disjunction between the West's increasing economic power, especially in energy, and its lack of electoral power in Ottawa, "the West . . . felt vulnerable and feared that its new-found wealth would be confiscated and its control over its rich resources stripped away."[61]

The Progressive Conservative government formed by Brian Mulroney after the 1984 election was the first regionally balanced federal government in Canada since the Diefenbaker government of 1958–62.[62] In fact, westerners were approximately equal in number to the Ontario and Quebec delegations in the government caucus. But this still meant that

---

Canadian Electoral System," *Canadian Public Administration*, vol. 23 (Fall 1980), pp. 427–57. For a review of recent reform proposals, see William P. Irvine, "A Review and Evaluation of Electoral System Reform Proposals," in Peter Aucoin, research coordinator, *Institutional Reforms for Representative Government* (University of Toronto Press, 1985), pp. 71–109.

61. Alan C. Cairns, "The Politics of Constitutional Renewal in Canada," in Cairns, ed., *Disruptions*, p. 75.

62. Regional balance is defined here as no region having less than half of the percentage of seats in the government caucus that it had in the House of Commons. The Trudeau Liberal government elected in 1968 came the closest to regional balance, but it heavily underrepresented the Atlantic provinces. It should be noted that although Quebecers were strongly represented numerically in Diefenbaker's 1958 government, they had limited influence. See Peter C. Newman, *Renegade in Power: The Diefenbaker Years* (Toronto: McClelland, 1963).

TABLE 1. Regional Representation in Canadian Government Caucus,
1945–88

Percent

Year and party in power[b]	Seats				Over- or underrepresentation[a]			
	West[c]	Ontario	Quebec	Atlantic[d]	West[c]	Ontario	Quebec	Atlantic[d]
1945 Liberal majority (125/245)	15.2	27.2	42.4	15.2	52.5	81.3	159.8	137.9
1949 Liberal majority (190/261)	22.6	29.5	34.7	13.2	83.2	92.7	124.2	101.0
1953 Liberal majority (170/265)	15.9	29.4	38.8	15.9	58.5	91.7	137.2	127.5
1957 Progressive Conservative minority (112/265)	18.8	54.5	8.0	18.8	69.0	169.8	28.4	150.6
1958 Progressive Conservative majority (208/265)	31.7	32.2	24.0	12.0	116.8	100.4	84.9	96.5
1962 Progressive Conservative minority (116/265)	42.2	30.2	12.1	15.5	155.5	94.1	42.6	124.6
1963 Liberal minority (129/265)	7.8	40.3	36.4	15.5	28.5	125.7	128.7	124.5
1965 Liberal minority (131/265)	6.9	38.9	42.7	11.5	25.3	121.4	151.0	92.0

they were outnumbered two-to-one by "central Canadians" together.
And despite important concessions to the West—notably repeal of the
Trudeau government's hated national energy program—there were important symbolic slights: Mulroney, like Trudeau, was a Quebecer; his
political agenda was dominated by consolidating the party's gains in that
province and winning Quebec's acceptance of the constitution through
the Meech Lake Accord; and he was perceived by westerners to favor
Quebec in awarding federal contracts.[63]

63. The most widely criticized example was the federal cabinet's 1986 decision to
award a maintenance contract for the CF-18 fighter plane to a Montreal-based firm rather
than one based in Manitoba's capital city of Winnipeg, despite the latter firm's lower bid.
See Campbell and Pal, *Real Worlds of Canadian Politics*, 1st ed. (1989), pp. 19–52.

TABLE 1 *(continued)*

Percent

	Seats				Over- or underrepresentation[a]			
Year and party in power[b]	West[c]	Ontario	Quebec	Atlantic[d]	West[c]	Ontario	Quebec	Atlantic[d]
1968 Liberal majority (155/264)	17.4	41.3	36.1	4.5	67.7	123.9	128.9	37.1
1972 Liberal minority (109/264)	6.4	33.0	51.4	9.2	24.2	99.1	183.6	76.0
1974 Liberal majority (141/264)	9.2	39.0	42.6	9.2	34.7	117.1	152.1	76.0
1979 Progressive Conservative minority (136/282)	44.1	41.9	1.5	13.2	161.5	124.3	5.6	116.8
1980 Liberal majority (147/282)	1.4	35.4	50.3	12.9	5.0	105.1	189.1	113.8
1984 Progressive Conservative majority (211/282)	28.9	31.8	27.5	11.8	101.9	94.3	103.4	104.4
1988 Progressive Conservative majority (169/295)	28.4	27.2	37.3	7.1	97.4	81.1	146.6	65.5

SOURCES: For 1945–65: Alan Frizzell, John H. Pammett, and Anthony Westell, *The Canadian General Election of 1988* (Ottawa: Carleton University Press, 1989), table A3, p. 135; for 1968–72: Richard M. Scammon, "Appendix: A Summary of Canadian General Election Results, 1968–1974," in Howard R. Penniman, ed., *Canada at the Polls: The General Election of 1974* (Washington: American Enterprise Institute for Public Policy Research, 1975), pp. 292–97; for 1974–88: Harold D. Clarke and others, *Absent Mandate: Interpreting Change in Canadian Elections*, 2d ed. (Toronto: Gage, 1991), table A2, p. 158.

a. Each region's share of seats in the governing party's caucus relative to its share of seats in the House of Commons. Figures over 100 percent indicate overrepresentation, and those under 100 percent indicate underrepresentation.

b. Numbers in parentheses are the number of seats the party in power held and the total seats in the caucus.

c. The provinces of Alberta, British Columbia, Manitoba, and Saskatchewan.

d. The provinces of New Brunswick, Newfoundland, Nova Scotia, and Prince Edward Island.

Strong regional cleavages have also limited another potential opportunity associated with single-member districts and plurality elections, their tendency to lead to single-party majority governments that are able to make difficult decisions and avoid stalemate. In regions where either the Liberals or Conservatives have ceased to be competitive, third parties have often risen up to challenge the regionally dominant national party, claiming that this dominant party is not really representative of regional interests.[64] Because the Canadian system rewards rather than punishes parties with a strong regional base, only thirteen of the twenty-one general elections in Canada since 1921 have produced single-party majorities.[65] From January 1962 through the end of 1991, there was a majority government only 72 percent of the time.

A Westminster-Style Parliamentary System

One of the most important Canadian institutions is its British system of parliamentary government in conjunction with single-member districts and plurality electoral rules. Instead of a separately elected chief executive, as in the United States, a government is formed by a party or parties in the legislature that can maintain the confidence of a majority in the House of Commons. If it fails to maintain that confidence, it must either call new elections or resign in favor of another group that might hope to win the confidence of a majority. Strong requirements for party discipline generally ensure that the parties vote as blocs on crucial issues. Requirements of cabinet solidarity—all members of the cabinet must support government policies even if they disagree with them—ensure that the government speaks with a single voice.

Canada deviates from the pure Westminster model in some important ways. Parliamentary supremacy is limited both by the British North America Act's grant of exclusive jurisdiction in some legislative areas to the provinces and—more recently—by the constitutionally embedded Charter of Rights and Freedoms. But on most matters, so long as the governing party in Ottawa has a majority (an important qualification to be examined further below) and maintains party discipline, the executive—the cabinet and the prime minister—will exercise a dominant influence in federal policymaking. Moreover, the cabinet has broad discretion to make many decisions through Order-in-Council (that is, by cabinet order) without any legislation at all. And most federal regulatory agencies' decisions are subject to ratification by the cabinet.

This concentration of power provides obvious opportunities to avoid the policy stalemates so common in the United States. A clear expression

64. The classic argument on this point is Maurice Pinard, *The Rise of a Third Party: A Study in Crisis Politics*, enlarged ed. (Montreal: McGill-Queen's University Press, 1975).

65. This effect tends to be cyclical: unless a regionally based party manages to gain significant success, notably by winning control of a provincial government as the Cooperative Commonwealth Federation did in Saskatchewan and Social Credit did in Alberta, it is likely to die out after a few elections.

of this occurred with the free trade debate in 1988. The Mulroney government had negotiated, and strongly endorsed, a free trade agreement with the United States before the election, while the opposition Liberals and New Democrats opposed it. With the anti–free trade vote divided among the two opposition parties, Mulroney's Progressive Conservatives were able to win 57 percent of the seats in the House of Commons with only 43 percent of the vote and implement the agreement.[66]

Some less obvious limitations and risks of Westminster institutions should also be noted, however. First, because power is centralized, accountability is centralized as well. The knowledge that most regulatory decisions can be reversed by the cabinet weakens the ability of regulatory agencies to function as arbitral bodies, shielding elected politicians from electoral pressures on regionally sensitive issues such as closure of rail branch lines in the Prairie provinces.[67] Whereas regulatory agencies in the United States are worried primarily about having their decisions survive judicial review, in Canada they must be worried about having them survive political review from a cabinet highly attuned to regional concerns (indeed, selected in part to be sensitive to them).[68]

A more important limitation of the Westminster system, however, is the inhibitions that it imposes on expression of regional interests—especially when those interests cross party lines. Because MPs in the

66. Of course, the majoritarian opportunities to avoid policy stalemate associated with a Westminster-style parliamentary system are likely to be realized only if one party is able to form a single-party majority government and thus be ensured of surviving its full term in office without falling victim to a vote of no confidence. As noted above, this has often not been true in Canada.

67. On the limited applicability of the American "independent regulatory authority" model to Canada, see G. Bruce Doern, "Regulatory Processes and Regulatory Agencies," in G. Bruce Doern and Peter Aucoin, eds., *Public Policy in Canada: Organization, Process, and Management* (Toronto: Macmillan, 1979), especially pp. 168–69. Canadian governments are not without opportunities to shirk accountability—referring controversial matters to nonpartisan royal commissions is a favorite technique—but even in these cases it is more difficult than in the United States simply to bury the reports if they make recommendations that the government disagrees with or finds politically inconvenient. Another common shirking technique is for the federal government to defer to provincial government action or vice versa. See Kathryn Harrison, "Federalism, Environmental Protection and Blame Avoidance," paper prepared for the 1991 annual meeting of the Canadian Political Science Association.

68. I am grateful to George Hoberg for this point. On the continuing importance of regional ministers in the cabinet and the distributional consequences, see Herman Bakvis, *Regional Ministers: Power and Influence in the Canadian Cabinet* (University of Toronto Press, 1991). For a historical perspective, see Frederick W. Gibson, ed., *Cabinet Formation and Bicultural Relations: Seven Case Studies*, vol. 6 of *Studies of the Royal Commission on Bilingualism and Biculturalism* (Ottawa: Information Canada, 1970).

governing party must support the government to keep it from falling, they cannot openly represent those interests if they clash with the party position.[69] Even though they may be vociferous spokespersons for regional interests in closed forums such as the party caucus or cabinet, their loyalty and legitimacy as defenders of their region is open to question—opening the door for other regional champions, notably provincial governments, to play the role.

Single-Party Cabinets

In Canada, as in most parliamentary systems, the cabinet is at least in theory the ultimate decisionmaking body. Cabinet formation in Canada is a complex balancing process of ensuring representation of provinces, language groups, religions, and even, within the two largest provinces (Ontario and Quebec), subregions, roughly in proportion to their share of the overall population.[70] As a broadly representative collective body, the Canadian cabinet is a logical forum for a consociational process of centralized bargaining across major social divides.

The ability of the cabinet to perform this function is weakened, however, by the tendency of the Canadian electoral system to produce tremendous underrepresentation for some regions in the caucus of the largest party in the House of Commons (table 1). Regional underrepresentation in the governing party caucus means that few MPs from that region are available to serve in the cabinet and underscores symbolically the apparent exclusion of the region from governmental power. There are several potential ways around this problem: cabinet members could be appointed from outside Parliament, oversized coalition governments could be used to ensure representation across regional lines, or members of the appointed Senate could be used to fill out the cabinet to ensure adequate regional representation. In Canada, only the last of these methods is used. Unlike cabinet ministers in some European systems, those in Canada are drawn exclusively from members of Parliament.[71] Perhaps the most interesting

69. Gibbins, *Regionalism*, chap. 3.
70. See W. A. Matheson, *The Prime Minister and the Cabinet* (Toronto: Methuen, 1976); and Richard J. Van Loon and Michael S. Whittington, *The Canadian Political System: Environment, Structure and Process*, 4th ed. (Toronto: McGraw-Hill Ryerson, 1987), pp. 440–45.
71. There are rare exceptions. Occasionally individuals will be brought into the cabinet from outside Parliament, but the expectation is that they will seek a seat as soon as one becomes available in a by-election, and resign if they lose the election.

constraint in the Canadian system is the complete absence of coalition governments at the federal level, even in periods of minority government. This is purely a matter of convention: the party that wins the most seats has almost invariably formed a minority government and relied on support from minor parties to stay in power, often in exchange for concessions on specific policies.[72]

Reliance on single-party cabinets adds to the already substantial symbolic barriers that party discipline and cabinet solidarity pose to using the cabinet as a consociational bargaining mechanism: because ministers from each region are required to defend the government's actions, they are likely to be seen as "sellouts" not truly representative of their region—especially if they are senators.

Another risk posed by the current norms and rules of cabinet formation is that the channeling of intense regional alienation in the West and Quebec into independent regional parties may lead to a weak minority government in Ottawa coincident with a constitutional crisis. Thus far this has not happened. Canadians' luck may be running out, however: the extraordinary unpopularity of the Mulroney government has fueled the growth of regional parties in both the West (the Reform) and Quebec (the Bloc Québécois) to compete with the three traditional parties— the Liberals, Progressive Conservatives, and New Democrats. It is quite possible that after the next election not only will no single party be able to form a majority government, but no two parties together may hold a majority. In such a situation, the inexperience of federal politicians at forming and governing in multiparty coalitions may be very costly indeed.

A Weak Second Chamber

Second chambers are a common feature of many federated or strongly divided societies. Often they provide extra representation for smaller political units—for example, small states in the United States. The Canadian Senate, the second chamber in Canada's federal Parliament, has very

---

72. Formal coalitions have taken place at the provincial level, notably in British Columbia and Manitoba. A federal Conservative-Liberal coalition was formed during World War I, although the Conservatives held a majority of seats in the House of Commons at the time. Prime Minister W. L. Mackenzie King did not resign after the 1925 election, even though the Conservatives won more seats. See Ian Stewart, "Of Customs and Coalitions: The Formation of Canadian Federal Parliamentary Alliances," *Canadian Journal of Political Science*, vol. 13 (September 1980), pp. 451–79, especially pp. 455, 467.

little in common with the American institution with which it shares a name. Canadian senators are appointed by the federal prime minister, rather than being elected, and serve until age seventy-five. The Senate was originally intended as a conservative check on the House of Commons (there is a property qualification for service) as well as a way to represent Canada's regions more equally.[73] In theory, the Senate adds arbitral, limited-government, and consociational elements to Canada's governing institutions (arbitral because the unelected senators need not cater to the whims of political majorities, limited-government because the Senate is an additional veto point for actions by the Commons,[74] and consociational because it makes more regional representatives available for the cabinet). In fact, it performs none of these roles very well. Lacking legitimacy because of their appointive status, senators have followed party discipline on matters of concern to their House of Commons counterparts when the Senate's partisan majority has been the same as that of the government. When its majority has differed from that of the Commons, the Senate has been reluctant to do more than delay (hoping to force some compromise) rather than simply turn down government initiatives. This reluctance is due to a fear that a defiance of the government would provide the catalyst that would finally give force to ever-present calls for the Senate's abolition or reform.[75] Thus the institution is neither perceived as above politics nor serves as an effective check on government.

73. Currently the constitution calls for a Senate of 104 members: 24 each from Ontario and Quebec, 24 from the Western provinces (6 each from British Columbia, Alberta, Saskatchewan, and Manitoba), 30 from the Atlantic provinces (10 each from New Brunswick and Nova Scotia, 6 from Newfoundland, and 4 from Prince Edward Island), and 1 each from the Yukon and Northwest Territories. In 1990 the Mulroney government named 8 additional senators, following the procedure in a never-before-used section of the British North America Act intended to break deadlocks between the Senate and House of Commons.

74. Since the 1982 constitutional reform, if the Senate does not ratify a constitutional amendment within 180 days after the House of Commons has done so, the House can bypass the Senate by passing another resolution of support.

75. There have been a few partial exceptions, but they ultimately confirmed the Senate's impotence. In 1988, for example, the Liberals used their majority in the Senate to delay consideration of the free trade agreement with the United States until after the general election. But after the Liberals lost the election in November, they did not attempt further delay even though they retained their majority in the Senate. In 1990, the Liberals, still with a slender majority in the Senate, blocked the government's proposed goods and services tax, revisions to the unemployment insurance program, and revisions to Canada's old age security (basic pension) program for several months. The impasse ended when Prime Minister Mulroney employed the authority noted in footnote 73 to name eight additional Progressive Conservative members to the Senate. Although Liberals protested

In recent years, the primary function of the Senate has been to supply cabinet ministers from regions where the governing party is weak, promoting at least the appearance of broad representation of interests. As noted earlier, however, the legitimacy of such ministers is highly suspect, and Senate appointments to the Cabinet underline the regional weakness of such governments. The importance of the limitations of the Canadian Senate should not be underestimated, given the concern of "outer Canadian" interests with increasing their representation in central institutions and the risk that electoral laws may prevent this from occurring in the House of Commons. Indeed, Roger Gibbins has argued that the major difference between regionalism in the United States and Canada is that equal representation of states in the U.S. Senate—along with weaker party lines, decentralization of power, and seniority systems in both U.S. chambers—has allowed regional tensions to take less divisive forms because legislators are freer to defend local interests. In turn, "the very effectiveness of territorial representation [in the United States] allowed the national government to prosper and expand."[76] The failure of the Canadian Senate to perform any of its potential conflict management roles very well has led to repeated calls, especially from the West, that it be replaced by a body that provides "elected, effective and equal" (or "triple E") representation for the provinces.[77]

Federalism

Federal arrangements provide an opportunity to limit central agendas and allow many decisions to be made by smaller, presumably more homogeneous, communities. Although the British North America Act of 1867 set up a federal system, it was a strongly centralizing document.[78] Policy areas were divided into those that were deemed to be of a national

---

this move, they were unable to prevent it. See the account in Campbell and Pal, *Real Worlds of Canadian Politics*, 2d ed., pp. 394–408.

76. Gibbins, *Regionalism*, p. 77.

77. In the 1970s, proposals for Senate reform focused more on the German *Bundesrat* model, in which members of the second chamber are appointed by and follow the instructions of provincial governments. A problem with such an approach is that it involves the provinces directly in—and gives them a potential veto over—decisionmaking in areas of exclusive federal jurisdiction. On Senate reform, see Donald V. Smiley and Ronald L. Watts, *Intrastate Federalism in Canada* (University of Toronto Press, 1985), chap. 7.

78. For a comprehensive history of the evolution of federalism in Canada, see Richard Simeon and Ian Robinson, *State, Society, and the Development of Canadian Federalism* (University of Toronto Press, 1990).

character and were to be under the jurisdiction of the federal government (for example, banking and currency, trade, interprovincial and international railways and shipping, bankruptcy and criminal law), and those of a "merely local or private nature in the province."[79] Nevertheless, the provinces did maintain ownership of natural resources and important powers over "property and civil rights" including, in the case of Quebec, its distinctive civil law. The provinces also held primary jurisdiction over education, although provincial autonomy to alter existing arrangements relating to denominational schools was restricted by the British North America Act, which gave Ottawa authority to enact remedial legislation on behalf of religious minorities who felt that their educational rights and privileges had been denied by provincial government action.[80] Unlike the American Constitution, the Canadian act gave residual authority to the federal government, which could "make laws for the peace, order, and good government of Canada" in all areas not explicitly reserved to the provinces.[81] In addition, the act gave the federal government enormously powerful tools, known as "reservation" and "disallowance," which would allow Ottawa either to prevent acts passed by the provincial legislatures from becoming law or to overturn them within a year once they had become law.[82]

Formal constitutional provisions inevitably contain ambiguities and are subject to a number of evolutionary forces. In Canada the central power was significantly eroded over the first seventy years of confederation. Decisions by the Judicial Committee of the British Privy Council— the final court of appeal for Canada until 1949—interpreted the "peace, order, and good government" clause of the British North America Act very narrowly, limiting the scope of federal action.[83] In addition, reservation and disallowance powers have fallen into disuse over the past fifty years.[84] There is today a near consensus that the nonuse of these powers

79. British North America Act, 1867, sec. 92. Section 95 placed immigration and agriculture under concurrent jurisdiction, so long as provincial statutes did not clash with federal ones.

80. British North America Act, 1867, sec. 93.

81. British North America Act, 1867, sec. 91.

82. On disallowance, see J. R. Mallory, *Social Credit and the Federal Power in Canada* (University of Toronto Press, 1954), chap. 2.

83. See Mallory, *Social Credit and the Federal Power in Canada*, chap. 3. See also Alan Cairns, "The Judicial Committee and Its Critics," *Canadian Journal of Political Science*, vol. 4 (September 1971), pp. 301–45.

84. Reservation and disallowance powers were used many times in the early years of confederation, not just to overturn provincial government actions that were outside their legal jurisdiction under the British North America Act, but also to prevent provincial

for such an extended period has created a binding convention that they are no longer legitimate.[85] Even if this were not the case, use of disallowance by the federal government against Quebec language legislation, for example, would clearly provide a huge boost to separatist sentiment in the province. Disputes between provincial governments and the federal government are now generally settled either by negotiation or through recourse to the courts.[86]

A number of developments since the end of World War II have both altered the operation of federalism and fostered calls—especially by the provinces—for further changes. After the war, the federal government increased use of its spending powers to create conditional grant programs in jurisdictions that were constitutionally the realm of the provinces, such as postsecondary education, health care, and income transfers. By 1960, however, a number of provincial governments became more assertive, seeking to exercise increased powers and increased tax resources to promote provincial interests.[87] This was especially the case in Quebec, where cultural as well as economic development concerns were critical. Some other provinces—but not all—also sought a revision of jurisdictions. In a number of important areas, provincial demands were accommodated by allowing provinces to opt out from federal programs—to run their own programs with compensation from Ottawa. In practice, only Quebec has taken this opportunity with most programs, retaining the facade of equal treatment of provinces while giving Quebec de facto special status.

There is no question that having subnational governments has significantly aided Canadian political stability by allowing policy diversity corresponding to the diversity in Canadian society and by allowing franco-

actions that clashed with important policy concerns of the federal government. For example, the federal government disallowed chartering of railways by the province of Manitoba that Ottawa felt would threaten federal policies and lead to a north-south rather than east-west flow of trade. On expansion of the terms of disallowance in the 1880s, see Vipond, "Constitutional Politics and the Legacy of the Provincial Rights Movement," pp. 275–88. Both of these powers were formally retained when Canada's constitution was reformed in 1982. In fact, however, the federal disallowance power has not been used since 1943 and reservation has been used only once (in 1961) since 1937.

85. See Andrew Heard, *Canadian Constitutional Conventions: The Marriage of Law and Politics* (Oxford University Press, 1991), p. 103.

86. See Mallory, *Social Credit and the Federal Power in Canada*, p. 22.

87. On this process of "province building," see Edwin R. Black and Alan C. Cairns, "A Different Perspective on Canadian Federalism," *Canadian Public Administration*, vol. 9 (1966), pp. 27–44; and R. A. Young, Philippe Faucher, and André Blais, "The Concept of Province-Building: A Critique," *Canadian Journal of Political Science*, vol. 17 (December 1984), pp. 783–818.

phones to take actions within Quebec to promote their language. In short, it has both increased minority representation in decisionmaking and helped to prevent stalemate. But it should also be noted that responsiveness to regional political majorities does carry with it risks of oppression—real or perceived—of minority rights, which may in turn may further exacerbate political cleavages. Certainly the actions of the anglophone provinces with respect to denominational schools had this effect in the nineteenth and early twentieth centuries, and the actions of recent Quebec governments with respect to provincial language laws have similarly increased anglophone hostility to Quebec both inside and outside the province. In addition, as David Elkins and Richard Simeon have noted, the current federal system has created a bias in the representation of political interests in Canada toward those with a strong territorial base: "The federal system . . . ensures that regional loyalties will be given effective political expression; other interests and cleavages are blurred, frustrated and denied a political base."[88]

Executive Federalism

One of the most important elements of the Canadian system of conflict management is not mentioned anywhere in its constitutional documents at all: negotiations between federal and provincial executives, in which either the "first ministers" or federal and provincial ministers responsible for a particular policy area meet together to work out policy change.[89] These negotiations have been the most important venue for constitutional reform proposals in Canada in recent years. There is, of course, virtually no parallel in the United States: meetings between the president and the governors are generally perfunctory occasions for speechmaking rather than serious legislating. Why is it different in Canada? One obvious difference is the small number of Canadian provinces: eleven officials can sit around a table and negotiate, fifty-one cannot. Another is the overwhelming centralization of legislative power that a parliamentary system gives Canadian political executives in comparison with their U.S.

88. David J. Elkins and Richard Simeon, *Small Worlds: Parties and Provinces in Canadian Political Life* (Toronto: Methuen, 1980), p. 293.

89. See Richard Simeon, *Federal-Provincial Diplomacy: The Making of Recent Policy in Canada* (University of Toronto Press, 1972). Both the Meech Lake Accord and the federal government's September 1991 constitutional proposals would entrench executive federalism in the constitution.

counterparts. The Canadian prime minister and provincial premiers generally can deliver legislative assent for their policy proposals, so long as their party has a legislative majority; American governors and the president have no such certainty and may in fact face hostile majorities in one or both chambers of their legislatures. Finally, as noted earlier, because party discipline and cabinet solidarity in the federal Parliament deny federal MPs full leeway to act—and equally important, to be seen to act—as provincial spokespersons, provincial governments have greater legitimacy as spokespersons for regional interests.[90]

But what effects has this mechanism had on management of political conflict in Canada? Executive federalism certainly provides an important opportunity to prevent stalemate through a centralized, consociational bargaining process, especially if it is conducted in a low-profile setting among officials who have common perceptions of sectoral problems. But executive federalism also poses risks. One that clearly has been realized as a result of the high-profile environment of federal-provincial first ministers' conferences is the elevation of provincial leaders' stature as spokesmen for regional interests. Indeed, "in the absence of effective regional voices in Ottawa, provincial Premiers have increasingly assumed the role of spokespeople not only on the provincial matters for which they were elected but on federal affairs."[91] Moreover, they have had strong incentives to take intransigent positions for fear of being criticized by the opposition parties at home, and hence to create stalemate. This is particularly true, Stefan Dupré has argued, when they are dealing with constitutional issues which, "being symbolic and abstract rather than tangible and quantifiable, are not amenable to readily measurable trade-offs."[92] Moreover, the growth of executive federalism has undercut further the already tenuous legitimacy of the federal cabinet as the primary locus of consociational bargaining. Finally, executive federalism has an important limitation: interests that do not have the federal government or one of the provincial governments as a strong advocate are likely to be ignored. Indeed, native peoples and women's groups have become

90. On this point, see Donald V. Smiley, *The Federal Condition in Canada* (Toronto: McGraw-Hill Ryerson, 1987), p. 85.

91. Tom Kent, *Getting Ready for 1999: Ideas for Canada's Politics and Government* (Halifax: Institute for Research on Public Policy, 1989), p. 41.

92. J. Stefan Dupré, "The Workability of Executive Federalism in Canada," in Herman Bakvis and William M. Chandler, eds., *Federalism and the Role of the State* (University of Toronto Press, 1987), p. 248.

alienated from the constitutional reform process in Canada because they do not feel that their interests are adequately represented.[93]

Courts and the Charter

Constitutionally entrenched rights and an independent judiciary are both important mechanisms for limiting majority rule. Entrenched rights are a limited-government mechanism: they may forbid or limit some actions by government, mandate others, and keep some issues off the agenda entirely. An independent judiciary is an arbitral mechanism: its members do not have to be responsive to political majorities to maintain their jobs. In practice, of course, the two are closely intertwined: the scope of judges' actions is determined in part by the scope given them by an entrenched bill of rights.

Canada and the United States differ both in the nature of their judiciary and in the nature of constitutionally entrenched rights. Canada's Supreme Court is not entrenched in the constitution but is rather a creature of parliamentary legislation (indeed, the Supreme Court was not even the final court of appeals for Canada until appeals to the Judicial Committee of the British Privy Council were abolished in 1949). It is thus at least theoretically possible (albeit highly unlikely) that a federal government could "circumvent adverse constitutional rulings of the Court simply by altering its composition, removing its jurisdiction or even abolishing the Court."[94] Second, members of both the federal and the upper provincial judiciaries in Canada are appointed and paid by the federal government. Canada's Supreme Court Act requires that three members of the federal Supreme Court be members of the Quebec bar, primarily to ensure that the Court has adequate expertise in Quebec's civil law tradition rather than as a mechanism for regional representation per se. While appointments to the federal Supreme Court in fact show efforts to achieve regional balance, critics at the provincial level have often argued that the federal government's monopoly on judicial appointments, especially to the Supreme Court, is inconsistent at least with the perception, if not the reality, of judicial neutrality in conflicts between the federal government and the provinces; one commentator likened it to "a hockey game where one

93. See Michael D. Behiels, ed., *The Meech Lake Primer: Conflicting Views of the 1987 Constitutional Accord* (University of Ottawa Press, 1989), chaps. 7, 10.

94. Peter H. Russell, "Constitutional Reform of the Judicial Branch: Symbolic vs. Operational Considerations," *Canadian Journal of Political Science*, vol. 17 (June 1984), pp. 227–52, quote on p. 231.

team brings its own referees."[95] Thus increasing the Court's regional representativeness by providing for some provincial role in Supreme Court nominations has been a frequent element in recent rounds of constitutional proposals.[96]

Another important difference between the two countries is that Canada lacked a constitutionally entrenched Charter of Rights until 1982.[97] In the United States, the courts have long acted as a defender of individual rights against oppressive action by government, overturning some government actions as unconstitutional. In Canada, as in most parliamentary systems, the courts have tended to be very deferential to Parliament. Moreover, rights issues in Canada have historically focused more on collective rights of religious and language minorities than in the United States. The British North America Act assigned responsibility for the historically most important manifestation of these issues—denominational schools—to the federal cabinet (through its powers to disallow provincial legislation and propose remedial legislation) rather than the courts.[98] Thus Canadian courts have tended to limit government action primarily on the grounds that federal actions intruded on areas that were properly the jurisdiction of the provinces under the British North America Act or vice versa.

The entrenchment of a fundamental Charter of Rights and Freedoms in the Canadian constitution in 1982 dramatically increased the importance of Canada's courts both as policymakers and as managers of social conflict. But the federal and provincial governments hedged the charter in several important ways. The first section declares that all the enumerated rights are "subject only to such reasonable limits prescribed by law as can be demonstrably justified in a free and democratic society"—a potentially large loophole in a country where the courts have traditionally

95. Peter McCormick, "The Courts: Toward a Provincial Role in Judicial Appointments," in Gibbins and others, eds., *Meech Lake and Canada*, p. 45. For evidence suggesting that the Supreme Court has not been biased toward the federal government, see P. W. Hogg, "Is the Supreme Court Biased in Constitutional Cases?" *Canadian Bar Review*, vol. 57 (December 1979), pp. 721–39.

96. See the discussion in Russell, "Constitutional Reform of the Judicial Branch." On regional and linguistic representation on the Supreme Court, see Clare F. Beckton and A. Wayne MacKay, research coordinators, *The Courts and the Charter* (University of Toronto Press, 1985); and Peter H. Russell, *The Supreme Court of Canada as a Bilingual and Bicultural Institution* (Ottawa: Queen's Printer, 1969).

97. A bill of rights was passed by Parliament in 1960, but it was not entrenched in the constitution and thus could be altered by later federal legislation. Moreover, it applied only to actions by the federal government, not to those by provincial governments.

98. Simeon and Robinson, *State, Society, and the Development of Canadian Federalism*, p. 26.

been deferential to Parliament. In addition, both the federal Parliament and the provincial governments retained the right to pass legislation contravening many basic rights, "notwithstanding a provision . . . of this Charter," by a simple majority vote of their legislatures. (Any such use of this notwithstanding clause would expire unless renewed after five years.) However, some charter rights were exempt from the notwithstanding clause, notably official language rights in dealing with the federal government and the government of New Brunswick, minority language rights in education, voting rights, and mobility rights.[99]

The record of the charter and the courts in managing societal conflict has been quite mixed and has involved some especially clear trade-offs. The courts have been reasonably effective in protecting minority rights, insofar as it is in their power to do so, but court decisions have not definitively settled policy disputes. The Quebec provincial government has repeatedly—and under the Parti Québécois, routinely—invoked the "notwithstanding clause" to thwart actual or potential challenges under the charter. Nor has the charter fulfilled the Trudeau government's hope that it would be a unifying device—that a Canadian national identity based in part on charter rights (especially minority language rights) would supplant regional identities, especially in Quebec.[100] The effect of the charter on Canadians' identities has been confined largely to English Canada, and the charter has served as a flashpoint for linguistic conflict.[101] Supreme Court decisions challenging Quebec language legislation (most charter cases overturning provincial legislation have been aimed at Quebec) have undermined the legitimacy of the charter in Quebec and forced political elites to openly choose between its legitimacy and the collective aspirations of francophones in Quebec.[102] In addition, the charter has

99. Some of the Constitution Act's minority language guarantees do not come into effect until ratified by the Quebec National Assembly. See Constitution Act, 1982, especially secs. 23, 33, 59.

100. On this point, see Peter H. Russell, "The Political Purposes of the Canadian Charter of Rights and Freedoms," *Canadian Bar Review*, vol. 30 (March 1983), pp. 30–68.

101. See Kenneth McRoberts, *English Canada and Quebec: Avoiding the Issue* (York University, Robarts Centre for Canadian Studies, 1991).

102. On the Court's record, see F. L. Morton, Peter H. Russell, and Michael J. Withey, "The Supreme Court's First One-Hundred Charter of Rights Decisions: A Statistical Analysis," *Osgoode Hall Law Journal* (forthcoming); an abbreviated version appears in Fox and White, eds., *Politics: Canada*, pp. 59–79. The delegitimization of the charter in Quebec should not be overstated. As Charles Taylor has noted, "The Charter was favourably seen [by Quebecers] until it came to be perceived as an instrument for the

given rise to notions of individualism, popular sovereignty, and constitutionally recognized group rights (for women, aboriginals, language minorities, multicultural groups, and the disabled), expanding both the cast of participants demanding a role in policymaking and the policy agenda.[103] Thus the charter has called into question the legitimacy and feasibility of executive federalism as a mechanism for consociational bargaining, much as executive federalism earlier undercut the cabinet as a consociational mechanism—but this time, nothing was left in its place. This has special implications, as will be discussed below, for constitutional reform.

A Constitutional Amending Formula

Stringent constitutional amending formulas are one of the most obvious limited-government mechanisms for protecting minorities. They may prevent majorities from changing either fundamental rights or representative institutions in ways that are harmful to minority interests. But such protections are not without costs, for they may also allow "minorities of the majority" to prevent changes intended to address minority concerns and simply prolong stalemate on important national concerns.

Perhaps the simplest thing that can be said about the history of Canada's constitutional amending formula is that it went from unwritten to unwieldy without ever passing through understandable. No formal amending formula was included in the British North America Act; it was simply assumed in 1867 that the Canadian government would petition the British Parliament for any needed changes. Several amendments were made by this procedure in the nineteenth and early twentieth centuries, using varying degrees of consultation with and approval by the provincial governments.[104] A limited amending formula giving the federal Parliament exclusive jurisdiction was adopted in 1949, but it was drawn so narrowly, and with so many explicit exclusions, that it had little practical effect.[105]

---

advancement of the uniformity of language regimes across the country. Even now its other provisions are widely popular." Taylor, "Shared and Divergent Values," in Ronald L. Watts and Douglas M. Brown, eds. *Options for a New Canada* (University of Toronto Press, 1991), p. 59.

103. See especially Cairns, "Constitutional Minoritarianism in Canada."

104. See Stevenson, *Unfulfilled Union*, p. 238.

105. This amending procedure—sec. 91(1) of the British North America Act—has been used to change the distribution of seats in the House of Commons, largely in response to population shifts, and to make minor changes in the Senate—adding a mandatory retirement age and adding single seats for the Northwest Territories and the Yukon. In 1980, the

A convention emerged that most important amendments, especially those involving changes in the distribution of jurisdictions between the federal government and the provinces, required unanimous consent of those governments.

The amending formula finally enacted in the 1982 Constitution Act—after prolonged wrangling that will be discussed below—is notable both for its complexity and for its loopholes. Rather than a single amending formula as in the United States,[106] Canada has four distinct formulas that are a complex hybrid of delegatory, consociational, and limited-government principles. The main amending formula requires the approval of the House of Commons, the Senate, and the legislatures of two-thirds of the provinces containing at least 50 percent of Canada's population. (Because this formula currently requires the approval of seven provinces, it is known as the "7/50" rule.) This formula applies specifically to the major organizing principles and powers of the House of Commons and Senate, among other subjects. But there are several important loopholes to amendments made under this provision. If an amendment limits provincial powers, provincial legislatures that have not approved the amendment may opt out by passing a resolution of dissent. Moreover, provinces that choose to opt out are to receive compensation from Ottawa if such an amendment transfers power over language and culture from the provinces to Ottawa.[107]

Three other amending formulas can also be found in the 1982 Constitution Act, however. Some constitutional revisions—including those affecting the offices of the queen, governor general and provincial lieutenant governors, the use of English and French, the composition of the Supreme Court, and the various amending formulas themselves—require the consent of all of the provincial legislatures as well as of Parliament. Second, constitutional amendments that apply only to a subset of provinces (entrenching language rights in a specific province, for example) require the approval only of Parliament and the affected provinces. Finally, the Constitution Act says that Parliament alone may amend the constitution

---

Supreme Court of Canada issued a ruling confirming that amendments made under sec. 91(1) could not alter the "essential characteristics" of federal institutions. See Peter H. Russell, Rainer Knopff, and Ted Morton, *Federalism and the Charter: Leading Constitutional Decisions*, new ed. (Ottawa: Carleton University Press, 1989), pp. 693–705.

106. The U.S. Constitution does provide for a constitutional convention as an alternative mechanism for constitutional amendment, but it does not apply to a distinctive category of subjects, as the Canadian formulas do. Moreover, the constitutional convention device has never been used.

107. Constitution Act, 1982, secs. 38(3), 40.

"in relation to the executive government of Canada or the Senate and House of Commons, except where otherwise limited." In fact, the limits placed by other sections of the Constitution are so sweeping that there is little of importance that can occur under this section. Most of the critical and controversial decisions are made under the unanimity or 7/50 rules.

Both the unwritten amending formula in effect before 1982 and the current formula have posed important risks for the central tasks of fostering political resolution of conflicts and giving political leaders incentives to affirm in word and deed the existing institutional order. Before 1982, the presumed requirement of provincial government unanimity for amendment not only fostered policy stalemate and inaction, it also placed enormous pressures on provincial politicians not to consent to any amendments that could be seen as sacrificing provincial interests—including preservation of the unanimity rule as a bargaining lever. Such concerns twice led premiers of Quebec to back away from deals for an amending formula for Canada's constitution after they had tentatively given their assent. Equally important, the unwritten nature of the unanimity provision both meant that it was subject to challenge and created incentives for an aggressive federal government to ignore it. When the Trudeau government did so in 1980–82, the predictable results were that the legitimacy of resulting amendments was open to question, and there were strong electoral incentives for politicians in the excluded provinces to take the lead in questioning the legitimacy of the federal initiative—if only to preempt rival politicians from doing so.

The 1982 Constitution Act altered the incentives and constraints influencing constitutional reform in Canada in two important ways that were not fully appreciated at the time. First, the new amending formulas required that agreements must be approved by provincial legislative assemblies. This new system created additional veto points and lengthened the ratification process, giving opponents time to mobilize. The new procedure is of little consequence, and a relatively closed consociational bargaining process between the eleven "first ministers" can be preserved, so long as premiers have strong control over their assemblies. But if they do not have a legislative majority, or feel electorally threatened, or are defeated during the ratification process, a painstakingly negotiated compromise can fail. (Nor does the Canadian electoral system provide a biennial "window" immediately after elections in which politically dangerous negotiations can be conducted, since each of the eleven governments is on its own electoral cycle rather than clustering most elections, as the United States does.) The new amendment process also provided an opening for groups and individuals motivated by a second critical change in the 1982 constitutional reform: the new Charter of Rights. The charter led many Canadians—the "new voices" such as aboriginals and language minorities, in particular, but many English Canadians more broadly—to view the constitution as "the people's document," which should not be subject to ratification by the prime minister and ten provincial premiers without any popular input.[108] The danger, of course, is that increased popular involvement will both lead to stalemate and heighten the salience of cleavages that might otherwise be muted by elite cooperation.

Restructuring Institutions

Political institutions evolve constantly, albeit informally, in response to changing societal demands. Sometimes these changes are embodied in widely held conventions about which political actions are permissible, regardless of what formal constitutions may say. This was the case when the federal government's power of disallowance became illegitimate through disuse.

Formal restructuring of institutional relationships through constitutional amendment is a much less frequent phenomenon. In Canada, only the 1980–82 round of constitutional negotiation has actually resulted in substantial constitutional change in the past forty years, despite persistent and widespread complaints about the functioning of various institutions. When reform has taken place, moreover, it has simply led to new grievances, stimulating demands for additional rounds of reform to address these grievances.[109]

108. See Alan C. Cairns, "Citizens (Outsiders) and Governments (Insiders) in Constitution-Making: The Case of Meech Lake," in Cairns, *Disruptions*, pp. 108–38; and Russell, "Can the Canadians Be a Sovereign People?"

109. The literature on constitutional reform in Canada is immense. An overview of the negotiations from the Trudeau period through the failure of the Meech Lake Accord can be found in David Milne, *The Canadian Constitution: The Players and the Issues in the Process that Has Led from Patriation to Meech Lake to an Uncertain Future*, 2d ed. (Toronto: James Lorimer, 1991). Clarkson and McCall, *Trudeau and our Times*, vol. 1, focuses on the Trudeau period; see also Roy Romanow, John Whyte, and Howard Leeson, *Canada . . . . Notwithstanding: The Making of the Constitution, 1976–1982* (Toronto: Carswell/Methuen, 1984); Robert Sheppard and Michael Valpy, *The National Deal: The Fight for a Canadian Constitution* (Toronto: Fleet Books, 1982); and Keith Banting and Richard Simeon, eds., *And No One Cheered: Federalism, Democracy and the Constitution Act* (Toronto: Methuen, 1983). The Meech Lake period is discussed in Patrick J. Monahan, *Meech Lake: The Inside Story* (University of Toronto Press, 1991); Andrew Cohen, *A Deal Undone: The Making and Breaking of the Meech Lake Accord* (Vancouver: Douglas

Constraints and Strategies

Constitutional reform efforts in Canada have been hindered by incompatible views among the participants over which conflict management tasks need to be addressed (for example, broadening representation or protecting minorities) and the institutional changes that need to be made. Individual politicians have brought their own agendas to bear, and strategic considerations have also led to shifting agendas and preferences.[110] But three conflicting reform agendas have dominated recent rounds of policymaking: a devolutionist agenda from Quebec, a western agenda focusing on the reform of central institutions, and a rights-oriented agenda sponsored by the Trudeau government.

Quebec governments have stressed the need to protect the collective survival of the francophone minority and have argued that Quebec is the only viable vehicle for that survival. They have sought devolution of powers to themselves, as well as a symbolic recognition of the province's special status within Canada, and have resisted reforms that would inhibit their ability to negotiate bilateral agreements with Ottawa or weaken their influence (assumed to be a veto before the 1982 Constitution Act) over the reform of federal institutions.

The western provinces originally had little interest in constitutional reform, but their apparent exclusion from power and resource jurisdiction battles with Ottawa during the Trudeau years led to increased concern both for greater western representation within central institutions (especially through Senate reform) and continued and expanded control over their natural resources. Other "division of powers" issues and language policies had a much lower priority.[111] At the same time, they have resisted

---

and McIntyre, 1990); and Pierre Fournier, *A Meech Lake Post-Mortem: Is Quebec Sovereignty Inevitable?* trans. Sheila Fischman (Montreal: McGill-Queen's University Press, 1991). See also the overview by Richard Simeon, "Why Did the Meech Lake Accord Fail?" in Watts and Brown, eds., *Canada: The State of the Federation 1990*, pp. 15–40. For a discussion of constitutional negotiations focusing on the role and aspirations of Quebec, see Alain-G. Gagnon and Mary Beth Montcalm, *Quebec: Beyond the Quiet Revolution* (Scarborough, Ont.: Nelson Canada, 1990), chaps. 6, 7.

110. For example, Prime Minister Trudeau shifted from opposing constitutional reform to supporting unilateral initiative in 1980-81, while Premier Lévesque "was reduced to a pragmatic and tactical defense of the existing constitution" in response to the defeat of the 1980 referendum and Trudeau's constitutional initiative. Cairns, "Politics of Constitutional Renewal in Canada," p. 67.

111. See Roger Gibbins, "Constitutional Politics and the West," in Banting and Simeon, eds., *And No One Cheered*, pp. 119–32.

special status and other measures that are perceived at home as pandering to Quebec or diminishing their own relative status.[112]

Ottawa's constitutional agenda during the period that Pierre Trudeau exercised dominant influence—as justice minister in 1967 and as prime minister beginning in 1968—was profoundly hostile both to Quebec's aspirations for special status and to general provincial demands for increased powers. Its focus was on the protection of individual and minority rights through a federal Charter of Rights. This was supposed to increase citizens' identities as Canadians and their identification with federal institutions, but most provincial governments saw it as an infringement on their power. Other actors brought additional issues to the bargaining table. Governments in the economically dependent Atlantic region have sought above all to ensure that Ottawa would be strong enough to transfer resources to the poorer provinces. Ontario, for very different reasons flowing from its status as Canada's economic center, also generally sought to preserve federal power. Of course, the terms under which amendments would be allowed—and the consequent leverage that would be provided—were an issue of concern to all parties, but with very different interests.

Canada's constitutional amending rules have been an additional constraint on constitutional reform. Constitutions are rarely written on a clean slate, and powerful interests with a vested interest in preventing change usually grow up around existing institutions. In the case of Canada, high barriers for approval of amendments tend to hamper change, especially for the most contentious amendments, which have the stiffest rules for adoption.

The combination of conflicting objectives and an amending process that makes it difficult to impose losses on any of the eleven participating governments creates strategic dilemmas for would-be constitutional reformers. Few, if any, proposed reforms in Canada are "Pareto optimal" (that is, few make at least some participants better off without making any worse off).

A package that responds to the agendas of only one or two governments is unlikely to be adopted because other participants have both the incentives and the means to block it. One way around this problem is to adopt a sequential approach, combining a relatively simple agenda with a promise that other demands will be addressed in future rounds of

112. See Monahan, *Meech Lake*, p. 52.

negotiations. This approach faces two problems: first, it may not be seen as a credible promise, given the high hurdles to adoption of constitutional proposals and the uncertain status of the politicians making the commitments (since they are subject to being thrown out by their own electorate); second, it may not be adequate for these politicians' publics. A third strategy is to develop proposals giving all important participants a stake in provisions that they very much want, so that they will be willing to accept things that they do not like but feel are less important than the things they do want. As reform proposals become more complex, however, more provisions must be included that are likely to be perceived as undesirable by some participants. Politicians may have electoral incentives to reject proposals even if they believe the proposals offer more gains than losses to their constituents. The reason is that constituents tend to be more sensitive to losses than to gains. Politicians in turn tend to view avoidance of blame as the safest position.[113]

Each of these three strategies has been tried in recent rounds of constitutional negotiations: the limited agenda several times by the Trudeau government, a sequential strategy by the Mulroney government with the Meech Lake Accord, and complex proposals in the current round of negotiations. In each case, the problems with the strategy quickly became apparent.

The 1980–82 Round

Throughout the 1960s and 1970s, intermittent constitutional negotiations repeatedly foundered on participants' conflicting interests and agendas.[114] That the impasse over constitutional reform was finally broken in the early 1980s reflects both the personal importance placed on the issue by Prime Minister Trudeau and his willingness to exploit ambiguities and break with consensual norms. After the Liberals lost the 1979 general election, Trudeau had already resigned as party leader when Liberal strategists engineered the defeat of Joe Clark's minority Progressive Conservative government on a motion of nonconfidence in the House of Commons. Threatened with running a general election and a divisive party leadership campaign simultaneously, Trudeau was prevailed upon to rescind his resignation, and when the Liberals won the ensuing election

---

113. See R. Kent Weaver, "The Politics of Blame Avoidance," *Journal of Public Policy*, vol. 6 (October–December 1986), pp. 371–98.
114. See Simeon, *Federal-Provincial Diplomacy*, chap. 5.

in February 1980, constitutional reform was made one of the new government's top priorities. An additional impetus to reform was Trudeau's pledge just before the Quebec referendum, a scant three months after his reelection, that negotiations on reformed federalism would occur if Quebecers rejected the Quebec government's sovereignty-association proposal.

Putting constitutional reform on the agenda and securing agreement on a reform package are two very different matters, however. Here the new Trudeau government faced not only the traditional difficulty of securing agreement from provinces with very different agendas and interests, but the special problem of the Parti Québécois government in Quebec. Even in the unlikely event that an accommodation could be reached between the positions of Pierre Trudeau and René Lévesque, there were few incentives for the PQ to reach a constitutional agreement. Consent by the Quebec government to a constitutional reform package would run counter to the party's position that no satisfactory renewal of federalism was possible. Consent might also undercut support in Quebec for sovereignty. It would, moreover, lead to charges of a sellout by hard-line factions in the party. On the other hand, given the PQ's precarious political position after the referendum defeat, they did not want to be seen as bargaining in bad faith.[115]

In this round, the Trudeau government had the political will to proceed unilaterally—that is, to ask the British Parliament for approval of a reform package without provincial consensus. Given the Trudeau government's emphasis on strengthening pan-Canadian identity as an alternative to Quebec nationalism, it is not surprising that patriation of the constitution (that is, ending the vestigial role of the British Parliament in the constitutional amendment process) and addition of a Charter of Rights were the centerpieces of the proposal. While unilateral action clearly was not Ottawa's preferred course of action, it was useful both as a stick to encourage the provinces to cooperate rather than be excluded from decisionmaking and as an ultimate weapon if those negotiations did not produce results to the liking of the Trudeau government. In using this strategy, the federal government was buoyed by opinion polls showing that the Charter of Rights and patriation enjoyed very broad popular support.

Quebec, on the other hand, sought to build a common front of the provincial premiers in opposition to Ottawa's proposals in order to de-

---

115. See Sheppard and Valpy, *The National Deal*, p. 47.

prive the federal government of legitimacy for its package. This would make unilateral reform politically unfeasible even if it was not, strictly speaking, unconstitutional. For quite a while, it appeared that at least the first part of Quebec's strategy (a common provincial front) was in fact working. Through the fall of 1981, Quebec and seven anglophone provinces remained together in opposing constitutional proposals put forward by Ottawa, and they developed an alternative proposal of their own. Only Ontario and New Brunswick sided with Ottawa. But the federal government refused to back down; instead it announced that it would proceed to London with a request for approval of its package without provincial consent. The provinces promptly challenged the move in provincial courts. Two provincial appeals courts (Quebec and Manitoba) backed Ottawa, while Newfoundland's court ruled that provincial consent was indeed required. All were appealed to the Supreme Court.

The decision ultimately announced by the Court was decidedly mixed. The justices ruled by a six-to-three margin that there was a convention requiring "substantial" provincial consent to constitutional amendments affecting their powers, but they also declared by a seven-to-two margin that this convention was not legally binding. Thus Ottawa could proceed alone with its package, but its actions would be highly suspect, giving ammunition to opponents of the package who hoped to block it in the British Parliament. But since the justices did not say that unanimous provincial consent was required, the Trudeau government had substantial leverage to break up the provincial coalition: those that agreed to support Ottawa might win approval for measures that their governments favored. And that is indeed what happened: on the night of November 4, 1981, the federal government and the nine predominantly anglophone provinces negotiated an agreement that was subsequently enacted as the Constitution Act of 1982.

The central thrusts of the Constitution Act were a strengthening of individual and minority rights vis-à-vis governments at all levels through the charter and a strengthening of *federal* arbitral institutions (the courts) plus addition of an "all-Canadian" set of amending formulas. While approval of the Constitution Act was regarded as a victory for the federal government, it should be noted that each of these provisions also incorporated important "provincializing" qualities in order to gain "substantial" provincial assent. The Charter of Rights and Freedoms was made subject to provincial override through the notwithstanding clause, while the multitiered amending formula guaranteed and institutionalized a provincial role in constitutional amendments and gave them a limited opt-out option for amendments they did not like.[116] The act also clarified provincial jurisdiction over natural resources and energy in a detail that is sometimes amusing: Canada is probably the only country in the world that has embedded in its constitution the rule that management and taxation of "sawlogs, poles, lumber, wood chips, sawdust or any other primary wood product, or wood pulp" are under provincial jurisdiction.[117]

The revised constitution is, however, also notable for what it did not include. There was no veto for Quebec over most constitutional amendments. The constitutional package neither transferred to provincial jurisdiction any of the powers sought by the Quebec government nor recognized symbolically any special status for Quebec.[118]

Thus the "renewed federalism" that had been promised at the time of the Quebec referendum turned out to exclude not only the Lévesque government, but also goals widely shared by Quebec elites. The Quebec government responded by challenging the constitutionality of this agreement in the courts (it lost),[119] and by passing a blanket exemption of its statutes under the charter's notwithstanding clause and applying the clause to all new provincial legislation.

The Meech Lake Accord

Clearly this situation was not tenable in the long run, and both the federal Progressive Conservative government elected in 1984 and the Quebec Liberals who defeated the Parti Québécois in the 1985 provincial election were determined to change it. The new Quebec provincial government headed by Robert Bourassa set forth five conditions that would be needed for Quebec to agree to a constitutional accord: a constitutional recognition of Quebec's status as a "distinct society"; constitutionalization of Quebec's preeminence in controlling immigration to the province

116. In addition, the final set of amending formulas did not include the option originally proposed by the Trudeau government of allowing the federal government to call a national referendum on an amendment if Ottawa and the provinces could not come to an agreement. See Clarkson and McCall, *Trudeau and Our Times*, vol. 1, p. 294; and Cairns, "Citizens (Outsiders) and Governments (Insiders)," p. 110.

117. Constitution Act, 1982, secs. 50, 51.

118. Simeon,"Why Did the Meech Lake Accord Fail?" p. 18.

119. The Quebec government argued that its approval was required on the basis of Quebec's status as the principal home of one of Canada's two linguistic groups. For the Supreme Court decision, see Russell and others, *Federalism and the Charter*, pp. 760–70.

(already being exercised under a federal-provincial agreement); restrictions on federal spending in areas of provincial jurisdiction; a Quebec veto over constitutional amendments involving changes to federal institutions (for example, the Supreme Court or the Senate) and extension of Quebec's right to opt out with compensation from amendments transferring jurisdiction from the provinces to Ottawa; and Quebec participation in naming some Supreme Court of Canada judges.[120] These conditions became the basis for the accord reached by the federal prime minister and ten provincial premiers at Meech Lake at the end of April 1987 and embodied in a detailed amendment proposal in June of that year.

Although the Quebec government had sought to have the "Meech Lake round" focus on Quebec's concerns, a few measures were included in the final accord to respond to the grievances of other provinces, notably a provision giving the provinces authority to nominate people to fill new Senate vacancies until comprehensive Senate reform could be initiated.[121] In addition, Quebec's province-specific demands were generalized to the other provinces to preserve the principle (especially cherished in the West) of equal treatment of all provinces: thus they all, for example, could negotiate immigration agreements with the federal government, all were to have a veto over constitutional amendments affecting the Supreme Court and the Senate, and all were to participate in the nomination of Supreme Court justices.

Two features of the accord are noteworthy for this analysis. First, unlike the 1982 Constitution Act, which focused on arbitral and limited-government mechanisms to guarantee individual liberties, the Meech Lake Accord lacked an overall institutional theme. Instead, a variety of mechanisms were used. Additional power was delegated to the provinces in controlling immigration. Limited-government guarantees were strengthened by increasing the hurdles to constitutional amendment and use of federal spending powers and potentially weakened through the "distinct-

---

120. See Gil Rémillard, "Quebec's Quest for Survival and Equality via the Meech Lake Accord," in Behiels, ed., *The Meech Lake Primer*, pp. 28–42; and Monahan, *Meech Lake*, chap. 3. Under section 40 of the 1982 Constitution Act, provinces that choose to opt out from constitutional amendments transferring jurisdiction from the provinces to the federal government can obtain financial compensation from Ottawa only for amendments affecting "education or other cultural matters." The Meech Lake Accord would have extended this to all such transfers.

121. Because the Meech Lake Accord also made Senate reform subject to the unanimity amending rule, the prospects were high that the provinces would retain their power to appoint senators (subject to cabinet approval of provincial nominees).

society" clause.[122] Additional regional input was given to the appointment of an arbitral institution, the Supreme Court. The theme of Meech Lake was rather a substantive one, gaining Quebec's acceptance of the constitution. Second, there was a tremendous disjunction between the way the Meech Lake Accord was negotiated and the way that it was to be ratified. The negotiation was a classic example of executive federalism, essentially limited to the eleven first ministers and their closest aides. But ratification of the accord was to be the first test of the new amending formula under the 1982 Constitution Act, with its clear requirement for provincial unanimity in some areas (including the changes to the amending formula), its requirement for approval by provincial legislatures as well as premiers, and its three-year time limit for ratification.

Despite the severe institutional hurdles, the Meech Lake Accord initially appeared almost certain to be ratified. It won approval not only from the prime minister and all provincial premiers but also from leaders of the federal opposition parties. Only Pierre Trudeau, now retired from electoral politics, took a position of unyielding opposition, arguing that the package constituted a massive giveaway to the provinces in the areas of immigration, spending powers, and the courts, a weakening of the Charter of Rights, and the end of his dream of "a single Canada, bilingual and multicultural."[123] Trudeau himself might seem to be a dubious rallying figure, given his own unpopularity when he left office.[124] But his critique, especially of the "distinct-society" portion of the accord, did resonate with English Canadians, who saw the clause as an embodiment and symbol of repeated "preferential treatment" for Quebec.[125]

122. The extent to which the distinct-society clause in the Meech Lake Accord could have been used to erode charter guarantees by the Quebec government is a subject of widespread disagreement among experts and politicians; indeed, politicians' widely differing suggestions about its effects were one of the major sources of suspicion about the clause among anglophone Canadians inside and outside Quebec.

123. See Pierre Trudeau, "Say Goodbye to the Dream of One Canada," in Donald Johnston, ed., With a Bang, Not a Whimper: Pierre Trudeau Speaks Out (Toronto: Stoddart, 1988), p. 9.

124. Alberta premier Don Getty stated, "While I knew that the accord was good, after Mr. Trudeau's intervention I'm certain it's one hell of a deal." Quoted in Roger Gibbins, "Introduction to Constitutional Politics," in Gibbins, ed., Meech Lake and Canada: Perspectives from the West, rev. ed. (Edmonton: Academic Printing and Publishing, 1989), p. 7.

125. See Michael Adams and Mary Jane Lennon, "The Public's View of the Canadian Federation," in Watts and Brown, eds., Canada: The State of the Federation 1990, pp. 97–108. On Trudeau's role, see Cohen, A Deal Undone, chap. 8.

Anglophones within Quebec were particularly concerned that the "distinct-society" clause would be used by Quebec governments as a mechanism to further erosion of their language rights. As Dion shows in his chapter, anglophone concern inside and outside Quebec was fueled in late 1988 by disputes over Quebec legislation regulating the use of English in commercial signs.

Other groups joined in the criticism. Aboriginal leaders, in particular, were critical of the lack of progress made in a series of first ministers' conferences mandated by the 1982 Constitution Act to address aboriginal concerns; the Meech Lake Accord once again appeared to place their concerns on the back burner. During the three-year ratification period, both of the federal opposition parties—the Liberals and the New Democrats—acquired new leaders who opposed the Meech Lake Accord.[126] Public opinion in English Canada moved against the accord and the closed way it had been negotiated. Most decisively, however, three provincial governments whose premiers had signed the accord (Manitoba, New Brunswick, and Newfoundland) were defeated during the ratification period. In each of the three provinces, the incoming premiers had deep reservations about the accord (Newfoundland's Clyde Wells was particularly hostile). In Manitoba, Premier Gary Filmon had the additional handicap of heading a minority government, thus needing to consult with leaders of the two opposition parties, one of whom was strongly opposed to the accord.

By the spring of 1990, with the deadline for ratification of the accord set to run out in June, the prospects for ratification appeared bleak indeed. A final week-long round of negotiations in early June failed to win a clear commitment of support from Premier Wells of Newfoundland, and in any event, procedural delays by Elijah Harper, a native member of the Manitoba legislature, prevented a final vote in that province. The accord was dead, and it appeared that Canada might be as well.

A Last Chance for Canada?

The collapse of the Meech Lake Accord unleashed an unprecedented surge in pro-sovereignty sentiment in Quebec, as Dion shows in his chap-

126. Jean Chrétien did not officially become leader of the Liberal party until immediately after the failure of the accord, but his selection had been a foregone conclusion for several months.

ter. In addition, a number of Quebec MPs in Prime Minister Brian Mulroney's Progressive Conservative caucus, led by Mulroney's former Quebec lieutenant, left to form a new pro-sovereignty Bloc Québécois in the House of Commons. And within English Canada, there was a widespread, albeit minority, sense that it might after all be best to "let Quebec go."[127]

Potentially the most critical moves were made by the Quebec provincial government. Quebec Premier Robert Bourassa responded to the upsurge in nationalist sentiment by announcing that Quebec would boycott federal-provincial conferences and deal only with Ottawa on constitutional issues. Thus the traditional route to constitutional agreements was foreclosed. Bourassa also sponsored a resolution in the provincial legislature that requires a referendum on sovereignty in 1992. The Bourassa government may have limited political wriggle room to amend the legislation (notably by calling a referendum instead on a "binding" constitutional reform offer by Ottawa and the other provinces), but such a move would be very risky politically.[128] Thus the Quebec referendum legislation counterbalances the bias toward the institutional status quo inherent in the current amending rules. Before, if no offers for reform were made that were acceptable to Quebec, current institutions would remain in place; now, if no acceptable offer is received, it is quite possible that Quebecers will vote for sovereignty.

The high stakes and short deadlines for constitutional reform might suggest a return to the centralized bargaining style of constitutional negotiation used for the Meech Lake Accord. But lingering public anger over the Meech Lake process, which appeared to exclude everyone but the prime minister and provincial premiers, and Bourassa's decision to boycott federal-provincial conferences led the Mulroney government to pursue a very different constitutional process.

Broad input was pursued through several channels. A citizens' commission held hearings throughout the country and issued a report, while Constitutional Affairs Minister Joe Clark consulted not only with provincial premiers but also with leaders of the native peoples. Only at the end of these processes did the government release its tentative proposals in

---

127. See David Jay Bercuson and Barry Cooper, *Deconfederation: Canada without Quebec* (Toronto: Key Porter, 1991).

128. On the Bourassa government's limited room for maneuver, see Patrick J. Monahan, "Closing a Constitutional Deal in 1992: A Scenario," in Douglas Brown, Robert Young, and Dwight Herberger, eds., *Constitutional Commentaries: An Assessment of the 1991 Federal Proposals* (Kingston: Queen's University, Institute of Intergovernmental Relations, 1992), pp. 101–06.

September 1991.[129] This in turn triggered hearings by a joint Commons-Senate committee composed of members of the three main federal parties (the Progressive Conservatives, Liberals, and New Democrats). The federal government is planning to issue a final set of proposals in March or April 1992. Provincial and territorial governments and native groups also established public consultative mechanisms, and some have advanced their own proposals.[130] The province of Ontario, for example, proposed a "social charter" of citizenship rights such as health care and unemployment assistance.[131]

Even if the federal agenda were a narrow one, the challenge of integrating the federal proposals and decisionmaking process with those occurring at other levels would be immense. But the federal government's tentative proposals addressed the concerns of a much wider range of constituencies than the Meech Lake Accord (although some issues appeared to be included merely as bargaining chips to be traded away at some future point.)[132] There were also important differences from the Meech Lake Accord in the proposals' substance and vulnerability to veto. For those who favored a stronger federal union, there was to be an enhanced federal power to override provincial laws or practices of provincial governments that restrict the movement of capital or labor within Canada, but only with substantial provincial support, and with an opt-out option for up to three provinces.[133] For supporters of an increased role for the provinces, Ottawa offered to cede to the provinces residual power over areas not specifically delimited in the constitution.[134] It also proposed creation of a new body, the Council of the Federation, which would be composed of representatives of the provincial, federal, and

129. See Government of Canada, *Shaping Canada's Future Together: Proposals* (Ottawa: Minister of Supply and Services, 1991).

130. See Manitoba Constitutional Task Force, *Report*, October 28, 1991.

131. See Robert Sheppard, "A Deal for Provinces or for People?" *Globe and Mail* (Toronto), December 17, 1991, p. A17.

132. See Geoffrey York, "Property Rights Seen as Bargaining Ploy," *Globe and Mail* (Toronto), September 26, 1991, p. A6.

133. The federal government's power could be used only with the approval of the governments (not legislatures) of at least two-thirds of the provinces having 50 percent of Canada's population. The legislature of a province that had not approved a specific use of the "common market" power could override that use for a three-year period by a vote of 60 percent of its members.

134. However, because the federal government would retain its jurisdiction over "national matters and emergencies" under the "peace, order, and good government" clause, and the provinces already have residual authority over non-national matters, many observers viewed this concession as an empty gesture with no practical import.

territorial governments and would essentially institutionalize and provide a firm voting rule (two-thirds of the provinces having 50 percent of the population) for formerly ad hoc arrangements of executive federalism.

The government promised aboriginal peoples that they would participate in the constitutional process, that a justiciable right to native self-determination would be negotiated (although it would not come into force for up to ten years to allow time for negotiations), and that the native peoples would be guaranteed some representation in a reformed Senate. For westerners and adherents of the populist Reform party, there was a proposal for a directly elected Senate with more equal representation of provinces (although clearly fewer powers than the House of Commons),[135] as well as parliamentary reforms to allow more "free votes" (without requirements for party discipline) in the House of Commons and entrenchment of property rights in the Charter of Rights and Freedoms. For proponents of charter rights, the threshold for invoking the "notwithstanding" clause was to be raised from a simple majority to 60 percent of a legislature's members.

On Quebec's demands addressed in the Meech Lake Accord, there was a decidedly mixed response. This was determined in large part by the Mulroney government's focus on provisions that did not require unanimity in order to avoid a repeat of the Meech Lake scenario, in which one or two small provinces could hold up the package by withholding their consent. The new package included the distinct-society clause, because it did not require unanimity, although the context of the clause was altered and its content clarified vis-à-vis the Meech Lake package to make it more palatable to anglophone Canadians.[136] Giving Quebec (and potentially other provinces) an increased role in immigration—another nonunanim-

135. The proposal did not call for complete equality, nor did it state whether senators should be elected from single-member districts or larger districts. Only the House of Commons could bring down the government on a motion of nonconfidence. The powers of the Senate would be limited to a six-month suspensive veto in some areas, whereupon a vetoed measure could become law if repassed by the House of Commons. In other areas (notably taxation and appropriations), it would have no vote at all. The Senate was also given authority to ratify the appointment of the heads of some federal agencies—notably the Bank of Canada.

136. In the Meech Lake Accord, symbolic recognition of the status of Quebec as a "distinct society," along with recognition of regional majority and minority languages, was placed in a new section 2 of the 1867 Constitution Act as an "interpretive clause" stating that the constitution of Canada should be interpreted in light of these fundamental factors. In the government's September 1991 proposals, symbolic recognition of Quebec's status as a distinct society in a new section 2 was to be embedded in a broader "Canada clause" recognizing a number of other characteristics of Canadian society, such as

ity item—also was in line with the Meech proposals. And in the area of federal spending programs, the federal government not only promised, as it had in the Meech Lake Accord, to allow opting out with compensation for all new shared-cost programs, it also promised not to undertake any such initiatives without the support of at least seven provinces representing at least 50 percent of the country's population.

The story was quite different in areas where unanimous provincial consent was required for constitutional amendment. On the constitutional amendment provisions, the government reiterated its support for the Meech Lake proposals, but stated that proposals should move forward only if unanimous support developed around them. On the question of entrenching the Supreme Court and specifying its regional composition and a provincial role in appointments in the constitution, the government proposed moving only on the provincial role in appointments, since the other items required unanimity. But the proposals did make some additional concessions to Quebec, notably by transferring jurisdiction over labor market training and proposing increased consultation in areas such as broadcast licensing. The proposals also suggested that on matters on language and culture, Senate votes be subject to a new double-majority voting requirement.

Given the wide-ranging nature of the government's proposals, there was something for almost everyone to like–and dislike. Not surprisingly, most participants focused on the things that they did not like. Quebec Premier Bourassa, for example, rejected the enhanced "economic union" powers for Ottawa, while generally expressing a willingness to negotiate in good faith.[137] Native leaders were even more critical. And the public appeared to be lukewarm at best. In a poll conducted at the end of October 1991, only 28 percent of Quebecers approved or strongly approved of the proposals as a whole, while 52 percent disapproved or strongly disap-

---

recognition of gender equality, aboriginal rights, and the contributions of immigrants from many countries. The government proposal suggested placing the "interpretive clause," stating that the charter should be interpreted in a manner consistent both with Quebec's status as a distinct society and the preservation of linguistic majorities and minorities inside and outside Quebec, in the charter itself (where it would follow a similar provision on aboriginal rights), rather than in the 1867 Constitution Act. Moreover, a clause was added clarifying that the attributes of Quebec's distinct society relevant to interpretation "include (a) a French-speaking majority; (b) a unique culture; and (c) a civil law tradition." Government of Canada, *Shaping Canada's Future Together*, p. 11.

137. See Rhéal Séguin and Patricia Poirier, "Bourassa Rejects Economic Plan," *Globe and Mail* (Toronto), September 26, 1991, p. A1, and Patricia Poirier, "Quebec Editorials see 'Power Grab,' " *Globe and Mail*, September 26, 1991, p. A7.

proved; comparable figures in the rest of the country were 28 and 37 percent, respectively. Only 28 percent of those polled outside of Quebec approved or strongly approved of the revised wording of the "distinct-society" clause.[138] The same polls showed the ruling Progressive Conservatives remained a distant third in national polls, with only 16 percent support among decided voters. Clearly the Mulroney government had its work cut out for it to avoid a Quebec referendum on sovereignty that— the same poll showed—would win if it were held at that time.

Proponents of Quebec's remaining within Canada had grounds for both optimism and pessimism as the critical year of 1992 dawned. On the optimistic side, a poll released in the first week of 1992 showed that while the critical distinct-society clause remained very popular in Quebec, a majority of Quebecers would accept a constitutional package without the clause if necessary to obtain a constitutional agreement; similarly, a majority outside Quebec would accept the distinct-society clause if required to adopt a reform package.[139] It is unclear whether this spirit of compromise reflects the traditional Canadian genius for muddling through on constitutional reform or simply an enhanced fear of change spawned by the current deep recession in Canada.

On the pessimistic side, there is an awareness that the institutional inertia that has always favored the constitutional status quo in Canada may now work against it. The addition of an action-forcing mechanism— Quebec's deadline for a provincial referendum on sovereignty by the fall of 1992—means that unless a constitutional agreement acceptable to the Bourassa government can be reached, the breakup of Canada is assured a place on the agenda. If that institutional inertia confronts a strong political momentum—Quebecers' frustration and anger at English Canada's inability to meet their demands for reform—the seemingly endless Canadian capacity to muddle through constitutional crises may finally have run its course.

Evaluating Institutional Management of Conflict in Canada

At the beginning of this chapter, I asked three questions about Canada's political institutions. Have they contributed to Canada's constitutional

138. See Hugh Winsor, "Canadians Cool to Proposals for New Constitution," *Globe and Mail* (Toronto), November 4, 1991, pp. A1, A6.

139. Nancy Wood, "Breaching the Barriers: Common Ground Appears on the Constitution," *Maclean's*, January 6, 1992, pp. 52–55.

discontents—in particular, to the phenomena of Quebec separatism and western alienation? Have they prevented a resolution of these discontents? Are there any "institutional fixes" available that might lessen these discontents and make conflict management less divisive?

None of these questions can be answered definitively,[140] but this chapter suggests several lessons about how to make such assessments. First, there is no such thing as a purely "institutional" effect because the effects of institutions vary depending on the social context in which they operate. The tendency of the Canadian electoral system to underrepresent some regions in the government caucus and overrepresent others, for example, would not occur in the absence of powerful regionally based political cleavages. Second, it makes no sense to measure the performance of existing institutions against opportunities provided by alternative mechanisms that could not function well or at all in Canadian conditions. For example, although a "legislative union" (abolishing provincial legislatures) would eliminate jurisdictional conflicts and might reduce risks for oppression of regional minorities, Canada's diversity makes that no more feasible an option today than it was in 1867. Third, every institutional option for managing conflict carries with it risks and limitations as well as opportunities. Entrenching a Charter of Rights, for example, has undercut the legitimacy of traditional consociational bargaining mechanisms and increased Quebecers' doubts about whether their collective aspirations are compatible with those of the rest of Canada. Finally, it is clear that choosing one institutional option over another is likely to mean that some conflict management values are advanced while others are sacrificed. A more powerful second chamber, for example, might provide more effective representation for some regions, but at increased risk of institutional deadlock.

An overall assessment of the effects of Canadian institutions on social discontents must be quite mixed. In some respects, Canadian institutions have proven to be remarkably adaptable and responsive to the conflicting, even incompatible, demands being placed upon them. Where institutional options pose potential risks, modifications and compromises have often

140. Most obviously, one cannot know with certainty what would have happened if a different set of political institutions had been in place. Moreover, each of the questions posed suggests a comparison with a specific institutional alternative, and there are an almost infinite number of possibilities, each with a unique set of trade-offs. In addition, observers' judgments are likely to be biased against the status quo: the failings of current arrangements are obvious; not so apparent are potential conflict management problems that are resolved smoothly by current institutions but might be exacerbated by alternative arrangements.

been made to mitigate those risks. For example, the use of the "opt out" provision in many federal programs and in the 1982 constitutional amending formula is an ingenious adaptation to the conflicting demands of Quebec for devolution of powers and the resistance elsewhere in the country to special status for Quebec. Other institutional compromises—for example, the coexistence of the Charter of Rights and the "notwithstanding" clause—similarly represent social compromises on deeply divisive issues.

It is nevertheless clear that a number of aspects of Canadian institutions do pose serious risks and limitations for conflict management. The most obvious and serious institutional deficiency is the combination of Canada's majoritarian electoral rules for the House of Commons and its impotent Senate. Canada's electoral rules, along with the tradition of single-party cabinets, facilitated serious underrepresentation of western Canada in the governing party caucus of the House for most of a generation, and Quebec was intermittently underrepresented. Patchwork solutions to address this concern, notably the use of senators in the cabinet, were not effective because they were not perceived as legitimate by the public in those regions. There is little doubt that the West's underrepresentation, and the fact that it coincided with numerous battles between Ottawa and the western provinces over control of natural resources, strengthened western alienation, increased the credibility of provincial premiers as spokespersons for their regions, gave rise to calls for institutional reforms incompatible with the claims of Quebec, and made it harder for English Canada—and especially the West—to comprehend and sympathize with Quebec's claims. "Why are they complaining," westerners ask, "when they are always in power in Ottawa?"

There is a great irony here. It is Quebec, the region that has benefited most over the past quarter century from the Canadian electoral system's tendency to overrepresent some regions in the federal governing party caucus, that is considering leaving the country, while the West, which was seriously underrepresented for most of the same period, is not.[141] It would be a mistake to conclude that institutional effects are unimportant, however; instead, this irony underscores the limitations of any type of central political institutions—whether majoritarian, limited-government, consociational, or arbitral—in dealing with some types of social divisions. It is likely that western Canadian alienation could be diminished by institutional reforms ensuring the region a greater voice in Ottawa. But

141. I am grateful to Stéphane Dion for this point.

Quebec francophones' distinctive language concerns and fear of assimilation have led them to focus primarily on devolutionary mechanisms that would give them greater control over the territory where they are a majority, rather than an increased say in central institutions. (However, there is little doubt that persistent underrepresentation of Quebec in the federal governing party caucus would have given pro-sovereignty forces a huge boost.) Quebec's concerns will always make it sit uneasily within Canada—indeed, within overwhelmingly English-speaking North America. The fears that flow from this permanent minority status can be mitigated, but there are no institutional "fixes"—not even Quebec sovereignty.

Current institutions also have serious shortcomings with respect to resolving discontents through constitutional or legislative settlements, the subject of my second question. Once again, however, the effects of institutions and social conditions are almost impossible to separate. The requirement that most constitutional amendments be ratified by either seven or ten provincial legislatures does provide a number of veto points at which amendments can be blocked. But first ministers' conferences also provide a consociational mechanism to circumvent these roadblocks and avoid stalemate, as was seen in the Meech Lake round. In Westminster systems, approval in such a forum is normally tantamount to ratification. The failure of the Meech Lake Accord was not the result of a tiny minority using veto points to block an agreement supported by a near consensus in Canadian society, for no such consensus existed. Rejection of the accord reflected the basic incompatibility of the Quebec and western constitutional reform agendas and the delegitimization of traditional consociational arrangements (notably executive federalism) that had enabled elites to make deals on matters where there was no consensus, with very little input from average Canadians. This delegitimization in turn resulted in large measure from the constitutional changes of 1982, notably the charter and the new amending formula.

The interaction between social and institutional constraints on constitutional reform is also evident in the absence thus far of use of the amending formula added to Canada's constitution in 1982. Section 43 allows constitutional amendments affecting "one or more, but not all" provinces to be concluded simply by an agreement between the federal Parliament and the legislatures of the provinces involved. This is an extraordinarily veto-free amending procedure. Although there is some disagreement about the legal scope of amendments that could be concluded under this formula, it does offer a potential vehicle for at least some forms of assymetrical federalism between Quebec and Ottawa. That it has not been used at all almost certainly reflects political constraints (notably the resistance to "special status" for Quebec in the rest of the country) as much as institutional ones. If Ottawa and Quebec moved toward entrenching assymetrical federalism through bilateral amendments, it certainly would hamper the ability of the federal government to win approval from other provinces for a broader constitutional settlement, and it would give Quebec less reason to bargain.

In considering my third question, the question of "institutional fixes" (or at least improvements on the status quo), I must begin by reiterating that there are no solutions to conflict management in the Canadian system that will benefit some parties without harming others. Nor, given the conflicting reform agendas of Quebec and the West, can institutional changes draw on only one of the conflict management options outlined at the beginning of this chapter. The basic question is whether these conflicting agendas can be harmonized at all—and if so, will the resulting mechanisms create unacceptable additional risks for conflict management?

It is not the role of this chapter either to summarize the immense literature on potential institutional reforms in Canada or to lay out a blueprint for constitutional reform.[142] A few comments concerning three central reform issues are nonetheless in order.

The first issue is underrepresentation of specific regions in the federal government, the central concern on the West's reform agenda since the 1982 constitution dealt with the issue of natural resources. Western proposals for ensuring broader regional representation in federal government decisions have focused largely on a broad set of changes in the Senate that would enhance its capacity to act as a limited-government mechanism while increasing representation of the smaller provinces. Reforms of the electoral system for the House of Commons that would diminish its majoritarian character have also been proposed by academics and some study commissions.[143]

---

142. For an overview and critique of institutional reform proposals, see in particular Aucoin, *Institutional Reforms for Representative Government*. For a review of specific constitutional reform proposals in tabular form, see Canada West Foundation, *Alternatives '91: A Roadmap for Constitutional Change* (Calgary, November 1991).

143. The federal government also proposed a "House of the Federation" representing provincial governments in its September 1991 constitutional proposals. On Senate reform, see Peter McCormick, "Canada Needs a Triple E Senate," and Eugene Forsey, "No—More Than a Triple E Senate Is Needed," in Fox and White, eds., *Politics: Canada*, pp. 435–

Reforms of the House and Senate have distinctive risks and limitations. Making the Senate more "equal, elected and effective" might increase the bargaining leverage of the peripheries, notably the West. But the West still might find itself politically isolated and outvoted in a more powerful Senate, and a more powerful second chamber carries with it a risk of institutional stalemate. Moreover, such a change might exacerbate linguistic fears by reducing Quebec's role in decisionmaking, and it would do nothing to ensure representation for Quebec in governments where the governing party was virtually shut out in that province, as happened under both John Diefenbaker's and Joe Clark's minority governments. Instituting some form of proportional representation in House elections would lessen problems of regional underrepresentation but would also benefit smaller parties, increasing the probability of minority or coalition governments and potentially weakening further the power of the center in Canada. The likelihood that proportional representation would hurt the two largest federal parties, the Progressive Conservatives and the Liberals, and the fact that it would do nothing for provincial governments have left this reform without powerful proponents in recent rounds of constitutional negotiations.

A second central constitutional issue comes from Quebec's reform agenda: recognition of a distinct status for Quebec within Canada and the precise form that status will take. I will focus here not on the symbolic recognition of Quebec as a distinct society, but rather on the institutionalization of a special status for Quebec in federal institutions and programs. The rejection of special status by English Canada has given rise to an alternative formula: generalizing to all provinces provisions sought by Quebec. Concerning federal programs, as noted earlier, this formula has in fact proven remarkably flexible, including provisions that in theory allow any province to opt out, not only of federal programs that touch provincial jurisdiction but also of constitutional amendments that would transfer jurisdiction from the provinces to the federal government (no such amendments have yet been proposed). Thus the fig leaf that Quebec is not receiving special status can be maintained.

Maintaining the fig leaf is harder when it comes to dealing with Quebec's demands for a role in federal institutions—for example, a Quebec veto over constitutional amendments. The Meech Lake Accord would

---

49, 440–46. On reforms for the House of Commons, see Irvine, "A Review and Evaluation of Electoral System Reform Proposals."

have followed the alternative formulation of treating all provinces equally by extending applicability of the unanimity constitutional amending formula to more categories of amendments rather than providing for a Quebec veto, and by giving all provinces the power to nominate Supreme Court justices. In the case of Supreme Court nominees, the risks of spreading the provincial power seem quite limited. When it comes to constitutional amendments, however, the risks of increasing constitutional rigidification are potentially quite severe. A more flexible, assymetrical formula that met Quebec's demand for a veto over changes in federal institutions would be a "7/50" formula in which Quebec necessarily was one of the approving provinces. This formula is currently unacceptable to most political leaders in English Canada, however.

Although political institutions are only partially responsible for blocking agreement on constitutional reform packages, the strong possibility that the 1991–92 round of constitutional reform may once again result in stalemate has triggered a great debate about alternative procedures for constitutional amendment—a third central reform issue. A common feature of the proposals for reform involves greater public participation, either through constituent assemblies or referendums. The most widely discussed proposal for breaking constitutional deadlock is to have the federal government call a national referendum; ratification would require either a simple national majority or majorities in each of the provinces or regions of Canada. Prime Minister Mulroney floated trial balloons about having a national referendum at the end of the current round of constitutional negotiations, but backed away largely under pressure from his Quebec caucus, which was fearful that such a referendum would be used—or at least portrayed by political rivals in Quebec—as a mechanism to force a constitutional settlement on Quebec. Use of a referendum is the device most favored by the public to ratify a constitutional accord, but it is not part of current amending formulas.[144] Thus a referendum could be used only as a supplement to current procedures— another veto point in a process that already presents many obstacles to the preservation of Canada. Even more important, the history of referendums in Canada suggests that such an instrument would be likely

144. On public opinion favoring the use of a referendum, see the Maclean's/Decima poll in "Cross-Canada Opinions," *Maclean's*, January 6, 1992, p. 65. For recent arguments in favor of a national referendum as part of the ratification process for the government's 1992 proposals, see Jeffrey Simpson, "It's a Blunt Instrument, but a Referendum Can Wrap up the Big Issue," and Richard Johnston, "Cutting the Gordian Knot," *Globe and Mail* (Toronto), November 28, 1991, pp. A18, A19.

to divide the population of the country along the lines of language and region.

There is no shortage of possible reforms of Parliament and federalism to address the current problems of Canadian confederation. Each has its own risks and limitations, however. Equally important, each would require some participants to sacrifice deeply held beliefs or power they currently hold. Preserving Canada, in short, is likely to force Canadians inside and outside of Quebec to compromise not just on institutional forms but also on the underlying values that those institutions tend to promote or diminish. This fact ensures that whatever the resolution of the current constitutional crisis, many Canadians will greet it as much with sadness for what has been lost as with joy and relief over what has been gained and retained.

STÉPHANE DION

Explaining Quebec Nationalism

NATIONALISM DERIVES from a sentiment of identity. It may lead, in some circumstances, to a political principle "which holds that the political and the national unity should be congruent."[1] The strength of such a political principle is striking today, when the world is experiencing the strongest fever of nationalism since the postwar decolonization movement. Many countries are facing ethnic tensions, and some (the Soviet Union, Yugoslavia, Ethiopia) may not survive the challenge of secession.

The Quebec-Canada question bears little similarity to these cases. Created in 1867, the Canadian confederation is not a decaying, totalitarian regime, a new democracy, or an unstable third world country; it is a wealthy modern welfare state. Free speech and voting rights have always been enjoyed in this liberal democracy. The secession of Quebec from Canada would be a new phenomenon: the first split in a modern welfare state. What are the closest cases? Norway and Sweden in 1905? Ireland and Britain in 1922? In neither case was a modern welfare state in place. Canada today has a massive mixed economy. About 45 percent of the gross domestic product is shared among the federal, provincial, and local levels of government. It has a full array of public services and goods as well as global communication and trade.

So why is secession an issue in Canada? To answer this question one must understand how Canada differs from the other twenty-three countries in the Organization for Economic Cooperation and Development (OECD).

The author wishes to thank his research assistant, Denis Saint-Martin. He is also indebted, for their comments on earlier versions of this paper, to Keith G. Banting, André J. Bélanger, Gérald Bernier, Alan C. Cairns, R. Kenneth Carty, Léon Dion, Roger Gibbins, Jonathan M. Lemco, Claire L'Heureux-Dubé, Laurence McFalls, Kenneth H. McRoberts, Alain Noël, François Vaillancourt, and Robert A. Young.
1. Ernest Gellner, *Nations and Nationalism* (Cornell University Press, 1983), p. 1.

First, it is easier for a minority group to achieve sovereignty if it controls a subnational government. Therefore all of the nonfederal liberal democracies are not comparable. Second, one may disregard all the homogeneous federal states where there is no minority linguistic group holding majority control of a subnational government. This leaves only Canada, Switzerland, and possibly Belgium, which in 1980 became a kind of centralized federation.[2]

The French speakers of Quebec are not part of a multilingual environment as in Europe. They are part of Canada, where English is the overwhelmingly dominant language outside of Quebec, and they are part of English-speaking North America, where they account for only 2.4 percent of the total population. No other linguistic minority combines to such an extent two features: a reason to fear assimilation and the ability to control a modern subnational government. And not any kind of subnational government: the province of Quebec is the most powerful subnational government in all of the OECD countries in terms of its share of resources and its scope of intervention.

In addition to this basic structural situation, one may add the historical fact that the French were the first Europeans to occupy the territory, the former Nouvelle-France. History has always been part of the nationalist credo in Quebec. The motto of the province of Quebec is "Je me souviens" (I remember). The "Québécois" share the same historical references of 456 years. They have their nationalist songs, their flag (the *fleur-de-lys*), and their celebrities unknown in other parts of Canada.

Yet Quebecers have elected pro-Canadian politicians since the beginning of the confederation. Until very recently, they have been disposed to accommodate their nationalist feelings within this confederation. This leads me to a second question: Why is Quebec nationalism challenging the unity of Canada today more than ever before? To answer, one needs to know more about Quebec and the roots of Quebec nationalism. Any secessionist movement is rooted in two antithetical feelings: fear and confidence. The fear is of being weakened or even disappearing as a distinct people, if it stays in the union; the confidence is that it can perform as well, or even better, on its own. To these two conflicting feelings, one may add a third one: a feeling of rejection, the sensation of no longer being welcome in the union. In Quebec the feeling of fear is a structural one, clearly connected with the linguistic issue. Quebecers are afraid of

2. John Fitzmaurice, "Belgium: Reluctant Federalism," *Parliamentary Affairs*, vol. 37 (Autumn 1984), pp. 418–33.

their language being diluted in an English-speaking ocean. The feeling of confidence is a more recent phenomenon, linked with important cultural changes in French-speaking Quebecers. The feeling of rejection is a sporadic phenomenon, expressed recently in the June 22, 1990, Meech Lake crisis, which I will discuss later in this chapter. To say that it is sporadic does not mean that it is less important; quite the contrary, such catalysts often generate great historical developments.

Fear, confidence, and rejection: these three feelings are strong in contemporary Quebec. I do not think that they are strong enough to create the first welfare state collapse in history, but I may be wrong. In any case they are the keys to the future of Quebec and of Canada. Before reviewing the roots of these nationalist feelings, I want to describe the variation in the support for the secessionist idea over the past three decades.

Measures of Quebec Nationalism

Nationalism has always existed in Quebec, but the secessionist idea ceased being politically marginal only in the 1960s. Not until 1990 did it attain majority support in Quebec.

I will use three measures to trace trends in secessionist sentiment since the 1960s. First, at the provincial level, I will review the popularity of the pro-sovereignty parties in comparison with the "federalist" ones—that is, those that support the Canadian federation. Second, I will describe the electoral behavior of Quebecers at the federal level. Third, I will outline trends in the popularity of the secessionist idea as measured in the polls.

The Course of the Parti Québécois

During the 1960s the two main parties in the provincial arena—the Parti Libéral and the Union Nationale—moved to a position demanding additional autonomy for the government of Quebec. However, both were still federalist parties. The small pro-independence parties at the time enjoyed little support from the voters. A terrorist group, the Front de Libération du Québec, was politically insignificant.

Then in 1968 the Parti Québécois was created. Its leader was René Lévesque, a credible and charismatic politician and a former star of the Liberal government as minister of natural resources. The raison d'être of the Parti Québécois has been labeled *souveraineté-association*—political sovereignty combined with economic association with Canada. This asso-

TABLE 1. The Electoral Record of the Parti Québécois, 1970–89

Percent

Item	1970	1973	1976	1981	1985	1989
Seats[a]	7	6	64	66	19	23
Votes	23	30	41	49	39	40

SOURCES: Gérald Bernier and Robert Boily, Le Québec en chiffres de 1850 à nos jours (Montréal: Association Canadienne-Française pour L'Avancement des Sciences, 1986); Robert Boily, "Profil du Québec," in Denis Monière, ed., L'année politique au Québec (Montréal: Le Devoir-Québec/Amérique, 1990), p. 212.
a. In the provincial legislature, the Assemblée Nationale.

ciation implies a common market with mobility of goods, services, capital, and people in a monetary union.[3]

The electoral record of the Parti Québécois from 1970 to 1989 is shown in table 1. It did fairly well in the first two elections in terms of votes received, but the Canadian system of single-member constituencies meant that the party won few seats in the provincial legislature, the Assemblée Nationale. Moreover, the stars of the party—notably Lévesque himself and the well-known economist (and current Parti Québécois leader), Jacques Parizeau—failed to win seats in the assembly. Then came the unexpected victory of November 1976, when the Parti Québécois won majority control of the provincial legislature with 41 percent of the vote. The remaining votes were split among three federalist parties. Reelected in 1981, the Parti Québécois shaped the government of Quebec until December 1985. Although it lost power to the Liberal party in 1985, it remained the official opposition party. In the 1989 election, the Parti Québécois retained 40 percent of the electorate's support.

To sum up, table 1 shows that the Parti Québécois remained a major political force during all these years, but that it never won an absolute majority of regular votes. What table 1 does not tell, however, is the extent to which support for the Parti Québécois was connected with its sovereignty option rather than with other factors, such as the charisma of its leader, its social program, its linguistic program, or variation in the popularity of the other parties. Here one must consider the electoral strategy of the Parti Québécois.

Since the Parti Québécois could count on the full support of all of the pro-independence forces, it sought to attract softer nationalists concerned with the economic consequences of secession. This electoral strategy was implemented in two ways: first, by emphasizing the "association" part of

3. Government of Quebec, La nouvelle entente Québec-Canada: Proposition du Gouvernement du Québec pour une entente d'égal à égal—la souveraineté-association (Quebec: Editeur officiel, 1979), pp. 62–71.

the sovereignty-association equation and second, by proposing a gradual schedule of achieving sovereignty. This is the "étapiste" strategy.[4] The étapiste strategy was gradually clarified. At the outset the Parti Québécois was divided between a radical wing, which asked for an automatic secession on the evening of an electoral victory, and a moderate wing, including René Lévesque, which argued that the decision about sovereignty should be made by a referendum following the election of a Parti Québécois government. During the first two elections in which the Parti Québécois took part, 1970 and 1973, the signal given to the electorate was not clear on this matter since the party itself was divided. But the moderate or "étapiste" wing finally won its point. The party focused the campaign of fall 1976 on issues other than sovereignty: integrity, good government, and good leadership.[5] It attempted to capitalize on the unpopularity of the Liberal premier, Robert Bourassa, and on his ambiguities regarding linguistic policy. The Parti Québécois promised not to implement sovereignty unless it received majority support in a referendum to be held later. The strategy paid off, and René Lévesque replaced Robert Bourassa as premier of Quebec.

After waiting four years, the Parti Québécois held the referendum in May 1980. Even then the sovereignty question was formulated in such a way as to postpone a final decision. Quebecers were asked simply to give the government of Quebec a mandate to negotiate sovereignty-association, a new arrangement with Canada that would then be submitted for approval in a second referendum. This second referendum was never held because 60 percent of voters in the 1980 referendum denied the government authority to initiate negotiation over sovereignty-association. Even with such a soft question, the pro-sovereignty politicians failed to muster more than a 40 percent level of support for their option. Even among French speakers, it seems that the "yes" position won only 48 percent of the vote.[6]

4. See Kenneth McRoberts, *Quebec: Social Change and Political Crisis*, 3d ed. (Toronto: McClelland and Stewart, 1988), pp. 237–62.

5. See Maurice Pinard and Richard Hamilton, "The Parti Québécois Comes to Power: An Analysis of the 1976 Quebec Election," *Canadian Journal of Political Science*, vol. 11 (December 1978), pp. 739–75, especially pp. 745–56.

6. Maurice Pinard, "Les francophones et le référendum: 52% contre 48%," *Le Devoir*, July 25, 1980, p. 9, cited in Stephen Clarkson and Christina McCall, *Trudeau and Our Times*, vol. 1: *The Magnificent Obsession* (Toronto: McClelland and Stewart, 1990), p. 241. See also Maurice Pinard and Richard Hamilton, "Les Québécois votent non: Le sens et la portée du vote," in Jean Crête, ed., *Comportement électoral au Québec* (Chicoutimi: Gaétan Morin, 1984), pp. 335–85.

The 1980 referendum disheartened the nationalist troops to the point that the idea of secession appeared dead. The Parti Québécois cautiously avoided discussing the sovereignty issue during the 1985 campaign, won by its old rival Robert Bourassa and the Liberal party. In the September 1989 elections the Parti Québécois made no substantial gains in either seats or votes (see table 1). However, by this time the party had as its head a clear pro-sovereignty leader, Jacques Parizeau, who had stopped the drift of the party's pro-sovereignty platform toward a position favoring autonomous status in the Canadian federation. In this way, the 1989 campaign underlines the renewal of the nationalist mood.

No other provincial elections have been held since 1989. However, following the Meech Lake failure in June 1990, the Quebec Liberal party switched to a far more nationalist platform. On March 27, 1991, Liberal members of the National Assembly endorsed the report of the provincial Commission on the Political and Constitutional Future of Quebec (the Bélanger-Campeau Commission). It recommended that a referendum be held in spring or fall 1992 on the constitutional future of Quebec. On March 10, 1991, the Liberal party had endorsed the Allaire report, which claimed for Quebec virtually every power possible, leaving to the exclusive care of the federal government only defense, customs, currency, post, the debt, and equalization payments to provincial governments.[7] This massive transfer of powers was described in the Allaire report as a necessary condition if Quebec was to stay in the federation. But Premier Bourassa rapidly put some distance between himself and the report by stating in June that Quebec's real purpose was to work with all Canadians to make the federation more manageable.

The law on the expected referendum enacted by the Liberal majority in the National Assembly is qualified by a preamble that allows Premier Bourassa too much leeway, in the opinion of the Parti Québécois.[8] All this suggests that the Liberal party, particularly Premier Bourassa, has not been seduced by the secessionist idea.

Since June 1990 the Parti Québécois has increased its popularity, however. It has either taken the lead or matched the Liberal party, de-

7. Quebec Liberal Party Constitutional Committee, *A Québec Free to Choose*, January 1991.

8. In particular, the preamble states that "the Government of Québec retains at all times its full prerogative to initiate and assess measures to promote the best interest of Québec" and that "the National Assembly continues to hold the sovereign power to decide on any referendum question and to pass appropriate legislation when necessary." Act 150, S.Q. 1991, C. 34, "An act respecting the process for determining the political and constitutional future of Québec," June 20, 1991, p. 4.

pending on the polls.[9] This time the Parti Québécois is promoting its sovereignty option. Yet its position regarding the association with Canada and the schedule of accession to sovereignty again gives some room to attract moderate nationalists. In particular, the party leaders clearly guarantee that the question of sovereignty will be resolved by a referendum on the new constitution and not only by an electoral victory.

Federal Elections in Quebec

The major parties of the National Assembly, the sovereignist Parti Québécois as well as the federalist Liberal party, identify the interest of the province with the government of Quebec. Both refer to what *le Québec* wants, what *le Québec* may not accept, and so on. This suggests that only the parliamentarians elected at the provincial level can speak for the people of Quebec. Yet Quebecers also elect parliamentarians at the federal level. The choices of Quebec voters in the federal electoral arena must also be taken into account to assess the strength of their nationalism.

During the 1970s the Parti Québécois never created a federal wing. René Lévesque did not believe that it could compete successfully with the established parties in the federal electoral arena. During the 1979 campaign a populist party enjoying some support in Quebec, Social Credit, changed its traditionally pro-federalist platform to a more pro-sovereignty one on the occasion of a change of leader. The new leader claimed to be sympathetic to the sovereignty-association option. The nationalist shift did not stop the party from losing all of its seats in the 1980 general election, however (see table 2). During the following elections, a pro-independence party tried without any success to elect members of Parliament, and it received very little support. The first pro-sovereignty MP was not elected to the Canadian Parliament until a by-election in the summer of 1990. This MP was elected under the label of the Bloc Québécois, a parliamentary group created by a former minister of the Mulroney government, Lucien Bouchard, who left the Conservative party during the Meech Lake crisis in the spring of 1990. Since that time the Bloc Québécois has become the most popular federal party in Quebec.

9. In mid-March 1990 a poll showed support of 51 percent for the Liberal party and 35 percent for the Parti Québécois. After the collapse of the Meech Lake Accord in June 1990, a poll showed 42 percent for the Liberal party and 46 percent for the Parti Québécois. Edouard Cloutier, "L'opinion politique québécois en 1989–1990," in Denis Monière, ed., *L'année politique au Québec* (Montreal: Le Devoir-Québec/Amérique, 1990), p. 168.

TABLE 2. Seats Held by Political Parties, Federal Elections, 1968–80

Party	1968 Quebec	1968 Rest of Canada	1972 Quebec	1972 Rest of Canada	1974 Quebec	1974 Rest of Canada	1979 Quebec	1979 Rest of Canada	1980 Quebec	1980 Rest of Canada
Liberal	56	98	56	53	60	81	67	47	74	73
Conservative	4	68	2	105	3	92	2	133	1	102
National Democratic	0	22	0	31	0	16	0	26	0	32
Social Credit	14	0	15	0	11	0	6	0	0	0
Independent	0	2	1	1	0	1	0	1	0	0
TOTAL	74	190	74	190	74	190	75	207	75	207

SOURCE: Frank Feigert, *Canada Votes 1935–1988* (Duke University Press, 1989), pp. 21, 166–67.

Thus competition at the federal level essentially was between federalist parties in the 1970s and 1980s. A striking point here is that until 1984 the Quebec electorate voted overwhelmingly for the federal party that was most supportive of a strong role for the central government—namely, the Liberal party. The Conservative party was more receptive to the government of Quebec's traditional demands. Quebec electors supported the centralist Liberal party even when the popularity of the Parti Québécois was at its peak at the provincial level. The cause of this contradictory behavior has a name: Pierre Elliott Trudeau, the flamboyant Liberal prime minister from 1968 to 1984 with a short interruption in 1979–80. Trudeau is still probably the Canadian best known by the outside world. What is less well known is that three out of Trudeau's four electoral victories were attributable to winning overwhelming majorities of the seats in Quebec (table 2). His most spectacular victory was in February 1980, when the Liberals won all but one seat only three months before the Parti Québécois lost the referendum on sovereignty-association. Trudeau won a plurality of seats in the rest of the country only once, in his first election campaign as prime minister in 1968. The rest of the country clearly expressed its dissatisfaction with his government three times: in 1972, 1979, and 1980.

Each of Trudeau's electoral triumphs was a humiliation for the nationalists in Quebec.[10] He was the champion of the federalist camp and the primary adversary of the independence movement. He tried to defend the central government against the appetite of the provinces and to obstruct any evolution toward a special political status for Quebec.

Trudeau's impressive electoral course contains an important irony. This well-known adversary of ethnic nationalism was elected and reelected thanks to the consistent support of his French-speaking compatriots. He was perceived by the francophones as "one of us." They were proud of "their" prime minister and impressed by his visibility at the international level. The spectacular popularity of Trudeau in Quebec is not only attributable to his personal charisma. His favorite themes also had some popularity with the electorate: the beauty of Canada, its good international reputation, the economic wealth of the federation, and the common links forged by history. At the same time that he institutionalized bilingualism in the federal government he stigmatized the Quebec separatist movement as inspired by ethnic intransigence.

---

10. For Trudeau's views, see Pierre Elliott Trudeau, *Federalism and the French Canadians* (Toronto: Macmillan, 1968).

The simultaneous popularity of Trudeau and Lévesque clearly expresses the double allegiance to Quebec and to Canada of the Quebec population. Since that time humorists have said that the dream of the Quebecer is to live in an independent Quebec—within a strong Canada!

Trudeau resigned in February 1984. He left behind a new constitution and a Charter of Rights and Freedoms, endorsed by every provincial legislature except Quebec's. The federal election in the summer of 1984 saw the downfall of his party and the triumphal election of the Conservative leader, Brian Mulroney, a bilingual Quebecer of Irish descent. Mulroney won an overwhelming victory in every region of the country, including Quebec, even though his party began the campaign with weak roots in the French province (see table 2). To get candidates, he welcomed personalities who had no links with the Conservative party. Some of them were acknowledged nationalists—members of the "yes" camp during the referendum campaign of 1980. During the 1984 campaign, Mulroney and his candidates actively courted the nationalists in Quebec, and they promised to pursue a constitutional revision that would be acceptable to Quebecers. The Meech Lake Accord of 1987 certainly helped Mulroney and his party keep their popularity in Quebec during the 1988 election, but the failure of that accord during the spring of 1990 opened the door to the Bloc Québécois.

Support for Sovereignty in the Polls

In addition to the strength of the pro-independence parties in Quebec, there is another way to measure support for the sovereignty idea—namely, the opinion polls. Using polls to capture all the nuances in public opinion regarding the secessionist idea is an art in Quebec. Answers vary strongly depending on the terminology used. The term "separatism" dramatically underlines the negative dimension of split and divorce, and accordingly it receives markedly less support than a more catch-all notion such as "sovereignty-association."

Edouard Cloutier of the University of Montreal aggregated the results of 134 polls testing support for the secessionist idea between 1960 and 1990, showing the periodic variation in support (see table 3). The results clearly point to the spectacular increase in support starting in 1987 with the Meech Lake crisis. Whatever the terminology, the new popularity of the secessionist idea is beyond doubt. Although the idea of "independence" got only 20 percent support during the early 1980s, it reached the 50 percent level for the first time in 1990.

TABLE 3. Support in Quebec for the Secessionist Idea, 1960–90[a]
Percent

Term used in polls	1960–64	1965–69	1970–74	1975–79	1980–85	1986–89	1990
Separatism	8	10	13	19	...	37	44
	(1)	(4)	(5)	(5)		(4)	(5)
Independence	...	...	27	20	20	32	50
			(1)	(2)	(4)	(3)	(3)
Sovereignty	...	...	...	...	18	41	55
					(4)	(3)	(7)
Sovereignty-association	...	...	32	31	39	46	58
			(2)	(25)	(8)	(2)	(9)
Mandate to negotiate sovereignty-association	...	...	...	49	40	...	68
				(17)	(19)		(1)

SOURCE: Edouard Cloutier, Jean H. Gay, and Daniel Latouche, *Le Virage* (Montreal: Québec/Amérique, forthcoming).
a. The numbers in parentheses are the number of polls used to compute the rate of support.

Support for sovereignty peaked at 70 percent in some polls during the second half of 1990. Support was even higher among francophones since the rest of the Quebecers (about 17 percent of the provincial population) are mainly strong supporters of the Canadian federation. However, the fervor of the movement cooled during the spring of 1991. Today the secessionist idea might not gain the support of a majority of voters. A CBC poll in April 1991 showed public opinion clearly divided. Ten percent agreed with the idea of full independence, 37 percent supported sovereignty-association, 36 percent asked for more power for Quebec but thought it should remain a province of Canada, and 16 percent supported the status quo. If no agreement were to be reached about a reform of the federation, 51 percent would opt for a sovereign Quebec, and 44 percent would prefer that Quebec stay in Canada.[11] Two subsequent polls showed support for sovereignty at 48 percent and 49 percent. But a poll taken at the end of May suggests a rekindling of the sovereignty fervor (57 percent).[12]

To sum up, public opinion polls confirm what I stated earlier: the secessionist idea has had substantial support since the 1970s. It enjoyed

11. Edouard Cloutier, Jean H. Gay, and Daniel Latouche, *Le Virage* (Montreal: Québec/Amérique, forthcoming).
12. Michel David, "Bourassa perd du terrain," *Le Soleil*, June 2, 1991, pp. A1–A2; and Pierre O'Neill, "La ferveur souverainiste persiste, révèle un sondage Multi Réso," *Le Devoir*, June 8, 1991, pp. A1–A4.

unprecedented popularity at the end of 1990 before declining in 1991. Three nationalist feelings—the fear of a disappearing linguistic tradition, a growing feeling of confidence, and the recent feeling of rejection—help explain this trend.

Fear of Disappearing: The Linguistic Issue

Nationalism has many roots: history, culture, territory. But the main reason why nationalist feeling has fueled a powerful secessionist movement in Quebec is the fragility of the French language in North America.

The Demolinguistic Situation

Canada is rightly known as a bilingual country, but most of its French-speaking population lives in Quebec (86.3 percent in 1986). The remaining contingent of French speakers is concentrated in Quebec's neighboring provinces, Ontario and New Brunswick. These three provinces held 96.9 percent of all French-speaking Canadians in 1986. French speakers accounted for less than 5 percent of the population in all of the provinces except Quebec and New Brunswick in 1986. That means that in eight out of ten provinces, the French presence is hard to perceive. Overall, the proportion of French speakers in the Canadian population dropped from 29.1 percent in 1941 to 24.2 percent in 1986.[13]

Francophone dominance grew, however, in Quebec. French speakers represented 82.9 percent of the total Quebec population in 1986, up 2.2 percentage points from 1971.[14] The decline of English speakers in Quebec is primarily the result of an exodus following the 1976 Parti Québécois election.[15] This emigration of Quebec's anglophone population, together with a lower capacity of the French province to attract and keep new immigrants and the spectacular drop of the French speakers' birthrate, decreased Quebec's demographic weight in the whole Canadian population from 29.0 percent in 1941 to 24.8 percent in 1986.[16] As a result, the share of MPs from Quebec in the federal Parliament dropped from 28.0

13. All the statistics in this paragraph are gathered from Statistics Canada, *Dimensions Series* (Ottawa: Minister of Supply and Services, 1988–89), Publications 93-151–57.

14. Conseil de la langue française du Québec, "Indicateurs de la situation linguistique au Québec," April 1991, pp. 2–3.

15. André Raynauld, "Les enjeux économiques de la souveraineté: Mémoire soumis au C.P.Q." (Montreal: Conseil du Patronat, October 1990), p. 68.

16. Statistics Canada, *Dimensions Series.*

percent of the total in 1974 to 25.4 percent in 1990. The same decline in Quebecers' weight will presumably occur in all federal institutions.

In short, Quebec is increasingly French, the rest of Canada is increasingly English, and the demographic weight of Quebec is decreasing within the federation. Everything suggests that the last two trends will continue in the foreseeable future. Thus it is not surprising that the French-speaking population of Quebec has a strong feeling of linguistic isolation in Canada and North America and a special loyalty for its provincial institutions, the only ones controlled by a French-speaking majority on the continent. Nationalism finds its central roots in this structural situation. The entire history of Quebec is haunted by the fear of anglicization, obsessed by the examples of Louisiana and parts of Canada where the French presence lives now only in folklore. The manner in which other Canadian provinces historically denied their French-speaking minorities any bilingual facilities, particularly regarding language of instruction in schools, did nothing to cool linguistic insecurity in Quebec.

Montreal is the financial and economic center of Quebec and a key to understanding the linguistic issue. The crucial Montreal area accounts for 44.7 percent of the total population of the province. English speakers living in Montreal represented a sizable majority (74.7 percent) of the English-speaking population of Quebec in 1986.[17] As a result of the English-speaking minority's control over corporations and financial institutions, together with the importance of American and English-Canadian enterprises in the Quebec economy, English was until recently the language of business in the province.

Another linguistic factor is the growing demographic importance of the immigrant population. Allophones—those whose native language is neither French nor English—increased from 3.7 percent to 6.8 percent of the population of Quebec between 1951 and 1986.[18] This immigrant population, once primarily from European countries such as Italy and Greece, now comes increasingly from third world countries. In Quebec as in other places, the insertion of these heterogeneous populations has created social tensions. In Quebec these problems are complicated by the language question. The attraction of the continental language is so strong that it is unlikely that many immigrants would join the French community without a compulsory law to protect the French language. By 1973–74, before such legal constraints, 88.6 percent of Montreal's allophone

---

17. Statistics Canada, *Dimensions Series.*
18. Conseil de la langue française du Québec, "Indicateurs," pp. 2–3.

schoolchildren received their instruction in English.[19] Because immigrants to Quebec, like English speakers, are concentrated in the Montreal area (at a rate of 90 percent), French speakers fear losing control of their metropolis. If Montreal became English, the rest of Quebec would no longer be in a position to shape a strong French community.

The Language Issue in Quebec and Canadian Politics

The linguistic context described above may easily become an explosive political problem. In reviewing the course of the nationalist movement since the 1960s, one finds a linguistic crisis at the beginning of each new outburst of nationalism.

The creation of the Parti Québécois occurred in a context of linguistic tension at the end of the 1960s. The conflicts were mostly linked to the control of school boards in some towns in the Montreal area.[20] The provincial governing party at that time, the Union Nationale, passed a law—Act 63—maintaining parents' freedom to choose French or English schools for their children.[21] Nationalists favored a law that would, at a minimum, have limited access to English schools to families with English backgrounds. Spectacular protests were mounted against Act 63. Nationalist feeling had never appeared so strong, especially among young Quebecers.

In an attempt to solve the language problem, Premier Bourassa abrogated Act 63 in 1974. He replaced it with a new law, Act 22, which was an attempt at compromise between the contradictory claims of English-speaking and French-speaking pressure groups.[22] The result dissatisfied both groups, however. The language issue was undoubtedly a factor in the electoral victory of the Parti Québécois in 1976, when an unusually large number of English-speaking voters, displeased with Robert Bourassa, gave their vote to the Union Nationale. This weakened support for the Liberal party and helped the Parti Québécois win a majority of seats in the National Assembly.[23] Moreover, the 1976 campaign occurred just after a new linguistic conflict that reinvigorated nationalist feeling. At

19. Marc V. Levine, *The Reconquest of Montreal: Language Policy and Social Change in a Bilingual City* (Temple University Press, 1990), p. 101.
20. William D. Coleman, *The Independence Movement in Quebec: 1945–1980* (University of Toronto Press, 1984), pp. 201–02.
21. An Act to Promote the French Language in Quebec, 1969, S.Q. C.9.
22. Official Language Act, 1974, S.Q. C.6.
23. See Pinard and Hamilton, "The Parti Québécois Comes to Power," pp. 758–60.

issue was the language to be used in controlling air traffic over the territory of Quebec.[24]

Only nine months after its election, the Parti Québécois government passed Act 101, a new law stipulating that French must be the usual language of work, instruction, communication, trade, and business in Quebec.[25] The English-speaking minority could retain its own language in publicly funded health care and social institutions, public schools, and universities, but access to English elementary and secondary schools was denied to French speakers and allophones. Act 101 automatically received full support from nationalist groups. English-speaking groups and the business community opposed it, and it was criticized as "retrograde" by Prime Minister Trudeau and the future leader of Quebec's Liberal party, Claude Ryan.[26]

Despite the protests, Act 101 was implemented. It rapidly appeared to be a success from the point of view of defense of the French language in Quebec. It generated a new perception of linguistic protection. But the cooling of linguistic insecurity had an effect unexpected by the Parti Québécois: it decreased secessionist sentiment and by doing so was an important factor in the defeat of the pro-sovereignty position during the 1980 referendum.[27]

Indeed, the Parti Québécois government inadvertently proved that it was possible to protect the French language adequately within the Canadian federation. This simple fact dissuaded many moderate nationalists from joining the sovereignty camp. This feeling of linguistic security remained strong during the years following the referendum, and it, along with the recession and demoralization created by the referendum defeat, maintained secessionist support at a very low level.

In fact, such a feeling of linguistic security was consistent with actual demolinguistic trends. The French-speaking population is growing relative to the English one in Quebec. Moreover, knowledge of French grew from 36.7 percent to 53.7 percent between 1971 and 1986 among the English population of Quebec, and from 47.1 percent to 66.3 percent among the allophones. In 1990, 90.2 percent of pre-elementary, elemen-

---

24. See Sandford F. Borins, *The Language of the Skies: The Bilingual Air Traffic Control Conflict in Canada* (Kingston and Montreal: McGill-Queen's University Press, 1983).

25. Charter of the French Language, 1977, S.Q. C.5.

26. Graham Fraser, *P.Q.: René Lévesque and the Parti Québécois in Power* (Toronto: Macmillan, 1984), p. 105.

27. McRoberts, *Quebec*, pp. 389–90.

tary, and secondary school students in Quebec went to French schools. The percentage among the allophones increased from 38.7 to 72.7 between 1980 and 1989. The effects of Act 101 are spectacular here. Because the compulsory effects of the law stop after secondary school, it is interesting to see what language of instruction allophones choose at the postsecondary level. Once again, the results are encouraging for the French language. The share of allophones registered in English-speaking colleges declined from 84.9 percent to 60.1 percent between 1980 and 1989. In short, use of the French language is increasing in Quebec.

Language is likely to remain a contentious political issue, however, because 46.3 percent of the English population and 33.7 percent of the allophones cannot speak French, and 70.3 percent of the French-speaking population cannot speak English. Moreover, many allophones still prefer English to French.[28]

The linguistic question was not an issue at all during the 1985 provincial campaign, and it was possible to assume at that time that a durable consensus had been reached on the matter. Then, the decision of the Supreme Court of Canada about the language of advertising in Quebec was announced on December 15, 1988.[29] The current crisis in Quebec and Canada may be properly described only when one keeps in mind that everything started, once again, from a language issue. Act 101 stipulated that, with a few exceptions, only French could be used on commercial signs in Quebec. The Supreme Court ruled that the unilingualism requirement was inconsistent with the Quebec and Canadian charters of rights because it violated freedom of expression. This decision was made in spite of the claim by the Quebec government that liberty of expression concerns the substance of a communication, not the language used, and that the "French only" requirement was for commercial public signs, obviously not for expression of religious, political, or ideological ideas. The Court added that a law requiring the use of the French language in signs, even in a dominant role, would be consistent with the Canadian and Quebec charters of rights so long as use of other languages was not prohibited.

To understand later events, it is necessary to say a word about the complexity of francophone public opinion regarding the language issue.

---

28. All the statistics in this paragraph are from Conseil de la langue française du Québec, "Indicateurs," pp. 4–5, 28–29, 36–37. On the language preferences of allophone Quebecers, see pp. 67, 75. Allophone Quebecers watch television in English 64 percent of the time. In Montreal they read their newspapers in English 67 percent of the time.

29. *Ford* v. *Quebec*, 54 DLR 4th 577.

It is important to distinguish between the strong support for Act 101 as a whole, which symbolizes the will to protect the French reality in Quebec, and the much weaker support for the specific compulsory measures of the law. Polls usually show an absolute majority contradicting itself by opposing any change in Act 101 yet supporting bilingual policies.[30] The prescriptions to banish other languages in many areas of public life were never popular. René Lévesque himself more than once professed to being "humiliated" by the need to resort to such legal restrictions.[31] Regarding the language of commercial signs in particular, the Act 101 policy of "French only" was never popular in public opinion polls; a policy of "French necessarily" received far higher support in the same polls.

The "French only" policy, however, has always enjoyed the full support of nationalist groups. For them a policy of unilingual French signs is very important, especially in Montreal, because a "French face" in the street is one way to signify to everybody—in particular the new immigrants—that things happen in French in Quebec. Even though they are a minority, the supporters of the "French only" policy are able to influence public opinion. Any agitation about language is likely to arouse the feeling of linguistic insecurity among the whole French-speaking population. At least, that is clearly the way that Premier Bourassa read the situation when he had to react to the Supreme Court's judgment.

Bourassa was pressed by nationalist groups to ignore the Supreme Court judgment. They urged him to use the "notwithstanding" clause—a provision of the 1982 constitution that allows governments to avoid conforming with Supreme Court decisions. But at that time, Bourassa was careful not to displease the other first ministers, since he needed the unanimous consent of all the provincial legislatures to ratify the 1987 Meech Lake Accord. Other first ministers said that use by the government of Quebec of the notwithstanding clause would be perceived as a hostile act. This added to Bourassa's usual concern about the equilibrium between the French-speaking and English-speaking lobbies within his own party. Consequently, he tried once again to find a middle way between the conflicting points of view. He used the notwithstanding clause but passed a new law, Act 178, on December 23, 1988, which legalized the use of languages other than French for commercial signs inside but not

---

30. Major polls of recent years on the linguistic issue were assembled in Edouard Cloutier, "L'opinion politique québécoise," in Denis Monière, ed., *L'année politique au Québec* (Montreal: Le Devoir-Québec/Amérique, various years).

31. Fraser, *P.Q.: René Lévesque and the Parti Québécois in Power*, p. 110; and René Lévesque, *Memoirs* (Toronto: McClelland and Stewart, 1986), p. 288.

outside commercial buildings, and only if they were in smaller letters than the French translation.[32] The so-called inside-outside bill angered English speakers in Quebec and elsewhere in Canada, and it contributed to the widening disenchantment with the Meech Lake Accord in English Canada and to its ultimate failure in June 1990. Act 178 also failed to cool the new nationalist fever in Quebec. In the context of the Supreme Court decision and Act 178, the pressure group Mouvement Québec Français was able to hold the biggest political meetings and demonstrations since the 1980 referendum, and the pro-sovereignty idea gained significantly in popularity in public opinion polls.

The Supreme Court's decision was not the first time that a federal institution attacked the Quebec government's language policy. In fact, language and nationalism issues are connected in Quebec in part because the policies of the federal and provincial governments contradict in some ways. The 1969 Official Languages Act was passed by the federal Parliament, with the support of all parties, in order to implement official bilingualism in federal institutions. This law was followed in 1974 by regulations on bilingual packaging and labeling. Trudeau's aim was to guarantee access to basic services in both French and English from coast to coast. This policy enjoyed a great deal of sympathy throughout the country, although many were skeptical about its feasibility.[33] The achievements are undeniable. Francophones represented 12.25 percent of all employees in federal institutions in 1945 and 26.7 percent in 1990 (30 percent at the chief administrative level), while French speakers are 24 percent of the national population.[34] But this federal policy did not make

32. An Act to Amend the Charter of the French Language, 1988, S.Q. C.54. Businesses with fifty or more employees did not have requirements for "French only" signs lifted under the new legislation.

33. Even in July 1990 after the Meech Lake failure, a poll showed that "65% of Canadians believe that the federal government should provide services to the public across the country in both English and French" and that "66% state that having two official languages throughout Canada better represents their opinion than the option of a French Quebec, with English as the sole official language in the rest of the country." Commissioner of Official Languages, *Annual Report 1990* (Ottawa: April 1991), p. 8.

34. Commissioner of Official Languages, *Annual Report 1990*, p. 125. The 1990 percentages include federal departments, public enterprises, Parliament (members and staff), the armed forces, and the Royal Canadian Mounted Police. For earlier data, see V. Seymour Wilson and Willard A. Mullins, "Representative Bureaucracy: Linguistic/Ethnic Aspects in Canadian Public Policy," *Canadian Public Administration*, vol. 24 (Winter 1978), pp. 513–38; and Jacques Bourgault and Stéphane Dion, "The Changing Profile of Federal Deputy Ministers, 1867 to 1988," report to the Canadian Center for Management Development, Ottawa, 1991, p. 4. Most francophone federal civil servants work essentially in English, and 88 to 93 percent of federal government jobs outside Ottawa, Quebec, and

the English-speaking provinces effectively bilingual, and it did not stop the assimilation of French-speaking communities outside Quebec. Federal policy did little to change the aspirations of the French-speaking population in Quebec—in Montreal in particular—which are to live daily life in French; to work, conduct business, buy goods, and go to the theater, all in French; and to secure the same French environment for future generations. Bilingualism in federal institutions is perceived positively by Quebec francophones, but it by no means ensures that they will be understood in French in all areas of Montreal, nor does it help to attract immigrant populations to the French community.

The federal government defined its role as the protector of linguistic minorities throughout the country. It considers its role in a strictly symmetrical manner—that is, that both minorities (the French outside Quebec and the English inside Quebec) must receive protection. In other words, federal policy has been to institutionalize the symmetry of the two languages, instead of to protect the sole endangered language, French. This symmetrical linguistic concept was enshrined in the Charter of Rights of 1982 without the consent of the government of Quebec. Act 101, with its unilingual prescriptions, contradicted federal policy, and its consistency with the charter was uncertain. Never has a law enacted in Canada been so contested in the courts. During the postreferendum years, when the feeling of language security was high in Quebec and nationalism low, it was possible for the federal legislature to enact the new constitution and the Charter of Rights, for the Supreme Court to invalidate parts of Act 101, and for the federal government to pass in July 1988 a law promoting minority languages everywhere in the federation. All this happened without giving rise to nationalism in Quebec. But with the emotional and visible issue of language in commercial signs, the storm began.

Two events during the winter of 1990 kept the language question at the fore of the crisis. First, sixty-two Ontario municipalities declared themselves English-unilingual in the first three months of the year, in spite of francophone protests. Such reactions had a tremendous effect on nationalist feelings in Quebec. Second, the Catholic school board of Montreal announced its intention to impose the exclusive use of French not only in classrooms but also in all school activities, even in schoolyards and during lunch hours. The board argued that such a rule was necessary to keep French as the language of some schools in the face of increasing

New Brunswick require no knowledge of French at all. Pauline Couture, "Racial Tension: No Simple Black-and-White Solution," *Globe and Mail* (Toronto), July 24, 1991, p. A13.

concentrations of young allophones systematically using English to com-
municate. Young allophone groups reacted by demonstrating with the
Canadian flag, and some young French speakers expressed their support
for the board's intention by displaying the Québécois flag. In the end the
board withdrew its proposal because of broad disapproval from both
allophones and French-speaking communities concerned about the effect
it would have on individual rights. The precarious situation of those
Catholic schools, however, was extensively publicized by the media.[35]
And all this occurred just before the collapse of the Meech Lake Accord
in June 1990.

The exact effect of these events on the French-speaking population is
hard to measure. Everything connected with the immigration and language issue is politically sensitive. The days when the French Canadians
had the highest birthrate in Western countries ended with the secularization and modernization of the province. The fecundity rate was 1.64
among French-speaking women of Quebec in 1981, when the rate needed
to replace a population is 2.1, according to demographers.[36] As in most
Western countries, the gap will be filled by immigration. Thus each event
suggesting that the integration of new immigrants into the French community is incomplete, fragile, or easily reversible nourishes the secessionist
feeling, whatever the official statistics may say about improvement of the
situation. It is easy to convince oneself that the security of the French
language would be strengthened if Quebec were an independent French-
speaking republic. Then the signal given to all inhabitants and new immigrants would be clearer.

Federal language policy unintentionally aided Quebec nationalism
throughout the 1970s and 1980s by challenging the Quebec government's
legislative efforts to protect French in Quebec. Francophone Quebecers
increasingly perceived the Quebec government as the collective protector
for French speakers and the federal government as a kind of intruder
state. This positive perception of the provincial government and negative
perception of the federal government extended from the linguistic issue
to cultural, social, and even economic areas. The language issue strengthened the idea that French Quebec is best served by a stronger Quebec
government facing the federal government. This strong identification with
the Quebec government has been facilitated by another factor: the new
self-confidence of French speakers in Quebec. Always concerned about

35. See, for instance, Francine Lalonde and others, "It's Time to Make French Schools
French," *Globe and Mail* (Toronto), May 14, 1990, p. A7.
36. Conseil de la langue française du Québec, "Indicateurs," pp. 10–11.

their survival in the Canadian federation, they now have a new confidence in their own abilities.

Feeling of Confidence: The Cultural Revolution

Three factors contributed to an unprecedented feeling of confidence among French-speaking Quebecers: the improvement of their economic situation relative to that of the English-speaking population in Quebec, the improvement of provincial institutions to the point where they reached the level of a quasi-state, and the increased perception that the Canadian federation—especially the federal government—was less helpful than in the past. This confidence, however, is fragile. It has been hurt greatly by the current recession.

The Economic Advancement of Francophones

Until the 1960s, English was undeniably the language of prestige in Quebec. The Royal Commission on Bilingualism and Biculturalism created in 1963 showed that in 1961 the wage gap between descendants of French- and English-speaking Quebecers was 35 percent (51 percent in the city of Montreal). Moreover, French speakers had little control of the ownership of the private enterprises operating in the province, and they were strongly underrepresented at managerial levels.

Two explanations of this economic gap have been suggested.[37] One points out the effect of the 1760 conquest of Nouvelle France. While the growing English population received resources, know-how, and capital from Britain, the French population was deprived of such structural advantages and found refuge in agricultural activities. The other explanation emphasizes the cultural orientation of the French population, assembled by a dominant French-Catholic elite opposed to capitalist values and industrial society. Although both factors are likely to have played a role, the cultural explanation is supported by events elsewhere in the world. One may easily be convinced of the truth of Max Weber's theory linking Protestantism and economic growth by looking at the situation at the beginning of the twentieth century. At that time in Europe the growth rate of the economy in Protestant countries topped that of Catholic

37. René Durocher and Paul-André Linteau, eds., *Le retard du Québec et l'infériorité économique des Canadiens français* (Montreal: Boréal Express, 1971).

countries by 152 percent.[38] Protestant minorities played a disproportion-
ate economic role in the wealthier Catholic countries, France and Belgium.
The Catholic countries did not close this gap until secularization occurred.
This pattern perfectly matches what happened in Quebec, except that one
must wait until the end of the 1950s to see an important move toward
secularization in Quebec. The death in 1959 of Maurice Duplessis, the
very conservative Union Nationale premier, was a major turning point.
Duplessis was in power from 1936 to 1939 and from 1944 until 1959.
The Liberal party took power from the Union Nationale in the election
of 1960, and it abruptly initiated major modernizing reforms. Specifically,
the provincial government took from the church essential control over
education, social services, and health care.

When this "Quiet Revolution" began, Quebec was already an urban
and industrial society, but the French-speaking population was clearly
lagging behind, as the statistics above show. The progress of the French-
speaking population has been spectacular in the past three decades. In
1952 the mortality rate per 1,000 births in Quebec and Ontario was 50
and 30, respectively. By 1974 both tied at 15 per 1,000 births. The
gap between the average total income of English-speaking and French-
speaking Quebecers decreased as well. An English speaker earned 44.7
percent more than a French speaker in 1970, but only 16.3 percent more
in 1980. The proportion of workers employed by francophone-owned
enterprises increased from 47.1 percent in 1961 to 61.6 percent in 1987.
French speakers accounted for only 30.5 percent of the managerial category of enterprises operating in Quebec in 1959, but 50.8 percent in
1988. Moreover, French-speaking large enterprises grew, and some of
their presidents became well-known figures.[39]

Antinationalist intellectuals of the 1950s, grouped around Trudeau
and the journal Cité libre, believed that the nationalist ideology would
largely disappear with modernization and the economic advancement of
the French-speaking population. Two good reasons may be found to
support such a view. First, radical nationalist intellectuals in Quebec until
very recently emphasized the economic alienation and exploitation of the

38. Ronald Inglehart, "The Renaissance of Political Culture," American Political
Science Review, vol. 82 (December 1988), pp. 1203–30.
39. Gary Caldwell and Dan Czarnocki, "Un rattrapage raté: Le changement social
dans le Québec d'après-guerre, 1950-1974: une comparaison Québec/Ontario," Recherches
Sociographiques, vol. 18 (January–February 1977), pp. 9–58; Conseil de la langue française
du Québec, "Indicateurs," pp. 60–61; and François Vaillancourt, "Demolinguistic Trends
and Canadian Institutions: An Economic Perspective," in Demolinguistic Trends and the
Evolution of Canadian Institutions (Ottawa: Commissioner of Official Languages, 1989).

Québécois in the Canadian federation. They described them as "an ethnic working class" and as "white niggers of North America."[40] Independence, these intellectuals believed, was the sole way to get out of poverty. Because such a perspective appeared increasingly in conflict with reality, it was logical to expect the secessionist temptation to decline.

Second, the economic advancement of French speakers was accompanied by the fading of the most obvious elements of Quebec's cultural distinctiveness. The Catholic church essentially lost its grip on education, social and health services, and the society in general. Weekly church attendance was 83 percent for Catholic Quebecers and 32 percent for Protestant Canadians in 1965, but the gap has disappeared since then. The majority of both confessional groups now believe, but practice only a little.[41] Quebec Catholic society in 1961 had the highest rate of clerics to faithful in the Western world. This rate dropped spectacularly in the following twenty years, leaving the church with a deep crisis of recruitment and aging.[42] Accordingly, morals and customs completely changed. The change can be shown most clearly in a single statistic: the birthrate, exceptionally high in Catholic Quebec until the 1950s, was similar to that of Ontario in 1975.[43] Many studies have shown that the values of Catholic French Canadians were more conservative and traditional than those of the average Canadian before the 1960s. Today, however, it would be difficult to identify consistent differences in attitudes on issues such as moral values, prestige ranking of professions, role of the government, workers' rights, aboriginal rights, equality between sexes and races, and conception of authority.[44]

40. Pierre Vallières, *White Niggers of America*, trans. Joan Pinkham (Toronto: McClelland and Stewart, 1971).

41. Reginald W. Bibby, *Fragmented Gods: The Poverty and Potential of Religion in Canada* (Toronto: Irwin, 1987); and Julien Harvey, "Le Québec, devenu un désert spirituel?" in Fernand Dumont, ed., *La société québécoise après trente ans de changements* (Quebec: Institut Québécois de Recherche sur la Culture, 1991) pp. 154–61.

42. Fernand Ouellet, "The Quiet Revolution: A Turning Point," in Thomas S. Axworthy and Pierre Elliott Trudeau, eds., *Towards A Just Society: The Trudeau Years*, trans. Patricia Claxton (Viking, 1990), p. 335.

43. Caldwell and Czarnocki, "Un rattrapage raté."

44. A. A. Hunter, "A Comparative Analysis of Anglophone-Francophone Occupational Prestige Structures in Canada," *Canadian Journal of Sociology*, vol. 2 (Spring 1977), pp. 179–93; Richard Simeon and Donald E. Blake, "Regional Preferences: Citizens' Views of Public Policy," in David J. Elkins and Richard Simeon, eds., *Small Worlds: Provinces and Parties in Canadian Political Life* (Toronto: Methuen, 1980), pp. 77–105; Richard Johnston, *Public Opinion and Public Policy in Canada: Questions of Confidence* (Toronto University Press, 1986); Richard Johnston and André Blais, "Meech Lake and Mass Politics: The 'Distinct Society' Clause," *Canadian Public Policy*, supp. 14 (September 1988), pp.

Of course, some subtle differences may escape the available measures of attitudes, but in the end the cultural convergence of French speakers and English speakers is striking. The same pattern occurred in the United States, where Catholics shared more authoritarian values than Protestants before the 1960s but lost their distinctiveness thereafter.[45]

Given the impressive economic advancement of French speakers and their cultural convergence with English speakers, why has Quebec nationalism become stronger than ever on the political scene? Why is it that when French speakers became more like their fellow citizens economically and culturally, they began to consider more seriously the possibility of political separation? An initial explanation is the language issue. As noted earlier, language has become the main source of cleavage between French Quebec and the rest of Canada with the fading of other cultural differences. Most French speakers judge the means mobilized to promote French in the country to be insufficient; many anglophones consider such means excessive.[46] No other attitudinal cleavage is nearly as strong as this one.

Language remains a high barrier between the two communities. Anglophone Quebecers choose French-language networks only 5 percent of the time that they spend watching television, and francophones watch English-language networks 14 percent of the time.[47] French-speaking artists look for recognition in Paris much more than in Toronto. The language difference is a strong incentive for both linguistic groups to create or strengthen their own associations rather than mix together. There are few English speakers in the public-sector bureaucracies of the government of Quebec. French speakers' accession to executive positions

---

25–42; Paul M. Sniderman and others, "Liberty, Authority and Community: Civil Liberties and the Canadian Political Culture," paper prepared for presentation at the 1988 annual meeting of the Canadian Political Science Association; Paul M. Sniderman and others, "Political Culture and the Problem of Double Standards: Mass and Elite Attitudes toward Language Rights in the Canadian Charter of Rights and Freedoms," *Canadian Journal of Political Science*, vol. 22 (June 1989), pp. 259–84; and Sylvia Bashevkin, "Solitudes in Collision? Pan-Canadian and Quebec Nationalist Attitudes in the late 1970s," *Comparative Political Studies*, vol. 23 (April 1990), pp. 3–24.

    45. Gerhard E. Lenski, *The Religious Factor: A Sociological Study of Religion's Impact on Politics, Economics and Family Life* (Doubleday, 1963); and Duane F. Alwin, "Religion and Parental Child-Rearing Orientations: Evidence of a Catholic-Protestant Convergence," *American Journal of Sociology*, vol. 92 (September 1986), pp. 412–40.

    46. The modal preference in terms of promotion of French among Canadian anglophones is for the status quo, but 42 percent believe that too much is done. André Blais, "Le clivage linguistique au Canada," *Recherches sociographiques*, forthcoming.

    47. Conseil de la langue française du Québec, "Indicateurs," pp. 74–75.

was accomplished essentially in francophone-owned enterprises rather than in English-speaking ones.[48] In other words, the two groups are increasingly similar in their behavior, and they interact on an equal basis more than ever. But they are still largely two parallel worlds broadly ignorant of one other, although more in competition than in years past.

Another factor to be considered is the distinction between cultural convergence and cultural identity. Alexis de Tocqueville foresaw that modernity would cause cultural convergence of populations and that it would encourage the placement of extreme value on cultural differences. As human groups lose their differences, they view them with nostalgia and put high value on the remaining ones. And since different groups increasingly share the same values, they compete more for the same goods and they envy each other more. This is exactly what happened in Canada. Most of the debate about the Meech Lake Accord focused on the opportunity to insert in the constitution a clause specifying that Quebec is a "distinct society" within Canada. The notion of distinctiveness reached quasi-unanimity in Quebec; some nationalist elites claimed that Quebec society was in many ways incompatible with English-Canadian society. And all this occurred precisely when the cultural dispositions of both societies were more similar than ever before.[49]

Cultural secularization and economic advancement gave tremendous confidence to the French speakers, in particular among the elites. It is striking to see how much the submissions by economists and other experts to the Bélanger-Campeau Commission in 1990–91 expressed the same optimistic perspective. They emphasized impressive economic progress, regardless of whether their conclusions were pro-Canada or pro-Quebec.[50] But while pro-federalism economists see in this progress the positive

48. Robert Grenon, "Présence francophone dans la haute direction des entreprises employant entre 500 et 999 personnes au Quebec en 1988" (Montreal: Office de la langue française, December 1988).

49. I expand this point in Stéphane Dion, "Le nationalisme dans la convergence culturelle: le Québec contemporain et le paradoxe de Tocqueville," in Raymond Hudon and Réjean Pelletier, eds., *L'engagement intellectuel: Mélange en l'honneur de Léon Dion* (Quebec: les Presses de l'Université Laval, 1991), pp. 291–311.

50. For pro-Canada conclusions, see Raynauld, "Les enjeux économiques de la souveraineté"; and Jean-Paul Murray and Gary Brazier, "Le Statu quo: un arrangement fonctionnel," report presented to the Commission on the Political and Constitutional Future of Quebec, October 1990. For pro-Quebec conclusions, see Pierre Fortin, "Le choix forcé du Québec: aspects économiques et stratégiques," report presented to the Commission on the Political and Constitutional Future of Quebec, November 1990; Pierre-Paul Proulx, "L'évolution de l'espace économique du Québec, la politique économique dans un monde de nationalismes et d'interdépendance, et les relations Québec-Ottawa," ibid., October

effect of belonging to the Canadian federation, pro-sovereignty economists argue for the possibility of a quiet and noncostly shift to sovereignty.
No one testified that there would be a significant short-term increase in
wealth following sovereignty. Many claimed, however, that there would
be no significant economic deterioration during the transition period and
probably an overall improvement in the long term. Even some important
business people have expressed this view. Almost half of 200 chief executives (48.5 percent) of the 500 biggest Quebec enterprises reported in a
poll that independence would have a positive effect in the long term, and
only 13.3 percent believed that there would be a negative effect. This
optimism is in stark contrast to the pessimism following the 1980 referendum, when most of the business class was hostile to the secessionist idea.[51]
In 1980 a pervasive argument against sovereignty was that it would cause
big business and foreign capital to flee Quebec. In 1990–91 many believed
that the new capitalist spirit in Quebec would inspire confidence and
credibility in international investors and that the local business class was
solid enough to support the transition costs.

Before the Quiet Revolution, traditional nationalism in Quebec was
mainly communitarian, centered on the Catholic church, and antistatist.
From 1960 until the 1980 referendum, nationalism was somewhat connected with the growth of the provincial government—called "the State
of Quebec"—and widely identified with the public sector and the new
middle class of artists and intellectuals. The pro-sovereignty position was
popular from the radical to the center-left part of the political spectrum.
But in 1990–91, with support from the business class and the unions,
sovereignty became a nonideological or catch-all idea and thus better
placed to seduce all groups and social classes.

Quebec as a Quasi State

Today the Quebec government and institutions form a quasi state with
exclusive or joint responsibility over education, health, welfare, natural
resources, municipal affairs, housing, culture, energy, immigration, industry, and language. This also strengthens the feeling of confidence in easy
and profitable sovereignty.

1990; and Rodrigue Tremblay, "Le statut politique et constitutionnel du Québec," ibid.,
November 1990.

51. *Les Affaires*, May 12, 1990.

Traditionally, it was the pro-federalists who argued that the decentralization of the Canadian federation allowed all the means necessary for development of Quebec society. In contrast, pro-sovereignty forces described the Canadian federation as centralist and as an oppressive iron collar. But in the 1990-91 debate, the pro-sovereignty camp instead pointed out that the move to political independence would be easy because Quebec institutions had expanded in all directions. Indeed, Quebec already has modern governmental bureaucracies, a complete educational system through the university level, public hospitals and social welfare organizations, financial institutions, public enterprises, and a network of municipalities regulated by the provincial government. Recently, the province has become home to large francophone-owned private enterprises. More than any other Canadian provincial government, Quebec has involved itself in diplomacy,[52] immigration policy, and autonomous fiscal policy. It is the only province with a full pension plan for its residents separate from the federal one that operates in the other provinces. A growing contingent of public servants, teachers, and intellectuals performs the varied responsibilities of this quasi state, and not surprisingly it has rapidly become the core of support for nationalism.

The strength of Quebec's provincial government is apparent if one compares Canada with the three other most decentralized countries—Switzerland, the United States, and the Federal Republic of Germany (see table 4). Canada has by far the weakest central government and the strongest second level of government. The most common indicator of decentralization is the relative autonomous fiscal capacities of different levels of government in a country. The gap between the fiscal weight of the federal government and the second-level governments is clearly lower in Canada than in Switzerland, the United States, and the Federal Republic of Germany. Canada is the only country of the four where the gap between the fiscal capacity of the federal government and that of the "states" significantly declined during the past decade. Moreover, the cake is divided among ten provinces in Canada, not fifty states as in the United States. Quebec is the second most populous province, and its government is involved in more fields than is the Ontario government. All of this suggests that Quebec already has the most powerful second level of government of all OECD countries.

52. Elliot J. Feldman and Lilly Gardner Feldman, "Canada," in Hans J. Michelmann and Panayotis Soldatos, eds., *Federalism and International Relations: The Role of Subnational Units* (Oxford University Press, 1990), pp. 176–210.

TABLE 4. Allocation of Public-Sector Revenues before Transfers, by Level of Government, Canada, Switzerland, United States, and Federal Republic of Germany, 1976, 1988

Percent

Level of government	1976				1988			
	Canada	Switzerland	United States	Germany	Canada	Switzerland[a]	United States	Germany
Federal	49.9	53.2	59.4	62.9	48.1	53.3	59.1	64.0
"States"	38.6	25.3	22.9	22.7	41.3	24.6	24.4	22.1
Local	11.5	21.5	17.7	14.4	10.6	22.1	16.5	13.8
TOTAL	100.0	100.0	100.0	100.0	100.0	100.0	100.0	99.9[b]

SOURCE: International Monetary Fund, *Government Finance Statistics*, 1985, 1990.
a. Data from 1984.
b. Numbers have been rounded.

A Federal Government in Bad Shape

Since the beginning of 1990, with secessionist sentiment higher than ever before, federal institutions have been under attack in French Quebec. More and more politicians and experts are confident that the help of the federal government is not essential. The counterargument has barely been developed mostly because the federal government decided to keep silent during extensive consultations initiated in response to the complaints in English Canada about the secretive way in which the Meech Lake negotiations had been conducted.

The opinion that "Canada does not work anymore" has gained extensive credibility among the Quebec French-speaking elite and within the French-speaking population as a whole, but to a degree more difficult to measure. The striking point is that none of these arguments was stressed during the 1980 referendum campaign. This attests to the new confidence of the French-speaking political and economic elites in their ability to independently manage a modern state without a decline in the standard of living.

There are six major lines of criticism leveled at the federal government during the current debate in Quebec. They were frequently heard at the Bélanger-Campeau Commission hearings and also broadly diffused in the media. As I said, the counterarguments were barely heard. The debate occurred when the popularity of the ruling federal party and prime minister was as low as 15 percent in national polls and when neither the Liberal party of Canada nor the New Democratic party was able to gain popularity in Quebec, even though the former chose a French-speaking Quebecer as its leader. The orientation of Quebec members of Parliament at the federal level was strongly nationalist or even, in the case of the Bloc Québécois, pro-sovereignty. This contrasts sharply with the situation in 1980, when federalist champion Pierre Elliott Trudeau was at the peak of his popularity in Quebec, three months after an overwhelming electoral victory in the province.

First, Quebec is not subsidized by the rest of Canada. During the 1980 referendum campaign, a major argument of the pro-federalist camp was that the Quebec government, institutions, and citizens were broadly funded by the rest of the country, mainly through equalization payments and the transfer policies of the federal government. This argument was not strongly voiced during the 1990–91 debate. In fact, the margin of difference in opinion between pro-federalist economists and pro-sovereignty economists regarding the gap between what Quebec taxpayers pay and get from the federal government was remarkably thin. No one claimed a figure higher than 1 percent of the Quebecers' total income as an estimate of the gain or loss of the province in its exchange of taxes and services with Ottawa.[53]

Second, the federal government is cutting payments to the provinces. The perception that a sovereign Quebec would be able to maintain the level of public services without necessarily increasing the fiscal burden was well served by the budgetary policy of the current Conservative government. In order to decrease its huge annual deficits, the federal government began to restrict the growth in the amount of money that it sent to the provinces for such services as health, welfare, and higher education and for equalization payments to the poorer provinces. It further reduced its economic role by privatizing important crown corporations. In doing so, it generated the perception that it will be less and less useful to Quebec if Quebec stays in the federation.

Third, the federal government duplicates provincial activities. The utility of the federal government was questioned in another way: the costly overlapping of its activities with provincial ones. Duplications occurred in up to 60 percent of spending programs, according to a broadly cited 1978 study.[54] The leader of the Parti Québécois, Jacques Parizeau, a well-regarded economist and former provincial minister of finance, claimed—with the support of many other experts—that under a sovereign Quebec, a lot of economies would be easily made by eliminating these massive duplications.

Fourth, the Canadian federation is paralyzed by incessant intergovernmental conflict. Nationalist supporters point out the political cost of managing the federation. Since so many federal and provincial jurisdictions overlap, new initiatives of the federal government inevitably lead to protests from provincial governments. In 1990–91 jurisdictional conflicts arose, for example, over communication and environmental policies. And even when the federal government acts in its own sphere of activity, it often faces recriminations from the provinces. Indeed, one of its major activities involves distribution of subsidies and public investments to the provinces. In a time of scarce resources, each choice that benefits one province tends to generate jealousy elsewhere in the country. By comparison, a sovereign Quebec would seem more homogeneous and better able

53. Fortin, "Le choix forcé du Québec," p. 13.
54. Germain Julien and Marcel Proulx, *Les chevauchements des programmes fédéraux et québécois* (Quebec: École Nationale d'Administration Publique, 1978).

to foster cooperation among the government, the regions, the unions, and the business class.

Fifth, the federation no longer offers useful economic protection in a time of trade globalization. It is likely that the 1989 free trade agreement with the United States helped to generate this opinion among many economists, business people, politicians, and citizens. The overwhelming popularity of free trade in Quebec reflects its cultural and economic self-confidence. The impression is that the future of the Quebec economy will be increasingly north-south. Regarding the west-east market, nationalists believe that access to this market is already secured by the free trade agreement, GATT rules, a mutual interest in commerce, and globalization of the economy, irrespective of whether Quebec remains a province of Canada or secedes. During the 1980 referendum campaign, this optimistic view was not really shared outside the circles of the Parti Québécois. In 1990 it probably would have rallied the majority of French-speaking economists in Quebec.

Sixth, the accumulated debt of the federal government proves that the federation is a financial failure. During the 1980 referendum campaign, the federal debt was not an issue at all. But in 1990, when the debt surpassed the C$400 billion mark, it became a target for nationalist critics. The federal debt soared from 37 percent of gross domestic product to over 60 percent between 1974–75 and 1989–90.[55] It devours a third of annual revenues compared with about a tenth in the early 1970s. Canada has one of the worst debt problems among OECD countries. Thus it is harder to perceive the Canadian federation as a useful financial deal. Many Quebec economists made this point in 1990–91. Some of them—and of course the Parti Québécois—blamed the growing debt on bad management at the federal level, and they pointed to the better state of the Quebec government's finances.

The Limits of the New Self-Confidence

So far I have reviewed the roots of the newfound self-confidence of French Quebec. Impressive economic advancement, the consolidation of a francophone business class, the development of modern institutions, and external factors (for example, free trade and the difficulties of the

55. H. Mimoto and P. Cross, "The Growth of the Federal Debt," *Canadian Economic Observer* (June 1991), pp. 3.1–3.34.

federal government) led to optimistic perceptions about sovereignty. But this optimism has had its limits. In particular, it has been strongly challenged by the deep economic recession that hit the eastern part of North America in 1990–91.

Unemployment in Quebec reached 12 percent.[56] Month after month, enterprises went bankrupt. Many new stars of the Quebec business establishment—Lavalin, Quebecor, Cascades, Malenfant—struggled financially. Moreover, the media began to emphasize what was wrong in the province—for example, the deterioration of health services and road transport, the high drop-out rates among students, forest depletion, and various problems with Hydro-Quebec. In short, a huge contrast arose between the optimistic nationalist language and tough daily reality. It is likely that this contrast contributed significantly to the drop in support for sovereignty in the spring of 1991.

Beginning in February 1991, prominent francophone business leaders in Quebec began to warn that independence would be "a very risky business."[57] Another sign of cold feet among the elite was the recommendation of the Bélanger-Campeau Commission to create a committee of experts on the profitability of sovereignty. The commission said that there was a lack of good empirical studies on the expected economic consequences of sovereignty and on the current advantages and costs of the Canadian federation. Indeed, many criticisms of the federal government are still impressionistic views rather than firm empirical facts.

Consider, for instance, the big savings expected from the elimination of program duplication. Although the federal government and the provincial governments are both involved in many sectors, they do not do the same things. No one has been able to identify a single program where the governments are performing the same task, strictly speaking. It may be that they harm each other in some ways, while complementing each other in other ways. The truth is that there are no studies on the matter. Because the evidence remains vague, arguments about expected savings have been weakened.

56. Albert Juneau, "La plaie du chômage," Le Devoir, February 13, 1991, p. A8.

57. The quote is from Bertin Nadeau of Provigo, in David Frum, "Quebec Nationalists Get Cold Feet," Wall Street Journal, July 19, 1991, p. A11. See also André Picard, "Sovereignty Studies Challenged," Globe and Mail (Toronto), April 1, 1991, pp. A1–A2; Miro Cernétig, "Beaudoin Issues Unity Battle Call," Globe and Mail, April 29, 1991, p. B3; and Clyde H. Farnsworth, "Separatist Fervor Fades in Quebec," New York Times, September 10, 1991, p. D1.

The optimistic theory is that an independent Quebec could significantly lessen political conflicts between the center and the peripheries and between economic agents. Yet, in their submissions to the Bélanger-Campeau Commission, representatives of the Quebec regions frequently complained about the allegedly centralized policies of the Quebec government, and they asked for a massive decentralization. A tripartite concord among the Quebec government, business, and unions has appeared at times in the past, but it would be for the most part a new pattern in a province that has more than its annual share of striking workers.[58]

Consider the access of a sovereign Quebec to foreign markets. It is true that the weight of the U.S. market is increasing in Quebec imports and exports, but Quebec is the most dependent of all provinces on the internal Canadian market.[59] Thus the assumption that the rest of Canada will not engage in protective policies damaging to the Quebec economy is all the more risky. The most important Quebec business association, the Conseil du Patronat, stressed its concern on this matter in its submission to the Bélanger-Campeau Commission.[60]

On the issue of government debt, one should not conclude too quickly that the federal government is the only guilty party. The provincial record is not very good either, and that is not only because the provinces— Quebec in particular—have accumulated a worrying debt (about C$170 billion). A recent study by Statistics Canada shows that one of the main factors in the growth of the federal debt was the transfer of personal and corporate tax points to the provinces between 1975 and 1977.[61] In assuming its huge deficit, the federal government may have lessened the financial difficulties of the provinces. After all, the provincial governments—Quebec in particular—used such an argument at the expense of their own municipalities. Indeed, after the recent cut of transfers from the federal government, some provinces cut their own transfers to municipalities, saying that it is at the municipal level, not at the provincial one, that expenditure cuts—or tax increases—can be most easily accomplished.

The debate about the currency creates a further impression of the fragility of secessionist arguments. One would expect that a confident

58. Robert Boily, "Profil du Quebec," in Denis Monière, ed., *L'année politique au Québec* (Montreal: Le Devoir-Québec/Amérique, 1989), p. 203.

59. Raynauld, "Les enjeux économiques de la souveraineté," pp. 13–14, 55.

60. Michel Bélanger and Jean Campeau, *Report of the Commission on the Political and Constitutional Future of Quebec* (Bibliothèque Nationale du Québec, 1991).

61. Mimoto and Cross, "Growth of the Federal Debt."

Quebec would be eager to create and control its own currency. In fact, even Parti Québécois leader Jacques Parizeau said that he would keep the Canadian dollar, even without the agreement of the Canadian Parliament and without holding any control over the central bank of Canada. The idea of an autonomous monetary policy is not popular.

Many other doubts have been raised about the profitability of sovereignty: the loss of economies of scale in national service delivery (for example, the post office), the cost of establishing embassies; the cost of economic support to the Quebec part of the national capital region, which is currently heavily dependent on the Canadian federal government;[62] and Quebec's share of Canadian assets and debts. The Parti Québécois committed itself to hiring in the Quebec civil service all Quebecers currently employed by the federal government, but the Liberal party said that that would be too costly.

The issue of sovereignty recently has been complicated by territorial issues. Territorial claims came from two fronts in 1990–91. First, native peoples—mostly the Crees in northern Quebec—warned with more insistence than ever that they would not allow their ancestral territories to be annexed to an independent Quebec. They started an intensive lobby to win international support for their cause. Second, English-Canadian intellectuals have argued that if Quebec secedes it should leave with only the territories it had in 1867 when the confederation began. All lands ceded to Quebec by federal laws in 1898 and 1912 should be given back, they claim.[63] These two claims mean that Quebec would lose three-quarters of its territory—all the northern land—with the natural resources and the hydroelectric dams and potential. In practice, it would be reduced to the Saint Lawrence River Valley.

Territorial objections to Quebec sovereignty are in many ways judicially and politically disputable. For instance, the Crees sold their rights to the territory for C$225 million in a treaty with the government of Quebec in 1975. Except for aboriginal groups, few in English Canada dispute Quebec's boundaries. But the Crees' position is gaining favor, and the territorial issue is likely to have a negative effect on secessionist support in Quebec.

In short, the new self-confidence extended optimism about the profitability of sovereignty, but not to the point of building a firm consensus blotting out numerous sources of doubt.

62. Bélanger and Campeau, *Report of the Commission*, p. 68.
63. David Jay Bercuson and Barry Cooper, *Deconfederation: Canada without Quebec* (Toronto: Key Porter, 1991).

Feeling of Rejection: The Meech Lake Crisis

The sudden increase in secessionist support since 1990 cannot be explained only by structural and long-term growth factors. Obviously, some catalyst is playing a role here. The identity of this catalyst is clear: the three-year debate over the Meech Lake Accord and its ultimate failure in June 1990.

English Canada's refusal to include in the constitution proposals that were almost unanimously viewed in French Quebec as minimum conditions had a very strong effect on public opinion in the province. It generated an intense feeling of rejection. A common interpretation was that *"les Anglais* do not want us any more."

The Meech Lake Failure

To fully understand French Quebecers' feeling of rejection in 1990–91, one must go back to the 1980 referendum campaign, when a feeling of rejection among French Quebecers was not perceptible. On the contrary, at that time, all the signals received from the other provinces led Quebecers to believe that the secession of Quebec would have been viewed as a disaster. Various groups claimed their attachment to the French-Canadian reality. In fact, the concern in Quebec was rather the reverse—that is, that English Canada would not let Quebec go.

At that time Trudeau pledged to renew federalism if the referendum of the Parti Québécois was rejected.[64] In Quebec the expression "renewed federalism" was broadly understood as synonymous with "new powers for Quebec in the federation." Since no gain of that sort for Quebec was included in the Constitution Act of 1982, many Quebecers felt betrayed by Trudeau. Later Trudeau said that he never promised a special status for Quebec, something evidently contrary to his political convictions. In spite of his justifications, the idea that Trudeau made a voluntary ambiguous statement in 1980 to attract the votes of soft nationalists is a major claim of the nationalist camp in 1990–91 and something barely denied by the federalist camp.

Another important event was the way that the Quebec government was isolated during the 1981-82 constitutional negotiations. The final negotiation occurred during the night of November 4, 1981, *la nuit des longs couteaux* (night of the long knives). René Lévesque, then premier

---

64. See Clarkson and McCall, *Trudeau and Our Times*, pp. 238–39.

of Quebec, was absent. Trudeauists argue that a separatist premier would never have agreed to any constitutional agreement, but the fact remains that the isolation of Lévesque was, to say the least, unfair, and is so perceived ten years later.

So the constitution was implemented in 1982 lacking only the consent of the province of Quebec. The next significant event is the federal electoral campaign of 1984. Brian Mulroney and Progressive Conservative party candidates endorsed the point of view that Trudeau's ambiguous statement in 1980 was an intellectual fraud, that the way Quebec was isolated in 1981–82 was a shame. Brian Mulroney solemnly committed himself to reintegrate Quebec in the constitution with "honor and enthusiasm."[65] In other words, the new prime minister of Canada legitimized the view that the rest of Canada owed reparation to Quebec. René Lévesque saluted this new Ottawa orientation as *"le beau risque"* (a risk that looks good).[66]

By 1987, it was not the secessionist René Lévesque who sat at the negotiating table, but the federalist Robert Bourassa, reelected in December 1985. Robert Bourassa brought the shortest list of constitutional demands ever requested by a government of Quebec: recognition of Quebec as a distinct society; a greater role over immigration; a role in appointments to the Supreme Court; limitation on federal spending power; and a veto on constitutional amendments. Bourassa was not in a position to ask for more because nationalist feeling was too low in Quebec at that time to concern the rest of Canada. His conditions roughly reflected the terms of the agreement reached at Meech Lake on June 3, 1987, between the prime minister of Canada and the ten provincial premiers. The government of Quebec, as well as the Quebec federal MPs of the Conservative party, and prime minister Mulroney claimed that they had indeed succeeded in reintegrating Quebec in the constitution with "honor and enthusiasm."

Yet the story did not proceed as hoped. The federal Parliament and ten provincial legislatures had three years to ratify the accord. Newly elected premiers in New Brunswick, Manitoba, and Newfoundland declared themselves not committed by the signature of their predecessors. Pierre Trudeau spoke out forcefully against the Meech Lake Accord,

---

65. Pierre Fournier, *A Meech Lake Post-Mortem: Is Quebec Sovereignty Inevitable?* trans. Sheila Fischman (Montreal and Kingston: McGill-Queen's University Press, 1991), p. 32.

66. Alain-G. Gagnon and Mary Beth Montcalm, *Quebec: Beyond the Quiet Revolution* (Scarborough, Ont.: Nelson Canada, 1990), p. 162.

saying that it would debilitate the central government and lead to a gradual secession of Quebec.[67]

The Meech Lake failure resulted, ultimately, from the refusal of two small provinces, Newfoundland and Manitoba, to give their assent to the accord. The eight other first ministers agreed with the accord, and one of the two hold-outs endorsed it at the end of a late round of negotiation. But it was not ratified because of the use of a procedural obstacle by an aboriginal member of the Manitoba legislature who was upset by the absence of any gains for aboriginal peoples in the accord. So one may think that it is not "English Canada," but only two small provinces, or even only one aboriginal MP, who rejected Quebec's minimal conditions. Such an interpretation would be misleading. There are too many polls showing that the fight by the premiers of Manitoba and Newfoundland against Meech Lake was supported not only by a broad majority of citizens in their own provinces, but also by a broad majority of citizens of all the English-speaking provinces.[68] During those three years of public debate, the opposition to the accord never stopped growing outside Quebec, while nationalistic feelings rose in Quebec.

I have already explained how much the language crisis over the Supreme Court decision interfered with this constitutional debate of 1982–90. The "inside-outside" Act 178 was opposed everywhere in English Canada and damaged the reputation of the Meech Lake Accord. It nourished anti-French and anti-Québécois attitudes. Events like the trampling of the Quebec flag in Brockville, Ontario; the rising of new, radical, pro-English groups and parties in New Brunswick, Ontario, and the western provinces; and the declaration by some municipalities in Ontario that they were English unilingual were commented on by the media in Quebec. Any manifestation of sympathy for French Quebec, on the other hand, was too discreet to be publicized.

No such manifestations of sympathies were evident after the Meech Lake failure on June 22, 1990, the deadline for ratification. Quite the contrary, a January 1991 poll indicated that nearly 70 percent of Canadians outside Quebec would not endorse further concessions to Quebec,

67. See Donald Johnston, ed., *With a Bang, Not A Whimper: Pierre Trudeau Speaks Out* (Toronto: Stoddart, 1988).

68. A March 1990 Gallup poll showed that 19 percent of Canadian English speakers favored the Meech Lake Accord and 51 percent opposed it. Among French speakers, 41 percent were in favor and 19 percent against. "Opposition to Meech Lake Reaches Highest Recorded Level," *Gallup Report* (Canada), May 18, 1990.

even if it meant that the province would separate.[69] Giving no more concessions to Quebec is exactly the platform of the Reform party, which enjoyed an impressive increase in support in the polls. The events since then have led to the impression that it will be difficult for Quebec to get substantial changes—maybe even any change—in the Constitution Act of 1982. This allows very little or no room at all between the status quo and complete independence. Softer nationalists have to choose between the polar opposites. From about February 1990 to February 1991, they seemed disposed to choose the secessionist camp.

Different Reactions to Meech Lake

Feelings of rejection grew in French Quebec in 1990–91 because the rest of the country, for the first time, seemed disposed to let it go. This shift in anglophone opinion is addressed in another chapter. I want to stress two points because they underline the different reactions of French Quebec and English Canada to the failure of the Meech Lake Accord.

The judicialization of politics. Much of the Meech Lake debate involved setting the rules that judges of the Supreme Court would use to make important collective decisions. In this sense, the Meech Lake Accord reflected the move toward judicialization of politics and policymaking in Canada and illustrates its difficulties. It is doubtful that French-speaking and English-speaking Canadians understood, or even cared, about the judicial quibbles of the never-ending constitutional debate. But they understood very simple ideas. Francophones believed that English Canada did not recognize Quebec's distinctiveness since it did not agree to enshrine in the constitution the obvious fact that Quebec is a "distinct society." English speakers believed that Quebec would get "something" that they did not have, and that "something" was superior to the human rights inscribed in the charter. Interpretations of the Meech Lake Accord varied widely. Some anglophone feminist groups feared that the distinct-society clause would allow the government of Quebec to oppress its female citizens by intransigent policies to increase the birthrate. This concern was received by feminist groups and public opinion in Quebec as an incredible ignorance of Quebec society.[70] One bad result of the judicializa-

69. Mentioned in Alain-G. Gagnon, "Everything Old is New Again: Canada, Quebec and Constitutional Impasse," in Frances Abele, ed., *How Ottawa Spends, 1991–92: The Politics of Fragmentation* (Ottawa: Carleton University Press, 1991), p. 99.

70. For a review of the debate, see Lynn Smith, "The Distinct Society Clause in the Meech Lake Accord: Could It Affect Equality Rights for Women?" and Donna Greschner, "How Not to Drown in Meech Lake: Rules, Principles and Women's Equality Rights," in

tion of politics is that it can set one population against another by presenting simplistic symbols and abstractions.

Such abstractions leave little room for compromise. An abstract idea confronting the Meech Lake Accord was the concept of "strict equality between provinces." It seemed impossible to accommodate such an egalitarian principle with a distinct-society clause that applied only to the province of Quebec. The truth is that Quebec has long had a special status. Since the beginning of the federation, it has had its own legal system based on the French civil code, and it has expanded its role in important fields since the 1960s, such as a pension plan, immigration policy, fiscal arrangements, and international relations. Such arrangements were negotiated with the federal government in recent decades in a piecemeal fashion. The focus was on means at least as much as on ends and on absolute principles. But when the time comes to speak about the constitution or Supreme Court interpretations, absolute principles take precedence in the negotiation. One hardly hears about concrete means and current realities.

Finally, judicialization of politics leads to government by judges. Constitutional experts were unable to say how the Supreme Court would interpret the distinct-society clause. One camp claimed that it would allow Quebec to extract more and more powers until the day it actually became a sovereign state. The other camp said that such a clause was an empty shell with nothing in it for Quebec. Meech Lake partisans did not agree either. Prime Minister Mulroney said that the clause would give no additional power to Quebec, while Premier Bourassa defended it as an essential extension of Quebec rights.

Canadian multiculturalism. For French-speaking Quebecers, Meech Lake was supposed to be their round, the "Quebec round," the reparation that English Canada owed to them. But very quickly, various feminist, aboriginal, ethnic, and regional groups complained that the accord gave them nothing. This was a powerful strike against Meech Lake in the English-speaking provinces. But reducing the Quebec question to "one among many others" gave a strong impetus to Quebec nationalist sentiment.

The failure of the Meech Lake Accord was the triumph of the multicultural vision of Canada over the bicultural one. The Meech Lake crisis stressed the multicultural-bicultural issue, but it did not invent it. In the

---

Katherine E. Swinton and Carol J. Rogerson, eds., *Competing Constitutional Visions: The Meech Lake Accord* (Toronto: Carswell, 1988), pp. 35–54, 55–63.

early 1960s the federal government instituted a royal commission called the Commission on Bilingualism and Biculturalism. Biculturalism refers to the "two founding nations," that is, the descendants of the British and the French. By the time the commission ended its activities, Trudeau was prime minister. He retained the idea of bilingualism, but decided to promote multiculturalism instead of biculturalism. English and French Canadians would have to give place to other cultural groups. The federal government promised to help these groups maintain and promote their cultures so that they would become fully part of the Canadian identity. Multiculturalism became an official policy. Enshrined in the Charter of Rights, it endowed ethnic communities with public money.

Nationalist Quebecers perceive multiculturalism as English Canada's way to dilute the Quebec question. Although there is a kernel of truth in their perception, multiculturalism is more than that. After all, 15 percent of Canada's population was born abroad. The same phenomenon is occurring in the United States, where the traditional melting pot notion is widely rejected. In Quebec, the governments of the province and the city of Montreal implemented their own multicultural policies with affirmative action programs for visible minorities, public funding for ethnic groups, and heritage-language courses in schools. But whatever the motivations behind Canadian multiculturalism, French-speaking Quebecers feared its effect—namely, that their specific concerns would weigh less and less in the Canada of tomorrow.

The Limits of the Feeling of Rejection

A strong feeling of rejection that appears so suddenly may also rapidly decline. There are some signs of this in the decline the secession idea has suffered in the polls since spring 1991. It suggests that the feeling of rejection is becoming less salient as it recedes into the memory. Obviously Quebecers' minds are shifting to other concerns, with the economic recession at the very forefront.

In normal times, outside exceptional crises, the relationship between English-speaking and French-speaking Canadians is not hostile or overwhelmingly negative. Comparative studies show that relationships between linguistic groups are less conflictual in Canada than in Belgium: mutual appreciation of the French and English in Canada did not deteriorate between 1968 and 1988.[71] The crucial question is whether the intense

71. Blais, "Le clivage linguistique au Canada."

resentment that has arisen since 1988 will be short-lived or long lasting enough to convince a majority of Quebecers that they have to leave.

But nationalism will benefit from any additional sign of rejection. A new increase in support for sovereignty seems likely if no proposals in response to Quebec requests are forthcoming from the rest of the country before May 1992.

Conclusion

I began this chapter by pointing out that the Quebec-Canada question has little to do with the nationalist explosions that threaten so many East European and third world countries. But one lesson may be learned from what has happened there: secession is less risky in democracy. Only during the 1980 referendum did many Quebecers consider an intervention by the Canadian army. In 1991 such a threat was lower than ever (although the territorial issue inspired some concerns of that sort).

If there is to be a secession of Quebec, the key decision will be made by Quebecers in a referendum. A few have already said that they will vote for sovereignty at any cost. We may become poorer, they say, but we will be happier. This is a highly respectable statement. It is also the slogan most likely to save the unity of Canada.

Only a combination of three factors is strong enough, perhaps, to change the historic French Quebec nationalism into a stable, majority-winning secessionist movement. The first is the fear of disappearing, or of being progressively weakened, in the Canadian federation, and thus raises the linguistic issue. The second is the new optimism in the profitability of sovereignty, inspired by a self-confidence rooted in the economic progress of francophones, the development of provincial institutions, and their condition relative to the federal one. The third is a feeling of rejection born from the Meech Lake crisis.

Quebecers' feelings of fear, confidence, and rejection explain the rise of support for secession; they suggest also the reversibility of such support. The fear that their linguistic heritage could disappear may not remain a strong impetus to separation, given the many signs that the future of the French language has been secured in the province of Quebec. It is doubtful that the new optimism is firm enough to lead to sovereignty because of the uncertainties the secessionist option still arouses. And the tensions reached in the middle of the Meech Lake crisis probably will decline, cooling the feeling of rejection.

One current issue is how to make Canadian federalism more manageable. I cannot assess the utility of switching specific sectors from the federal government to the government of Quebec (or to all the provincial governments). Serious empirical studies are needed to review individual sectors and programs where the federal and provincial governments overlap in their activities.

Another issue is the matter of the development and security of Quebec society. I have read and heard nothing to convince me of the necessity of a dramatic transfer of responsibilities from the federal to the Quebec government, nothing to prove that workers or professional Quebecers will better serve Quebec society if they follow the direction of Quebec City instead of Ottawa. I believe the development of Quebec is best assured if it retains the most powerful subnational government in the OECD countries. Quebec's specific conditions may lead to more provincial control in some sectors (language, immigration, culture, and communication). But one should not go too far in that direction. Then the rest of the country would question the role of federal MPs, ministers—and perhaps even a prime minister—from Quebec: it would seem too odd that those politicians would be involved in so many decisions that would not apply in their constituencies.

The key issue is and always will be language. The government of Quebec would better serve its citizens if it focused the negotiation on such a critical issue, instead of bringing on the table vague notions (distinct society) as it did during Meech Lake, or instead of demanding almost everything as it did after Meech Lake (the Allaire report).

If the French language is better protected in Quebec now, it is the result of the economic advancement of French-speaking consumers, workers, and investors. But it is also attributable to the language legislation of the province. There is no doubt that without Act 101 immigrants would massively have joined the English-speaking community. Yet the contribution of immigration is a necessity for the French-speaking community, considering demographic trends (low birthrate and aging).

It is a great pity that the debate about commercial signs and the outside-inside bill has so harmed the image of Quebec linguistic policy. A "French necessarily" policy would have been sufficient in this area, especially considering similar practices throughout the world.[72] But I also think that

72. Although many countries have legislation regarding commercial signs—38 percent of the sample, including the United States, where eighteen states have declared English to be the official language of the state in response to the growth of the Hispanic community—

the "French only" policy was a small discomfort for English speakers, that the widely shared concern of French speakers about the need to send signals to every citizen about the necessity of learning French is understandable, and that the Supreme Court's decision to mix all this with an assault on the freedom of expression is questionable. At any rate, the issue is hardly big enough to warrant splitting the country. The key issues are elsewhere, in the two major sections of Act 101: the language of instruction and the language of the workplace.

With respect to those sections, the Quebec language policy is both necessary for the majority and fair for the minority. Regarding the language of the workplace, the prescriptions of the law set a "predominantly French" policy and not a "French only" one.[73] The target of the language of instruction policy is the new immigrants, who are informed of the law when they come to Quebec. None of those legal requests injured the rights and the institutions of English speakers in the province. French Canadians in the other provinces can only dream about having such conditions.

Quebec policies regarding the language of instruction and the language of the workplace were not significantly weakened by the various judgments of the Supreme Court. They remain useful and necessary protection for French Quebec. Since the judgments have been issued, one may think that the survival of those policies is secured. In fact, nothing is less certain. The decisions of one group of judges may be overturned later by their successors. A Supreme Court might decide someday that denying the right of a new immigrant or of a francophone to go to an English school, when English speakers have such a right, is contrary to the Charter of Rights; the Court could invoke to this effect Article 15 prescribing legal equality of all citizens.[74] Such a judgment may seem unlikely today, but who knows for the next generation? The French presence will decrease as a

Quebec is the sole democratic and developed political entity that forbids an important minority the use of its language for commercial signage. See Jacques Leclerc, *La guerre des langues dans l'affichage* (Montreal: VLB Editeur, 1989), p. 50; and Paul Pupier, "Il est interdit d'interdire! Quelques droits linguistiques (et autres) à considérer par qui veut légiférer sur l'affichage," paper prepared for the 1991 World Congress of the International Political Science Association. In Florida, Dade County adopted an antibilingual ordinance in 1980 that forbids the use of Spanish except for some specified circumstances. Gilles-L. Racine, "The Language Question in Quebec," 1991 Quebec Summer Seminar, Center for the Study of Canada, Montreal, June 7, 1990.

73. Stéphane Dion, "The Problem Associated with the Extension of a Minority Language into the Private Sector," paper prepared for the International Seminar on Language Planning, Santiago de Compostela, Spain, September 28, 1991.

74. I thank Louis Massicotte, who pointed out this possibility to me.

demographic reality outside Quebec, and Quebec's weight will decline in Canada. Therefore, it is necessary to solidify language protections now.

Under the current constitution, the province of Quebec may use the "notwithstanding" clause to avoid the consequences of the Supreme Court's decisions. But recent experience shows that such a use is politically costly. Something more is needed.

Robert Young of the University of Western Ontario has recommended a unilateral devolution of power over language to the provinces to avoid the risk of destroying the country.[75] Such a reform would fully solve the Quebec problem. But it means that the French speakers outside Quebec would lose the protection of the federal government. Such a loss would hurt them terribly. This would be unfair to the Acadian community of New Brunswick, for instance, whose institutions are extensively funded by the federal government and which shows a strong resistance to assimilation. Such a reform asks French-speaking Quebecers to press their interest at the expense of other French speakers. It is doubtful that they would accept it. I would not accept it.

The best solution would be a unilateral devolution of power over language only to the legislature of Quebec and applied only to the Quebec territory. Such a policy would be justified by the fact that only the French language is in danger and needs protection. The rights of English speakers historically have been well respected by provincial laws and Quebec's Charter of Rights. The English-speaking provinces would not receive the same devolution of powers because it is the French language that needs protection, and because nothing in the history of those provinces suggests that they will perform such a duty.

Although such a solution seems reasonable to me, it probably would not to English Canada. One objection would be that English speakers of Quebec would be alone in receiving no protective status regarding language in the Canadian Charter of Rights and would be left facing a French-speaking majority. With the commercial signs affair still fresh in their minds, Canadian English speakers would not accept this solution. My three English-speaking coauthors have told me that they would not accept it.

So what can be done? I suggest including in the Canadian constitution a clause assigning to the legislature of Quebec the duty to protect the French-speaking character of the province. Such a clause would secure the

75. Robert A. Young, "How to Head Off the Crisis," *Globe and Mail* (Toronto), January 10, 1991, p. A17.

interests of the French majority in Quebec without harming the English-speaking Quebecers and the French speakers outside Quebec. With it, I do not think a Canadian court would strike down the current policies of the province regarding the language of instruction or the language of the workplace. And since minority linguistic rights are already included in the charter (in article 23), I do not see how it could be perceived as offensive.

In addition to the clause, the control of immigration that the province of Quebec already has must be included in the constitution for obvious reasons. Finally, the province of Quebec must hold a constitutional veto. It is likely that the nine other provinces would ask the same, which would make any ensuing modification of the constitution very difficult. Perhaps that would not be so bad: governments might be dissuaded from losing so much time and energy in never-ending discussions of constitutional reform.

This proposal is a remarkably modest demand coming from a francophone political scientist Quebecer. Still, a majority of Quebecers might approve of it. And I cannot imagine that it would be considered excessive by the rest of the country after a reasonable examination.

ANDREW STARK

English-Canadian Opposition to Quebec Nationalism

Canada is now "passing through the greatest crisis in its history."

Quebec's nationalists are "precursors and prophets" in the vanguard of an international trend.

COMMENTS LIKE these—which suggest that Canada is undergoing a crisis unique by the standards of its own past and of universal relevance given the spirit of the age—were not hard to come by in 1991.[1] In the eyes of many observers, Canada is finally approaching the moment of disintegration toward which its entire history has led, a moment that may even help inspire similar moments in other states. Despite Prime Minister Wilfrid Laurier's declaration in 1900 that the twentieth century belongs to Canada, Canada may, in fact, not survive the twentieth century.

In reality, of course, the universal import of Canada's situation may be considerably blunted by the fact that Quebec already represents the most powerful substate government within the OECD. Moreover, Canada itself is the only modern democratic welfare state to have been so seriously threatened by nationalist-based disintegration.[2] And the historical uniqueness of Canada's current predicament also dims when

The author would like to thank Alan Cairns, H. D. Forbes, Elliot J. Feldman, Timothy Woolstencroft, and his coauthors in this volume for their valuable comments on previous versions of this chapter. He also thanks Michael Ede, Roy Norton, and Andrew Pascoe for providing helpful information at various stages.

1. Jeffrey Simpson, "The Two Canadas," *Foreign Policy*, no. 81 (Winter 1990–91), p. 71; and Jacques Parizeau, quoted in Clyde H. Farnsworth, "Quebec Separatist Hails Baltics' Independence," *New York Times*, September 8, 1991, p. 14.

2. See the discussion in Stéphane Dion's chapter, p. 77.

one considers that in almost every recent generation, a royal commission has arisen to declare that Canada is "passing through the greatest crisis in its history."[3] Disagreement over the comparative and historical stature of Canada's current crisis will continue. But there is no disagreement about the existence of a crisis. Here all parties are in accord: Canada is in serious trouble.

Canada is in crisis because its English-speaking population recently found itself unable to accommodate within the federal structure even the more moderate aspirations of Quebec nationalism. Those aspirations are essentially twofold: (1) the desire that Quebec's distinct society be meaningfully recognized in the constitution (or that some other form of special constitutional status be accorded), and (2) the desire to devolve a limited number of federal powers to the Quebec government (here I include the claim that Quebec be allowed to opt out of certain federal programs and receive compensation for establishing its own equivalents). Quebec's demands, as embodied in the Meech Lake Accord, actually went beyond both those desires. They included an expanded Quebec veto over certain types of proposed constitutional amendments and the right of Quebec to participate in the appointment of Supreme Court justices. But for the purposes of simplicity—and to show that even a pared-down Quebec nationalism is at odds with much current thinking in English Canada—I will confine my definition of Quebec nationalism to the aspirations for distinct status and devolution. In any case, recent history suggests that these items are more central to Quebec's nationalist goals than the veto or appointment power.

"Quebec nationalism," as I use the term here, is thus distinct from Quebec separatism. As Richard Cleroux explains, "Nationalism says survival can be assured within the Canadian context or outside of it. Separatism goes one step further and says it has to be outside."[4] Of course, if Quebec nationalism continues to be frustrated in its attempt to survive within a Canadian context, Quebecers will have to choose between an unaccommodating Canada and the province's secession. My guess is that between unaccommodation and secession, Quebecers will choose secession—if not in 1992, then eventually.

3. See Citizens' Forum on Canada's Future [the Spicer Commission], *Report to the People and Government of Canada* (Ottawa, 1991), pp. 50–51.
4. Richard Cleroux, "Separatism in Quebec and Alberta," in Larry Pratt and Garth Stevenson, eds., *Western Separatism: The Myths, Realities and Dangers* (Edmonton: Hurtig, 1981), p. 105.

Four English-Canadian Ideologies

In what follows I attempt to explain English Canada's recently demonstrated inability to meet the aspirations of Quebec nationalism within a federal structure. This inability, I suggest, can largely be attributed to four sets of ideas that—although not necessarily with coequal strength, and not always coherently or explicitly—command the allegiance of many English Canadians, especially among elites. They are the political thought and policies of Pierre Trudeau; Canadian nationalism in its current, social-democratic cast; western Canadian alienation as manifested today by the Reform party; and some of the developing doctrines surrounding Canada's Charter of Rights and Freedoms.

At first it may seem (especially to an American reader) that I am grouping apples and oranges rather than comparable ideologies. After all, Trudeau is an individual, the Reform party is a political organization, the 1982 charter is a constitutional document, and perhaps only nationalism is immediately recognizable as an ideology. Ideologies, however, can have disparate origins and come to the fore through a variety of vehicles. Despite their differences in genesis, form, and substance, each of these four ideologies advances a theory of the state and a conception of the citizen that is incompatible with the aspirations of Quebec nationalism.

There is yet another sense in which these four ideologies represent comparable political forces. They are all, to some extent, based in established political organizations: Trudeau's political thought still dominates the current leadership of the federal Liberal party; Canadian nationalism finds a home primarily in the social-democratic New Democratic party and to some degree in the left wing of the Liberal party; the newborn Reform party is the primary conduit for western alienation; and the ideology of the charter is embodied in a multitude of "charter" groups—multicultural, linguistic-minority, and feminist, to name a few.[5] (In its approach to the constitution, Canada's other major federal political party,

---

5. During the debate on the Meech Lake Accord, the leaders of the Liberal and New Democratic parties—John Turner and Ed Broadbent, respectively—supported the accord. Nevertheless, their parties proposed amendments that would have mitigated the impact of the accord's devolutionist or distinct-society strands, and some members of each caucus ultimately voted against the accord. After the parliamentary vote, both parties chose new leaders—Jean Chrétien and Audrey McLaughlin—who opposed the accord and are fundamentally against distinct status and devolution for a variety of reasons. Although not all Liberals and New Democrats oppose the twin ideas of distinct status and devolution, the two parties are now under the control of those who do.

the governing Progressive Conservatives, espouses a variant of the one ideology with which these other four contend: the aspirations of Quebec nationalism within confederation. And certainly, there is a segment of English-Canadian public opinion that continues to support the accommodation of Quebec nationalism.)

All four ideologies incarnate historical traditions in Canadian political thought. Trudeau's approach to federalism has a long line of distinguished antecedents among Quebec political thinkers and politicians. Canadian nationalism in various forms has been around since the nineteenth century. The Reform party is the latest of an evolving species of western Canadian splinter parties, which over generations have given voice to a developing set of regional grievances. And the intellectual currents surrounding the charter—a belief in the rights of groups and individuals—are rooted in philosophies that are by no means new to the Canadian scene.

In other important respects, however, these four currents of thought differ from their historical antecedents. While Trudeau's ideological predecessors were mostly French-Canadian intellectuals and statesmen, only Trudeau was able to fashion their ideas into an explicit federal political program and create a following for them in English Canada. Indeed, Trudeau's ideas retain a strong following in English Canada even though they have been repudiated by many French-Canadian intellectuals, most of whom now are Quebec nationalists—at least in the modest sense in which I am using the term.

Canadian nationalism in its current form also differs from previous doctrines that have borne the name. For many decades a Tory and British-imperialist phenomenon, Canadian nationalism is now identified with a social-democratic and anti-American political outlook. For its part the Reform party represents a sharp break from the early 1980s, when western alienation was expressed—especially in Alberta—in a small number of fledgling western separatist parties and more established western provincial parties with strong decentralist views. Today the Reform party casts a relatively benign eye on the federal state, and it explicitly disavows western secession, devolution, and even the expansion of provincial government power at the center. Finally, although the view of state and citizen associated with the charter has been around for decades, the recent constitutional entrenchment of charter rights has given it a new political saliency.

In this chapter I describe the roots and structure of these four ideologies of state and citizen and the ways in which each conflicts with the aspirations of Quebec nationalism. Where warranted, I also discuss the ways in which each ideology either resembles or differs from the other three. Specifically, I examine Trudeau's influential belief in the strong federal state and the cosmopolitan citizen; contemporary Canadian nationalists' devotion to the social-democratic state and the identity-less citizen; the Reform party's version of the strong federal state and the "unhyphenated" citizen; and the charter ideology's promotion of the universalizing state and the group-affiliated citizen. English Canada's ability to accommodate the aims of Quebec nationalism within a revised federal structure is seriously impaired by these four ideologies, and it will stay impaired precisely to the extent that elite and popular opinion in English Canada remains influenced by them. Of course, there also exists within Canada a longstanding tradition that emphasizes the necessity (some would even say "exalts the virtue") of moderation, mediation, and compromise.[6] This tradition, however, did not prevail during the Meech Lake debate, and it may not be much in evidence at the moment. For the crisis to be resolved in any lasting way—and one in which Canada remains intact—there will have to be a significant change in the recent balance of ideological forces.

The Political Thought of Pierre Trudeau

With the exception of a nine-month interregnum in 1979-80, Pierre Elliott Trudeau served as Canada's prime minister from June 1968 to June 1984. Probably no other Canadian prime minister has been as governed by a coherent political theory.[7] In the area of constitutional politics, no other Canadian prime minister in this century has so dominated his cabinet and government. And only one Canadian prime minister in the twentieth century has enjoyed greater longevity in office. The power that ideas held over the man, the dominance that the man held over his government, and the influence of that government on a generation make an understanding of Trudeau's political thought necessary to an understanding of the current crisis.

6. See, for example, some of the discussion in Douglas V. Verney, *Three Civilizations, Two Cultures, One State: Canada's Political Traditions* (Duke University Press, 1986), pp. 47–57.

7. Some years ago Trudeau's colleague Gérard Pelletier correctly observed that Trudeau's writings constitute "the most serious effort to formulate a political theory for Quebec and Canada" made during his generation. See Gérard Pelletier, "Preface to the French Edition," in Pierre Elliott Trudeau, *Federalism and the French Canadians* (Toronto: Macmillan, 1968), p. xvi.

The first principle of Trudeau's politics is a passionate intellectual opposition to nationalism in almost all its forms. At the level of the state, Trudeau has thus always upheld the idea of federal entities whose borders embrace more than one historical or cultural nation. And at the level of the individual citizen, Trudeau has always been a cosmopolitan, averse to the idea of individuals rooting themselves too completely in their native ethnic and national identities.

The Federal State and Official Bilingualism

Although Trudeau deplored nationalism, he nevertheless believed that for a federal state to counter the ethnic nationalisms it contains, it must itself lay claim to the status of a nation and cultivate its own overarching, countervailing nationalist loyalties. This kind of nationalism at the federal level–which Trudeau has variously described as a "gum," a "glue," and a "heavy paste"—may be necessary to keep multinational federal states together.[8] Because loyalties to particular cultures and regions will be stronger than any allegiance to the federal structure, Trudeau argued that the government in a federal state such as Canada should cultivate a national spirit and invest "tremendous amounts of time, energy, and money in nationalism, *at the federal level.*" A "national image," he argued in 1965, "must be created that will have such an appeal as to make any image of a separatist group unattractive." To this end "resources must be diverted into such things as national flags, anthems . . . [and] film boards."[9] Of course, Trudeau's antipathy toward nationalism meant that "nationalism will eventually have to be rejected as a principle of sound government," by the federal state no less than by the nation-state. But even if "*in the last resort* the mainspring of federalism cannot be [nationalist] emotion but must be reason," at this historical moment, the federal state can bolster itself against its various internal nationalisms only by developing its own strong sense of nationhood.[10]

8. Pierre Elliott Trudeau, "Federalism, Nationalism, and Reason," in Trudeau, *Federalism and the French Canadians*, pp. 190, 188, 192.

9. Trudeau, "Federalism, Nationalism, and Reason," p. 193 (emphasis in the original). See also Richard Handler, *Nationalism and the Politics of Culture in Quebec* (University of Wisconsin Press, 1988), p. 97.

10. Trudeau, "Federalism, Nationalism, and Reason," pp. 194, 203. See also Pierre Elliott Trudeau, "New Treason of the Intellectuals," in Trudeau, *Federalism and the French Canadians*, p. 177. One of Trudeau's long-time scholarly observers has noted "the irony . . . that a professed anti-nationalist should have mastered the nationalist strategy to perfection." See Ramsay Cook, *The Maple Leaf Forever: Essays on Nationalism and Politics in Canada* (Toronto: Macmillan, 1977), p. 195.

It is not surprising, then, that more than twenty years after writing these words, Trudeau would insist, before a parliamentary committee during the Meech Lake debate, that any proposed alteration to the federal constitutional structure should not be "destructive of the national will," which statesmen over the previous century had so carefully built.[11] He flatly rejected the idea that a particular substate entity should be able to claim distinct national status, or depart from national standards in significant policy areas, or trump the expressed will of the nation in any way. In the name of nation building at the federal level, Trudeau and his followers thus resisted giving Quebec or any other province a constitutionally meaningful recognition of its distinct society, significant new federal powers (through the procedure of opting out or otherwise), and a veto over proposed constitutional amendments.

Of course, over and above flags, anthems, and film boards, the most important glue holding together the Canadian federal state—and resisting the pull of Quebec substate nationalism—would be its national language policy. "Not only did Quebec francophones have to see the federal government as 'their' government, they had to see Canada as 'their' country. They would do this, [Trudeau] argued, only if there were a meaningful Francophone presence outside Quebec."[12] Thus Trudeau instituted a policy of official bilingualism, thereby enabling francophones to enjoy federal services in French anywhere in the country. And he constitutionalized the rights of the French-language minorities in the provinces outside of Quebec, thereby placing them under federal protection. These two aspects of Trudeau's language policy—official bilingualism and the protection of linguistic minorities—flow directly from his desire to submerge Quebec nationalism within a strong, uncompromised federal state and national community. If the French language were being protected nationwide and at the federal level, then there would be no need to give Quebec the constitutional power to preserve and protect its "distinct society."

There is a further strand in Trudeau's thought that modifies, or rather supersedes, the importance he placed on submerging nations (like Quebec)

11. Trudeau, "Who Speaks for Canada?" in Michael D. Behiels, ed., *The Meech Lake Primer: Conflicting Views of the 1987 Constitutional Accord* (University of Ottawa Press, 1989), pp. 63, 74.

12. Kenneth McRoberts, "Making Canada Bilingual: Illusions and Delusions of Federal Language Policy," in David P. Shugarman and Reg Whitaker, eds., *Federalism and Political Community: Essays in Honor of Donald Smiley* (Peterborough, Ont.: Broadview Press, 1989), pp. 147–48. See also Keith Banting and Richard Simeon, "Federalism, Democracy and the Constitution," in Banting and Simeon, eds., *And No One Cheered: Federalism, Democracy, and the Constitution Act* (Toronto: Methuen, 1983), p. 12.

within strong federal states (like Canada): namely, ultimately submerging all states within a system of world federalism. If, as Trudeau once wrote, Quebec should be regarded as but a "sub-sub species" of the "sub-species Canada," then Canada itself should be regarded as "the envied seat of a form of federalism that belongs to tomorrow's world. . . . Canadian federalism is an experiment of major proportions; it could become a brilliant prototype for the moulding of tomorrow's civilization."[13] In other words, Canada is a kind of historical way-station, a showcase federal state that, by demonstrating the success of the federalist principle, would thereby prove to the world the pointlessness of the state itself. Even "if a Canadian nationalism does take form"—in other words, even if Canadian "ethnic communities succeed in exorcizing their own respective nationalisms"—then that Canadian nationalism "will have to be exorcized in its turn, and the Canadian nation will be asked to yield a part of its sovereignty to a higher authority, just as is asked, today, of the French-Canadian and English-Canadian nations."[14]

Trudeau has always kept in his hip pocket something of a "death wish"—or, more exactly, a "death indifference"—toward the country. For him, Canada is less important than the ideal of federalism that as a prototype or experiment it is meant to foster. If at any point the country cannot survive without compromising that federalist ideal—by giving in to Quebec nationalism—then it is the country, not the ideal, that must go. If the choice were between a new, weaker federal structure that could accommodate Quebec nationalism on the one hand and Quebec's complete separation on the other, Trudeau would prefer the latter. As he told the Canadian Senate's Meech Lake committee:

> If the people of Canada want [the Meech Lake Accord] . . . then let [it] be part of the Constitution. I, for one, will be convinced that the Canada we know and love will be gone forever. But, then, Thucydides wrote that Themistocles' greatness lay in the fact that he realized Athens was not immortal. I think we have to realize that Canada is not immortal; but if it is going to go, let it go with a bang rather than a whimper.[15]

13. Trudeau, "New Treason of the Intellectuals," pp. 161, 179; see also p. 154.
14. Trudeau, "New Treason of the Intellectuals," p. 155.
15. Trudeau, "Who Speaks for Canada?" p. 99. The reference to Thucydides—with which Trudeau approved Canada's disappearance, if need be, in the name of a greater global federalist principle—echoed a 1962 essay in which he anticipated the disappearance of French Canada in the name of the greater good of building a federalist Canada. "The nation of French Canadians will some day fade from view," Trudeau wrote not unhopefully,

This was not the first, nor was it the last, occasion on which Trudeau pointed out that states in general, and Canada in particular, are mortal; and that if the federal state has to choose between abandoning federalist principles (as Trudeau understood them) on the one hand and ceasing to exist as a state on the other, the latter is the correct course.[16]

The Cosmopolitan Citizen and Personal Bilingualism

Linked with his view of the federal state is Trudeau's conception of the cosmopolitan citizen. Indeed, this idea constitutes the second strand of his antinationalist political philosophy. Trudeau viewed all types of national culture that the world has to offer—all varieties of cultural tradition, language, race, and religion—as characteristics that any individual, regardless of origin, could pick up and discard, and mix and match, to create and re-create a self.[17] Trudeau was always more at ease with the idea of pluralism as a feature of individuals than merely of societies—and especially linguistic pluralism, or personal (as distinct from simply official) bilingualism. Trudeau thus urged both unilingual anglophones and unilingual francophones to learn the other tongue.[18]

To French Canadians, Trudeau's message was that they should see

---

adding the rhetorical flourish, then as now, that "it is to the lasting greatness of Thucydides that he was able to visualize a world in which Athens would be no more." See Trudeau, "New Treason of the Intellectuals," p. 177.

16. See, for example, Pierre Elliott Trudeau, "Quebec and the Constitutional Problem," in Trudeau, *Federalism and the French Canadians*, pp. 6, 37; and Trudeau, "The Values of a Just Society," in Thomas S. Axworthy and Pierre Elliott Trudeau, eds., *Towards a Just Society: The Trudeau Years*, trans. Patricia Claxton (Markham, Ont.: Viking, 1990), p. 377.

17. See the characterization of Trudeau in Christina McCall-Newman, *Grits: An Intimate Portrait of the Liberal Party* (Toronto: Macmillan, 1982), p. 62. There is a statement of Ernest Renan's Trudeau liked to quote in his early writings: "Man is bound neither to his language nor to his race; he is bound only to himself because he is a free agent." Trudeau, "New Treason of the Intellectuals," p. 159. See also Trudeau, "Values of a Just Society," pp. 363–64.

18. In a 1962 essay Trudeau warned unilingual Quebec francophone intellectuals that if they "refuse to master another language than their own, if they . . . recognize no loyalty but to their nation, then they may be renouncing forever their place among the world's intellectual élite" (Trudeau, "New Treason of the Intellectuals," p. 174). Trudeau equally scolded unilingual English-Canadian business people, refusing to accept it "when these insular people insist, with much gravity, that their jaws and ears aren't made for [French]. . . . No doubt, had English-speaking Canadians applied themselves to learning French with a quarter the diligence they have shown in refusing to do so, Canada would have been effectively bilingual long ago." Trudeau, "New Treason of the Intellectuals," pp. 163, 167.

language not so much as a constituent of, but rather as a cipher for, their indigenous personality—that they accept the idea that they can as easily express their being in English as in French.[19] And to English Canadians, he stressed that the main roadblock in becoming bilingual is not so much the need for long-term linguistic cognition, as it is for initial political enlightenment—and he suggested that they get on with it. Trudeau thus believed that realizing both a Canada and a Quebec of bilinguals was a desirable, if not a readily attainable, goal. While his belief in strengthening allegiances to the federal state led him to implement a policy of official bilingualism and support for linguistic minorities, his belief in the cosmopolitan citizen thus led him to encourage—in a more limited way, given the division of power and the magnitude of the task—personal bilingualism. During his tenure, Canada did make small but still remarkable progress toward becoming a nation of bilinguals. A quarter of a million Canadian schoolchildren are now enrolled in schools featuring immersion courses in the other tongue.

Trudeau encouraged his ideal of the culturally cosmopolitan and linguistically dualistic Canadian through rhetoric and abetted it to some degree through policy. This ideal, however, conflicts directly with the aspirations of Quebec nationalism and in particular with the idea of Quebec as a distinct society. Trudeau's conviction that Quebecers should aspire to embody other cultures and languages and not remain hidebound by their own runs flatly counter to the view advanced by one of Quebec's more ardent nationalist writers, Lionel Groulx. "Personality . . . cannot be composite, made up of disparate pieces," Groulx wrote. Instead, "an inner principle, an incoercible force, pushes a human being to become uniquely itself, just as the same law leads the maple to be nothing other than the maple."[20] While the cosmopolitan Trudeau wrote longingly of cultivating individuals "not coercible" by their ancestral cultures, Groulx, the nationalist, spoke sternly of ancestral cultures as "incoercible forces."[21] Similarly, the idea that Quebecers, as individuals, should surmount their loyalty to their own nation and become linguistic dualists— if not complete cultural cosmopolitans—runs directly counter to the linguistic philosophy expressed by former Quebec premier Jean Lesage, who

19. See Edward Andrew, "Pierre Trudeau on the Language of Values and the Value of Language," *Canadian Journal of Political and Social Theory*, vol. 6, nos. 1-2 (1982), pp. 143–55.

20. Lionel Groulx, *L'Appel de la race* (Montreal: Fides, 1956), p. 110, quoted and translated in Handler, *Nationalism and the Politics of Culture in Quebec*, p. 45.

21. Trudeau, "Values of a Just Society," pp. 363–64.

was a Quebec nationalist of a certain vintage. "Of all the languages currently spoken in the world," Lesage stated in 1961, "the French language is the one that fits us best because of our own characteristics and mentality. We could no longer be French Canadian if we spoke another language because then we would adopt means of expression produced in a foreign culture."[22] The ideas that Quebecers are meant to embody only one culture and speak only one language directly underlie the Quebec nationalists' argument that their society is distinct. Indeed, these ideas are central to most doctrines of Quebec separatism.[23]

Even his opponents would be (or, at least, they should be) hard-pressed to deny a certain nobility in Trudeau's "vision"—and the overused word does apply here. Certainly, it has been an influential vision. Members of various English-Canadian elites have adopted it wholesale as their own political philosophy—most prominently Clyde Wells, the premier of Newfoundland, and Sharon Carstairs, the former leader of the opposition in Manitoba, who were both instrumental in the defeat of the Meech Lake Accord. Others are committed to parts of Trudeau's vision on a more instrumental level. Middle-class English-Canadian parents who send their children to French immersion classes believe in Trudeau's vision of a country of bilinguals. Quebec anglophones, as well as many francophones outside of Quebec, have a strong stake in his vision because it argues for placing federal government resources on their side in a difficult cultural and linguistic situation. Accordingly, all oppose altering the federal structure to accommodate the demands of Quebec nationalism.

There is, though, an important difference between Trudeau and his many followers. Although his thought culminates in an impractical if appealing idealism—he sought, after all, nothing less than world federalism and the advent of "the unmatchable bicultural man"—Trudeau bal-

---

22. Jean Lesage, *Discours de Jean Lesage*, vol. 1 (Quebec City: Government of Quebec, 1961), p. 10, quoted and translated in Handler, *Nationalism and the Politics of Culture in Quebec*, p. 161.

23. Trudeau's cosmopolitan view of the individual led not only to the belief that individual Quebecers should try to embody cultures and languages other than their own, but also to the view that if Quebec culture and language were worthy enough, they would not need special constitutional protection, for then non-Quebecers would flock to embody them and keep them alive. With respect to Quebec culture, Trudeau urged that "if Quebec became such a shining example, if to live there were to partake of freedom and progress, . . . if the universities commanded respect and renown from afar," then special constitutional powers would not be necessary to ensure Quebec's cultural survival. "You don't protect a language," Trudeau wrote in a similar vein, "by a constitution"; it is secured only if "that language [is] the expression of a lively, important, cultured, wealthy, powerful group." See Trudeau, "New Treason of the Intellectuals," p. 180.

anced that idealism with a hard-nosed realism.[24] All along, even as he strenuously pursued his goals, he recognized their fundamental incompatibility with the aspirations of Quebec nationalism and hence with the survival of Canada in the long run. One wishes that his followers, who in so many other ways carry his tradition of state and citizen into the current debate, would make this last recognition as well.

Canadian Nationalism

Most English Canadians consider themselves nationalists in some sense. They feel pride in Canada's political culture, its government institutions, its social programs, its physical beauty, or other features of the country. This type of nationalist feeling, rooted as it is in a basic love of country, inclines all who share it to seek to keep Canada whole and independent.

Although many English Canadians consider themselves nationalists in this visceral sense, "Canadian nationalism"—as a recognized doctrine, an influential participant in the current debate, and (I will suggest) a key contributor to the ongoing crisis—has a narrower meaning. The term as it is most often used in current Canadian discourse refers to a specific and highly developed set of beliefs that by no means capture universal assent. Specifically, "Canadian nationalism" is a label that now refers to the thought of a particular group of English-Canadian politicians and intellectuals, most of whom are social democrats, anti-American (at least in some fashion), and associated with the New Democratic party and the left wing of the Liberal party.

In two key respects—in its desire to create a social-democratic state and in the peculiar conception of the "identity-less" citizen that it nurtures—this leftist nationalism, as a doctrine of political and intellectual elites, has helped to widen the gulf between English Canada and the aspirations of Quebec nationalism.

Contemporary Canadian Nationalism

For the past twenty years in Canada, those writers and politicians known as the "Canadian nationalists" have assumed the task of articulating a coherent and compelling nationalism, national identity, or national

24. On the bicultural man, see McCall-Newman, *Grits*, p. 62.

sense of self. As the following quotations show, their efforts have failed in a particular way.

—*Bruce Hutchison*: "On the evidence so far you might say that we have constructed a national character by refusing to construct one. . . . Perhaps the refusal to admit achievement is an achievement in itself."[25]

—*Robertson Davies*: "This refusal [on the part of Canadians] to admit to the possession of a national soul is itself evidence of the kind of national soul we have . . . It is a wistful, reticent, self-doubting soul."[26]

—*Hugh Hood*: "Imagine a Canadian dream, which implied that everybody in the world ought to share it! Imagine a Committee on un-Canadian Activities! You can't. Un-Canadianism is almost the very definition of Canadianism."[27]

—*George Woodcock*: "America's strengths as a state are its gravest flaws. Canada's weaknesses as a state are its greatest virtues."[28]

—*Margaret Atwood*: "Americans worship success; Canadians find it in slightly bad taste. In fact, Canadians find Canadians in slightly bad taste. . . . One could sum up the respective stances by saying that the typical American is unthinkingly and breezily aggressive, while the average Canadian is peevishly and hesitantly defensive."[29]

—*William Kilbourn*: "The Canadian identity—the phrase is both a chimera and an oxymoron."[30]

In sum, as Mordecai Richler has written, Canadians are "a reticent people, nicely self-deprecating."[31]

The extent to which Quebecers would see themselves in these various portraits—and the extent to which their English-Canadian authors were thinking of Quebecers when they were composing them—is an important question, but one that need not be answered here. It is enough to say that, on their face, these passages convey an accurate sense of the contemporary

25. Quoted in Andy Stark, "Canadian Conundrums: Nationalism, Socialism, and Free Trade," *American Spectator*, vol. 22 (April 1989), p. 21.

26. "Some Thoughts on the Present State of Canadian Literature," *Transactions of the Royal Society of Canada*, vol. 9 (1971), p. 263.

27. "Moral Imagination: Canadian Thing," in John Robert Colombo, ed., *Colombo's Canadian Quotations* (Edmonton: Hurtig, 1974), p. 265.

28. "Various Americas," in A. W. Purdy, ed., *The New Romans: Candid Canadian Opinions of the U.S.* (Edmonton: M. C. Hurtig, 1968), p. 76.

29. *Second Words: Selected Critical Prose* (Toronto: Anansi, 1982), pp. 372, 374.

30. "The Peaceable Kingdom Still," in Stephen R. Graubard, ed., *In Search of Canada* (New Brunswick, N.J.: Transaction, 1989), p. 1.

31. Mordecai Richler, "Canadian Identity," in Elliot J. Feldman and Neil Nevitte, eds., *The Future of North America: Canada, the United States, and Quebec Nationalism* (Cambridge, Mass.: Harvard University, Center for International Affairs, 1979), p. 55.

doctrinal English-Canadian nationalist's view of what it means to be a Canadian. Certainly, they distill a dominant outlook, one that many political scientists and historians have elaborated or explored in much greater depth.[32] What accounts, however, for this peculiar, oft-remarked-on national sense of self? How could a doctrine known as Canadian nationalism bear fruit in the seemingly self-defeating—to say nothing of self-deprecating—idea of an "un-Canadian" Canadian and a "non-nationalistic" nationalism?[33]

Like many left-wing, third world nationalisms today, Canadian nationalism is rooted in anti-American sentiment, or at least in various aversions to political culture in America. But unlike these other nationalisms, which are uncomplicatedly prideful, assertive, and aggressive, Canada's is distinctly diffident, hesitant, and reticent. And this is the case in large measure because—while in other countries pridefulness, assertiveness, and aggressiveness are seen as attributes of nationalism—in the eyes of Canadian nationalists, they are seen as attributes of Americanism.

Socialists and social democrats, of course, traditionally face theoretical, if not always political, difficulties in allying themselves with nationalism. But it is the way in which they have handled these theoretical difficulties that largely explains the peculiarities of the doctrine espoused by contemporary left-wing Canadian nationalists. In 1967, for example, political scientist Gad Horowitz attempted to reassure his fellow socialists that nationalism can be a friend, not an enemy, to socialism in Canada—but only, as it turns out, an unusually anemic kind of nationalism. As a general proposition, Horowitz observed, "nationalism has bathed the world in blood," but Canadians, and in particular social-democratic Canadians, need not fear the consequences of their own nationalism because

> there is no unique set of Canadian values which is to be . . . imposed on [others] by forceful persuasion. . . . It needn't be uniquely Canadian as long as it isn't a copy of the United States. [Otherwise,] it could be anything. [Canada] could be a replica of Sweden, or, if you

32. See, for example, Joseph Levitt, "English Canadian Nationalists and the Canadian Character 1957-1974," *Canadian Review of Studies in Nationalism*, vol. 12 (Fall 1985), p. 233; Lionel Rubinoff, "Nationalism and Celebration: Reflections on the Sources of Canadian Identity," *Queen's Quarterly*, vol. 82 (Spring 1975), pp. 1–13; and A. B. McKillop, "Nationalism, Identity and Canadian Intellectual History," *Queen's Quarterly*, vol. 81 (Winter 1974), pp. 533–50.

33. See Cook, *The Maple Leaf Forever*, p. 187. For an insightful critical exposition of contemporary Canadian nationalism, see Peter Brimelow, *The Patriot Game: National Dreams and Political Realities* (Toronto: Key Porter, 1986), pp. 117–75.

like, North Korea, Albania or Ireland, or Spain or Yugoslavia or Cambodia or all of them.[34]

Canada poses no threat to itself or the world in being nationalistic—in being assertive, prideful, or even forceful—but only because there is nothing unique or distinctive about its values. If there were, nationalism in Canada would be truly dangerous—chauvinistic, doctrinal, and racist. Horowitz went on to declare:

> Canadian socialists are nationalists because they are socialists. If the United States were socialist, then we would be continentalists at this moment. If the possibilities of building a socialist society were brighter in the United States than in Canada, or as bright, we would not be terrified by the prospect of absorption.

In other words, if succumbing to Americanism did not necessarily imply becoming aggressive, competitive, and jingoistic, there would be no need for Canada to struggle to remain unique and distinct. In such a situation Americanism would no longer be dangerous.

For contemporary left-wing Canadian nationalists, Canadians can be assertive and forceful and proud only if there is nothing unique or distinctive about them. And Canadians can justify remaining unique and distinct—that is, a separate country—only as long as the alternative is Canada's integration into a culture of aggressiveness, force, and pride. The inability to combine a sense of uniqueness and distinctiveness with a feeling of pride and assertiveness is the dilemma of contemporary Canadian nationalism. It is an exceedingly circumscribed kind of nationalism in which the creation of a social-democratic state is more important than Canada's continued existence as a distinct country, and in which an identity-less Canadian is a prerequisite for any feeling of national pride.

Social Democracy and Quebec Nationalism

Both the desire of English-Canadian nationalists to build a social-democratic state—a garrison against U.S. capitalism—and their unwillingness to forge a unique Canadian identity are contributing to Quebec's current bout of discontent within confederation.

34. Gad Horowitz, "On the Fear of Nationalism: Nationalism and Socialism, A Sermon for Moderates," *Canadian Forum*, vol. 46 (1967), pp. 6–7.

Because of their fundamental commitment to creating a social-democratic state in the northern half of North America, many prominent Canadian nationalists have built up a variety of grievances against Quebec. Some feel betrayed by Quebec's having decisively supported the free trade agreement with the United States when English Canada (so they claim) opposed it. Others are chagrined at the rise of a new entrepreneurial class in Quebec; not so long ago the province had appeared to them to be an incipient beachhead of North American socialism. Still others are alarmed by what they consider Quebec nationalists' preference for the rights of Quebec's francophone majority over the rights of women, aboriginals, and various ethnic and linguistic minorities.

Because they see Quebec variously as a pro-American, increasingly capitalist, and even crypto-authoritarian presence within the Canadian state, some Canadian nationalists have come to believe—certainly with great reluctance—that they can create a truly distinctive, social-democratic Canada only if Quebec leaves. More specifically, in Quebec nationalism's demands for a devolution of federal powers to the provinces, English-Canadian nationalists see a potential crippling of the Canadian state's ability to control the economy and shape the society in accordance with social-democratic principles.[35] In short, they prefer a smaller—but stronger—federal state to a larger but weaker one.

Although twenty years ago left-wing Canadian nationalists feared that the only thing that made Canada distinct from the United States might be Quebec, many now fear that Canada must let Quebec go to remain distinct from its southern neighbor.[36] Philip Resnick, a nationalist intellectual living in British Columbia, describes "a new hostility in the attitude of many English Canadian nationalists towards Quebec."[37] According to Resnick, English-Canadian nationalists are now prepared to show Quebec nationalism the same indifference that Quebec nationalists, for some time, have shown to the social-democratic aspirations of English-Canadian nationalists. If twenty years ago Gad Horowitz was prepared to join the

35. See, generally, Philip Resnick with a reply by Daniel Latouche, *Letters to a Québécois Friend* (Montreal: McGill-Queen's University Press, 1990), especially pp. 31, 32, 47, 51.

36. Levitt, "English Canadian Nationalists," p. 233.

37. Resnick, *Letters*, pp. 58, 66, quote on p. 58; see also Simpson, "The Two Canadas," p. 80. As Sylvia B. Bashevkin points out in *True Patriot Love: The Politics of Canadian Nationalism* (Don Mills, Ont.: Oxford University Press, 1991), however, mass opinion among those who can be considered Canadian nationalists displays considerably greater sympathy toward Quebec nationalism, and vice versa, than is displayed by nationalists among Canada's elites.

United States if it became a socialist state, today Philip Resnick is prepared to say good-bye to a Quebec that, in his view, never will. For both these nationalists, the integrity of Canada is less important than the creation of a social-democratic state.

If English-Canadian nationalists are beginning to view Quebec's continued presence within the confederation as an obstacle to their goal of establishing a social-democratic state, Quebec nationalists have for a long time chafed at English-Canadian nationalism's "identity-less" Canadian—a Canadian without "colour, sound, and flavour." Or, more exactly, Quebec nationalists chafe at what—exempting themselves as they usually do from the term "Canadian"—they see as English Canada's inability to articulate an *English*-Canadian identity. Quebec nationalism has always had a vested interest in the idea of a Canada comprising two distinct, self-aware founding peoples, French and English.[38] This "deux nations" concept of the country, according to which Canada should be seen not as ten provinces of which Quebec is one, but rather as two nations of which Quebec is one, logically "demands that the constitution [then] recognize [that] duality, and make it real and functional. For instance, to put both founding peoples on equal footing . . . would mean that Quebec must have power unilaterally to veto proposed constitutional amendments even if they are wanted by the English majority."[39] The idea of special status—that Quebec must be recognized as a distinct entity in a sea of English Canadians—also grows out of the two-nations concept.

Obviously, however, there could be no "revision of Confederation based upon a dialogue or bargaining process" between English Canada and Quebec, as long as one of them, in its own mind, depended on the other for its identity and could not exist apart from it.[40] After years of placing the entire burden of Canadian distinctiveness on Quebec, when some English-Canadian nationalists then turned around and opposed the distinct-society clause—claiming that Quebec was just as polyglot as English Canada—Quebec nationalists were doubly infuriated. As Quebec nationalist Daniel Latouche put the point in a recent reply to Canadian nationalist Philip Resnick:

38. Daniel Latouche, "Betrayal and Indignation on the Canadian Trail: A Reply from Quebec," in Resnick, *Letters*, p. 117.

39. Jane Jacobs, *The Question of Separatism: Quebec and the Struggle Over Sovereignty* (Random House, 1980), p. 79.

40. Kenneth McNaught, "The National Outlook of English-Speaking Canadians," in Peter Russell, ed., *Nationalism in Canada* (Toronto: McGraw-Hill, 1966), p. 61.

First, for years you maintained the fiction that English Canada did not exist, could not exist, and should not exist as a distinct cultural identity. . . . [This] allowed you to maintain the fiction that any political reconstruction of Canada along bi-national lines was doomed from the start, since one of the two supporting collective entities was entirely a figment of our imagination. . . . For years, you kept telling us that there were so few things that distinguished English Canada from the United States that you needed [Quebec] to make you feel different. . . . And now you have the *culot* of turning around and telling us that [Quebec is not a distinct society].[41]

At least when English-Canadian nationalists saw Quebec—even if they did not see the rest of Canada—as forming a distinct, articulable entity, the idea of a binational country, cherished by Quebec nationalists, was only one nation away. Now that Quebec's distinctiveness is denied as well, the idea of a binational nation is two nations away—further removed than ever.[42]

Two central dynamics are now at play between Canadian nationalism and Quebec nationalism. In the assertive, capitalistic, entrepreneurial spirit underlying the most recent round of Quebec nationalist feeling, English-Canadian nationalists have seen a betrayal of their dream to create a social-democratic state in Canada. And in the diffident refusal to articulate an identity for individual Canadians that lies at the heart of English-Canadian nationalism, Quebec nationalists have come to see an intellectual roadblock to their own nationalist aspirations. Put another way, in Quebec nationalism's specific demands for a decentralized federal state, Canadian nationalists see a threat to their ability to introduce social-democratic social programs with meaningful national standards. And in

41. Latouche, "Betrayal," pp. 115–17.
42. As Donald Smiley once observed, many prominent social-democratic English-Canadian nationalists, writing in the 1970s, not only recognized Quebec's distinctiveness but in fact actively supported its right to self-determination. They also evidently hoped that Quebec's strong sense of self would somehow rub off on English Canada—albeit less, so it seemed, for English Canada's sake than for Quebec's (that is, so that Quebec *indépendantistes* would have an entity to negotiate with). Now, by contrast, Canadian nationalists fully accept English Canada's lack of distinctiveness and would like to visit that description on Quebec as well. See Smiley, "Reflections on Cultural Nationhood and Political Community in Canada," in R. Kenneth Carty and W. Peter Ward, eds., *Entering the Eighties: Canada in Crisis* (Toronto: Oxford University Press, 1980), pp. 30–32. See also Abraham Rotstein, "Is There an English-Canadian Nationalism?" *Journal of Canadian Studies*, vol. 13 (Summer 1978), pp. 115, 117.

Quebec nationalism's demands for a constitutional recognition of Quebec's distinct society and veto power, Canadian nationalists have come to see a false—indeed, un-Canadian—pretension to distinctive nationhood, a pretension that they for decades have denied to the citizens of English Canada.

Western Alienation and the Reform

The Canadian Reform movement was established as a political party in 1987. There remains, however, a degree of ambiguity surrounding the extent to which "the Reform" is better understood as a movement ideology rather than a political party. Nowhere is this ambivalence more evident than in the fact that "party" is usually informally dropped from its appellation. Even Party leader Preston Manning continues to refer to his following as "the Reform movement" almost as often as he calls it "the Reform party."[43] And although it is rooted in western Canadian alienation, the Reform is also preponderantly national in its concerns and impact. It is of course true that the Reform has both a more defined partisan purpose, and a greater regional coloration, than either Trudeau's political thought or Canadian nationalism. Nevertheless, it is also, like they are, an ideological and a national movement.

From 1905, when the provinces of Saskatchewan and Alberta were created, until the late 1970s, alienated westerners typically formed integrationist, not recessionist, movements. They tried "to eliminate those conditions which hampered their integration into the Canadian mainstream," not to establish their own independent state.[44] The Canadian Progressive movement, for example, made the abolition of party discipline in the federal Parliament—with its attendant muzzling of regional voices—an important plank in its platform for the 1921 national election, in which it won all but four seats in Manitoba, Saskatchewan, and Alberta. Yet although they became important players on the national stage, Progressive and, later, Social Credit MPs continued to emphasize specifically western preoccupations such as freight rates, interest rates, and interprovincial trade.[45]

43. E. Preston Manning, "A Political Strategy for the West," notes of an address to the Edmonton Area Rally, September 26, 1988, p. 10; and Manning, "Preparing for the 21st Century," address, March 1990, p. 8.
44. Larry Pratt and Garth Stevenson, "Introduction," in Pratt and Stevenson, eds., *Western Separatism*, p. 12.
45. Roger Gibbins, "American Influence on Western Separatism," in Pratt and Stevenson, eds., *Western Separatism*, pp. 194–95.

But in the late 1970s and early 1980s, western alienation seemed to undergo a transformation. In the wake of a number of federal moves culminating in the Trudeau government's national energy program and constitutional package—which progressively alienated western public opinion—aggrieved westerners began to give up on the national center altogether. Abandoning its traditional integrationist thrust, western alienation found its loudest voice in two secessionist organizations, "West-Fed" and the Western Canada Concept, that briefly enjoyed a certain amount of regional popularity and national notoriety. Unlike the Progressives and Social Credit, which maintained federal parties throughout most of their lives, West-Fed and the WCC sought power exclusively at the provincial level. And although they turned out to be mere flashes in the pan, the political forces they represented did exert an enduring gravitational influence on the established provincial parties, particularly on the Progressive Conservative government of Alberta. In the early 1980s the Alberta government adopted a radically anti-integrationist stance. Western interests, it argued, could best be defended by devolving federal powers to the provinces, not by increasing regional representation at the center.

Although West-Fed and the WCC were secessionist in their orientation, their ideologies were not regionally restricted in scope. Interested in more than "traditional regional grievances of political impotence and economic exploitation," the western secessionist movements of the early 1980s vented western Canadian opinion on a range of issues "not directly related to western interests": bilingualism, gun control, capital punishment, metrification, and "many other aspects of modern Canadian life."[46]

Western alienation in its earlier (Progressive–Social Credit) guise was national in its political ambitions but regional in its concerns. In its later (West-Fed and WCC) guise, western alienation became regional in its political ambitions, while coming to concern itself with many items on the national agenda. Viewed from this historical perspective, the Reform emerges as a kind of synthesis of its two predecessors. It combines the national elements of both and hence aspires to be a truly national political movement.

In the first place, Reformers believe the Mulroney government not only has frustrated the aims of the region, but also has harmed the whole nation. Thus, in the spirit of early 1980s-style western alienation, Reform-

---

46. Gibbins, "American Influence," p. 202; Pratt and Stevenson, "Introduction," p. 16; and Lauren McKinsey, "Watching the Separatists," in Pratt and Stevenson, eds., *Western Separatism*, p. 215.

ers do not confine their movement to the traditional regional grievances of discriminatory freight rates, usurious interest rates, and unfair distribution of federal largesse. They also offer a complete menu of western positions on broader national issues such as bilingualism, multiculturalism, immigration, tax policy, and welfare. These positions stake out a deeply conservative populism and draw on a longstanding resentment of what are seen as past federal concessions to Quebec, and to central Canada more generally, in all these areas.

On the other hand, though—and more in the original spirit of older forms of western alienation—Reformers eschew the confined regional presence that satisfied the forces that led to West-Fed and the WCC. The Reform wants to play a role on the national stage. To the dismay of some members, party leader Preston Manning has in fact succeeded in barring the establishment of provincial Reform wings while expanding the party's national activities into Ontario and Atlantic Canada. According to Manning's reading of western Canadian history, the older protest movements, the Progressives and the Social Credit, "all started out aiming at Ottawa." Eventually, however, "they got discouraged, got into provincial politics, and none of them ever got around to the reforms in the federal arena that gave them their original reason for being."[47] The Reform is not going to make that mistake, Manning claims. In the next federal election his party expects to field candidates outside as well as throughout the West.

Some Reformers have complained that the movement's original regional voice has been diluted because of the national scope of its operations and concerns. After all, western Reform candidates now account for only a minority of the 200 the party conceivably could field nationally, and western concerns are now confined to a handful of paragraphs in the party's fifty-four-page policy booklet. Yet although the Reform possesses a more national center of gravity than have other western protest movements, it also claims to be structured to respond to regional concerns much more effectively than any other national political party.

The federal and provincial wings of Canadian parties often differ on important questions. In many cases they have even become officially separate organizations. This weakening of ties has meant that the provincial parties have usually felt completely free to voice regional interests, and to do so in an unalloyed way that their federal namesakes—concerned, as

---

47. Quoted in Stevie Cameron, "Reform Party: Looking for the Next Target," *Globe and Mail* (Toronto), October 25, 1989, p. A7.

they have had to be, with their parties' national standings—have been unable to match.[48] Within the federal parliamentary parties, however, party discipline, along with cabinet solidarity, remains a powerful imperative in Canada's British form of government. Because of this strong, unifying party control, members of the federal Parliament often provide less than effective voices for the competing interests of their various regions.

The Reform party seems bent on avoiding what it sees as the twin mistakes of contemporary Canadian parties: strong intraparliamentary party discipline and weak extraparliamentary (federal-provincial) party coherence. The Reform, which currently holds one seat apiece in the House of Commons and the Senate, has promised to break with long-standing parliamentary tradition and radically curtail party discipline, allowing its MPs to operate largely as regional or provincial—indeed, constituency—delegates. (Whether the Reform could then persist as a coherent party is, of course, an important question.)

The Reform also has taken steps to ensure the preeminence of its federal members as regional spokespersons. By quashing its incipient provincial organizations at its April 1991 convention, the party guaranteed that it will never be blindsided, undercut, or overshadowed by a provincial wing. Terminating its embryonic provincial wings was no empty gesture. Until the Reform's decision against pursuing the provincial option, polls showed that a provincial Reform party would likely have won the next Alberta election. Indeed, a lawsuit was even launched by one would-be provincial Reform party against the federal party, but with little success. Nevertheless, the federal Reform leadership realizes that the role to which it aspires—that of unchallenged aggregator and articulator of regional interests—would simply not have been served by the emergence of provincial Reform leaders with much better chances of coming to power. Hence, Manning actively intervened with the party grass roots to put an end to the fledgling provincial movements. Alone among its partisan competitors, the Reform party boasts a unitary, not a federal (let alone a confederal) extraparliamentary structure.[49] In promising to be an

48. See, for example, Alan C. Cairns, "The Governments and Societies of Canadian Federalism," in R. D. Olling and M. W. Westmacott, eds., *Perspectives on Canadian Federalism* (Scarborough, Ont.: Prentice-Hall, 1988), p. 111; and J. Stefan Dupré, "The Workability of Executive Federalism in Canada," in Herman Bakvis and William M. Chandler, eds., *Federalism and the Role of the State* (University of Toronto Press, 1987), pp. 236–37.

49. The unitary nature of the extraparliamentary Reform party is borne out not only in its structure, but also in its concentration of power in the leader. In February 1991

unprecedentedly fragmented party within Parliament, and an unprecedentedly unified party outside it, the Reform hopes to arrogate to itself a unique role in representing Canadian regional interests.

One can, as noted earlier, speak of a Reform ideology in much the same manner as one can speak of an ideology of Canadian nationalism or an ideology associated with Trudeau's thought. In each case the ideology goes well beyond a mere party platform, and those who subscribe to it are not restricted to membership in any one party.[50] According to the polls in mid-1991, the Reform would win a sizable block of seats in an election held anytime soon. But regardless of whether the party survives over the long run as the vehicle for Reform ideology, that ideology—and in particular its views of state and citizen—will continue to form a significant strand in English-Canadian political culture.

The Reform View of the State

Two key principles make up the Reform view of the Canadian state. The first derives from the idea that provincial and regional interests in a federal state are best pursued by increasing provincial and regional control over national institutions. Proponents of this view, including the Reform, typically call for a reconfiguration of the Canadian Senate to make it more responsive to regional interests, a greater role for regional ministers and regional representation in the federal bureaucracy, and guaranteed seats on the Supreme Court for representatives from the various regions.

While the Reform seeks added regional input to federal institutions, Quebec nationalists, like the assertive western governments of the early 1980s, seek to devolve federal powers to the provinces. These differences in approach to the federal state reflect the differing nature of western

---

Preston Manning announced that all would-be Reform candidates would be required to complete—to his satisfaction—a forty-page questionnaire detailing their political opinions and past behavior. This new policy represents a transfer of prerogative from the constituency party to leader that is unparalleled in the practice of other Canadian parties: the Reform leader has now positioned himself so as to be able to routinely overrule a constituency party's choice of candidate, although once candidates become MPs, the leader will relinquish his traditional prerogative of telling them how to vote and return that prerogative back to the constituency. Paradoxically, then, the party has begun to instill the moral equivalent of party discipline in the extraparliamentary party even as it proposes to abandon the actual practice within the intraparliamentary party.

50. In fact, Manning himself explicitly acknowledges those who, he claims, have chosen to pursue Reform goals through the vehicles of other parties. See "A Political Strategy for the West," p. 3.

and Quebec grievances. The regional concerns of western Canadians are largely economic (freight rates, the national transportation system, interprovincial trade, monetary policy) and hence fall more naturally under federal jurisdiction. The indigenous concerns of French Quebecers, by contrast, are largely cultural (language, communications, immigration) and thus fall—or could more easily be made to fall—under provincial jurisdiction.[51] Thus the Reform, in adopting the more traditional western approach to the federal state, has consistently found itself at odds with the devolutionist program of Quebec nationalism. At various points the Reform has explicitly opposed "a substantial transfer of powers from Ottawa to the provinces," voiced its "objections to the decentralization aspects of Meech Lake," and attacked the Quebec Liberal party's Allaire report of February 1991, which calls for the devolution of federal powers to the provinces.[52] The Reform's antidevolutionist approach to the federal state has placed it in direct conflict with the aspirations of Quebec nationalism for a significantly devolved federal structure.

A second major strand in the Reform ideology of the state concerns the question of whether some provinces should be allowed greater constitutional power than others. Although Reform ideology displays considerable ambiguity on this point, the Reform has opposed any kind of distinct status for Quebec.

In speech after speech Preston Manning speaks of the Reform's commitment to "a new constitutional foundation in which all provinces and Canadians are treated equally," pledges to uphold the "the constitutional equality of all Canadians and provinces," and calls for a governmental system that "recognize[s] the equality . . . of all provinces and citizens."[53] A belief in the constitutional equality of all provinces *and* citizens does, of course, afford a coherent basis for opposing distinct constitutional status for Quebec and Quebecers. After all, while some provincial pre-

51. Gibbins, "American Influence," pp. 196, 197.

52. Therese Arseneau, "The Reform Party of Canada: The Secret of Its 'Success,' " paper prepared for the 1991 annual meeting of the Canadian Political Science Association, pp. 11, 13; Stephen J. Harper, "The Reform Vision of Canada," speech to the party assembly, Saskatoon, Saskatchewan, April 5, 1991, p. 3; Preston Manning, "Reform Party Position on the Meech Lake Accord," May 18, 1990, p. 1; Reform Party of Canada, "Reform Party Response to the Allaire Report," January 30, 1991; and Cameron, "Reform Party."

53. E. Preston Manning, "Getting Our Constitutional House in Order," July 1990, p. 4; Manning, "Reform Party Position on the Meech Lake Accord," May 1990, p. 3. See also Manning, "The New Canada," notes of an address, November 1990, p. 6; and Manning, "The Road to New Canada," address to the 1991 assembly of the Reform Party of Canada, Saskatoon, Saskatchewan, p. 10.

miers objected to the distinct-society clause because it violated the "equality of provinces," various charter groups "objected to the distinct society on the ground that it violated the norms of equal citizenship."[54] The Reform claims to oppose special status on both grounds. It opposed the distinct-society clause during the Meech Lake debate, and it will oppose any other form of special status for Quebec in the future.

Yet when one moves beyond the question of the distinct society, a concept that unites the principles of provincial equality and citizen equality in active opposition, the two goals cease to coalesce. Indeed, Canada's biggest constitutional battles have been fought precisely between the proponents of provincial equality on the one hand and the defenders of citizen equality on the other. To take one recent example—as Trudeau succinctly put the point in a recent recollection of the 1982 constitutional negotiations—the amending formula favored by the provinces was that "all provinces were equal," whereas the opposing federal formula stated that "all Canadians would be equal."[55] Yet the Reform blithely speaks of upholding "the constitutional equality of all Canadians *and* provinces" and of doing the impossible, namely, creating "a new constitutional foundation in which all provinces *and* Canadians are treated equally."[56]

Indeed, on closer inspection the party appears to resemble the proverbial knight—the creation of Canadian humorist Stephen Leacock—who lept on his horse and rode off in all directions. In addition to upholding the constitutional equality of all provinces and citizens, the Reform also declares that "the demands . . . of all *regions* of the country should be entitled to equal status in constitutional and political negotiations."[57] Regional equality differs yet again from the principles of provincial equality and popular equality.

In articulating its position on constitutional reform, the party has thus at different times called for "constitutional conventions organized in each Province," demanded "constitutional conventions in every region," and insisted that "any new constitutional arrangements should be subject to a national referendum."[58] These three amending procedures—provincial,

54. Alan C. Cairns, "Constitutional Change and the Three Equalities," in Ronald L. Watts and Douglas M. Brown, eds., *Options for a New Canada* (University of Toronto Press, 1991), p. 81.

55. Trudeau, "Values of a Just Society," p. 378.

56. Manning, "Reform Party Position on the Meech Lake Accord," p. 3 (emphasis added).

57. Manning, "Preparing for the 21st Century," p. 5 (emphasis added).

58. Manning, "Preparing for the 21st Century," p. 5; and Reform Party of Canada, "Reform Party Position on the Meech Lake Accord," pp. 3, 4.

regional, and popular—rest on conflicting principles, and the Reform offers no means of arbitrating among them in the likely circumstance that they each ratify diverging constitutional proposals.

Tactical political imperatives may underlie this ambiguous aspect of the Reform's theory of the state. Westerners support provincial equality, while Ontario, where the Reform hopes to do well, naturally leans toward citizen equality. Nevertheless, both types of equality stand united in their opposition to special status for Quebec. The Reform, no less than Trudeau and the Canadian nationalists, would unhesitatingly bid adieu to Quebec rather than entertain compromises in the pursuit of what it sees as the ideal state.[59]

The Reform View of the Citizen

If leftist nationalism posits an "identity-less" citizen, and Trudeau's politics were premised on the idea of a cosmopolitan citizen, then the Reform explicitly advances the concept of an "unhyphenated" citizen. Canada's national symbol, Reformers believe, "is not the maple leaf but the hyphen. Its federal politicians talk incessantly about English-Canadians, French-Canadians, aboriginal-Canadians, ethnic-Canadians, but rarely about 'Canadians, period.' It has become patently obvious in the dying days of the 20th century that you cannot hold a nation together with hyphens."[60]

An aversion to hyphenated Canadianism has long roots in western Canadian political argument, most notably in the rhetoric of John Diefenbaker, the former Progressive Conservative prime minister. Unhyphenated Canadianism means, first and foremost, that Quebec should not have

---

59. Arseneau, "Reform Party," p. 4. It should be noted that the Reform view of the state does not itself sit particularly well with the theories of the state propounded by either Trudeau or the Canadian nationalists. True, both Trudeau and the Reform are opposed to devolution. But while the Reform insists that the regions have a role to play in a strong federal center, Trudeau believes that any such "intrastate federalism" impedes the construction of a strong federal state and hence runs athwart the creation of a national will. See Rainer Knopff and F. L. Morton, "Nation-Building and the Canadian Charter of Rights and Freedoms," in Alan Cairns and Cynthia Williams, eds., *Constitutionalism, Citizenship, and Society* (University of Toronto Press, 1985), p. 136. As for Canadian nationalists, most (as indicated above) wish to build an activist, social-democratic federal state, whereas the Reform—although it clearly tilts in the direction of federal rather than provincial power—is basically a conservative movement, bent on rolling back both levels of government in a host of areas.

60. Manning, "New Canada," p. 2.

distinct constitutional status that other provinces do not enjoy. It also means a significant curtailment of official bilingualism, an end to state-assisted personal bilingualism, the termination of government aid programs for multicultural, ethnic, or women's groups, revocation of the policy that allows Mounties who are Sikhs to wear turbans on duty, and other similar changes.[61]

Reformers claim that the movement is opposed only to state-recognized and state-assisted hyphenation, not to hyphenation itself. Or, to switch metaphors, Reformers believe that it is the state's business to provide only the backboard and the glue for the Canadian linguistic, cultural, racial, and sexual mosaic, and not to help manufacture the multicolored tiles themselves. Yet in Reform rhetoric there is an undercurrent that probably more accurately reflects the views of grass-roots Reformers—according to which national homogeneity at the official level is, in fact, the first step toward cultivating a long-sought national identity at the social level. An early draft position on multiculturalism, for example, states that "Reformers believe we should be working toward a *Canadian culture* in which we all share."[62]

This idea would not be shared by many Canadian nationalists, for whom "un-Canadianism" is the very definition of Canadianism. And there are obvious differences between the Reform's unhyphenated Canadian and the cosmopolitan Canadian that Trudeau posits as an ideal. In fact, if the Reform is in favor of unhyphenated Canadianism, then Trudeau and his followers are in favor of multihyphenated Canadianism: English-speaking French-Canadians, French-speaking English-Canadians, and so forth. Early on Trudeau scorned the idea of making everyone "good, clean, unhyphenated Canadians," and the Reform is explicitly opposed to the Trudeau government's bilingual and multicultural programs.[63] Yet the unhyphenated Canadian stands with the multihyphenated Canadian and the un-Canadian Canadian in providing its own basis of opposition to distinct status for Quebec.

61. See Reform Party of Canada, *Principles and Policies: The Blue Book, 1991* (Calgary: Reform Fund Canada, 1991), pp. 31, 32, 35. See also Manning, "Political Strategy for the West," and generally, Roger Gibbins, "The Reform Party and the Political Future of the Canadian West" (University of Calgary, n.d.); and Peter C. Newman, "Preston Manning's Contradictory Vision," *MacLean's,* June 24, 1991, p. 43.

62. Reform Party of Canada, "Draft Position on Multiculturalism," May 1990, p. 1 (emphasis in original). Interestingly, this politically problematic plank has been dropped from the latest (May 28, 1991) draft of the party's position on multiculturalism.

63. See Trudeau, "Federalism, Nationalism and Reason," p. 199.

The Canadian Charter of Rights and Freedoms

In 1982 the Charter of Rights and Freedoms became part of the Canadian constitution. A Bill of Rights had existed since 1960, but it was a legislative document and not part of the constitution. The opening sections of the 1982 charter guarantee for the first time a set of what Americans would recognize as "individual rights." They include the fundamental freedoms of conscience, religion, expression and association; the democratic right to vote in periodic elections; the mobility right to enter and leave Canada and to take up residence in any province; and various legal rights against unreasonable search and seizure, arbitrary detention and imprisonment, cruel and unusual punishment, and the like.

Other charter sections entrench rights that Americans do not find in their own Constitution. Although the precise meaning of the term is open to considerable dispute, it suffices here to label them "group rights." Thus the charter recognizes rights that implicitly or explicitly accrue to women, multicultural groups, linguistic minorities (francophones in English Canada and anglophones in Quebec), and aboriginals, as well as the disabled and the aged. Consequently, the charter has created "an environment in which [Canadians] are highly conscious of their identity as members of particular groups and are encouraged to organize and lobby for their [constitutional] interests."[64]

Some scholars now refer to the charter as the third pillar of Canadian government.[65] This is an apt description, not only because it accurately conveys the prominence the charter has gained in the company of the two more venerable pillars—the parliamentary system and the federal structure—but also because the charter was meant to act as a counterweight to them. Because the charter protects citizens' rights, it is widely held to have introduced Canada's first constitutional limitation on the supremacy of Parliament at the federal and the provincial levels. And because the rights in question are universal, that is, applicable equally to all Canadians, the charter is widely held to have introduced a pan-Canadian set of values that move against the centrifugal forces of a federal state.

---

64. Cynthia Williams, "The Changing Nature of Citizen Rights," in Cairns and Williams, eds., *Constitutionalism, Citizenship, and Society,* p. 125. Strictly speaking, aboriginals are not really a "charter group"; the bulk of the protection the 1982 constitution extended to them lies outside the charter itself. Nevertheless, aboriginals are very much a part of the new "group-affiliated" constitutional politics spawned largely by the charter, and so I will include them in my discussion here.

65. Williams, "Changing Nature," pp. 126, 128.

In this counterfederalizing vein, it is also often said that the charter has begun to supplant Canadians' traditional regional and linguistic identifications. That is, it has superimposed on the old, federally based divisions a new set of pan-Canadian attachments based on gender, religion, race, and age. Over and above Canadians' loyalties to their provincial governments, the charter is also said to have created a new allegiance to central institutions, especially the Supreme Court, which are ultimately charged with protecting charter rights.[66] More generally, both of the more established institutional pillars—the parliamentary system and the federal structure—are considered affairs of governments, not of people. Consequently, the charter has been described as appending a "people's constitution" to what was previously a constitution concerned exclusively with the structure of, and relations between, governments.

The charter represents an ideological innovation as well as an institutional innovation. Specifically, it has given salience to a new view of state and citizen—a view of the state variously characterized as "universalizing," "unifying," "homogenizing," or "centralizing," and a bipartite view of the citizen as both rights-bearing and group-affiliated. The 1982 debate on the charter, however, "emphasized special claims rather than those rights possessed by all Canadians," and by comparison with the previous nonconstitutional Bill of Rights, the charter itself represents a "shift in emphasis from the rights of individuals to the rights of special groups." I will therefore concentrate here on the charter's advent of "group-affiliated" citizens, citizens newly "conscious of their identity as members of particular groups."[67]

The Charter and the Other Two Pillars

Many observers have questioned the extent to which the charter represents both an innovative limitation on parliamentary supremacy and a unifying force in counteracting the centrifugal pulls of a federal system. Some scholars argue that a meaningful judicial culture of rights thrived in Canada before the charter and that the old Bill of Rights could easily have limited the power of Parliament more than the courts allowed it to

66. Knopff and Morton, "Nation-Building and the Canadian Charter of Rights and Freedoms."

67. Donald Smiley, "A Dangerous Deed: The Constitution Act, 1982," in Banting and Simeon, eds., *And No One Cheered*, p. 81; and Williams, "Changing Nature," p. 125, respectively.

do.[68] Others point to two important clauses in the charter—the "free and democratic society" provision, and the "notwithstanding clause"—that they believe mute its impact on parliamentary supremacy. Section 1 subjects all charter rights, and hence the ability of the judiciary to enforce them, to "such reasonable limits as can be demonstrably justified in a free and democratic society." Section 33 explicitly allows the federal and provincial parliaments to override certain charter rights (including the fundamental freedoms and the legal rights), notwithstanding their charter protection, simply by including an explicit override provision in the legislation in question. Neither of these clauses, of course, finds any equivalent in the American Bill of Rights, and the jury is still out on the question of whether they will significantly dampen the charter's effect on parliamentary supremacy.

There are also those who question the extent to which the charter can act as a unifying, universalistic force in counteracting the centrifugal pulls of a federal system. To be sure, the charter provides another set of cleavages—gender, ethnicity, and so forth—that crosscut the traditional federal (that is, linguistic and territorial) divisions of the country.[69] The charter, in other words, may well draw Canadians "away from territorial and linguistic identities to embrace new, trans-national identities based more on gender and race."[70] Yet these various new trans-national identities may themselves encourage a "serialized, fragmented concept of the people, the people sliced into individual and group instances."[71]

In particular, in the struggle over constitutional amendment and interpretation, charter groups have become rivals with very different imperatives. Some believe that the charter accords certain groups a higher status than others. Protections for linguistic minorities, for example, are immune from the notwithstanding clause, while protections for the disabled are

68. Ian Greene, "The Myths of Legislative and Constitutional Supremacy," in Shugarman and Whitaker, eds., *Federalism and Political Community*, pp. 267–90.

69. Alan C. Cairns, *Disruptions: Constitutional Struggles, from the Charter to Meech Lake*, ed. Douglas E. Williams (Toronto: McClelland and Stewart, 1991), p. 131; and John D. Whyte, "The 1987 Constitutional Accord and Ethnic Accommodation," in Katherine E. Swinton and Carol J. Rogerson, eds., *Competing Constitutional Visions: The Meech Lake Accord* (Toronto: Carswell, 1988), p. 269.

70. Gibbins, "Reform Party and the Political Future of the Canadian West," p. 6.

71. Reg Whitaker, "Commentary," in David E. Smith, Peter MacKinnon, and John C. Courtney, eds., *After Meech Lake: Lessons for the Future* (Saskatoon: Fifth House, 1991), p. 111. See also Deborah Coyne, "Commentary," in Smith, MacKinnon, and Courtney, eds., *After Meech Lake*, p. 141; Guy Laforest, "Interpreting the Political Heritage of André Laurendeau," in Smith, MacKinnon, and Courtney, eds., *After Meech Lake*, pp. 99–107; and Cairns, *Disruptions*, p. 133.

not.[72] Charter groups thus become competitors in the belief that "if you upgrade the rights of [some], by definition, you have lowered everyone else's."[73] Others fear that the rights of some groups will inevitably come into direct substantive conflict with the rights of others. Here, the most talked-about example is the possibility that the self-government rights of aboriginals could conflict with the equality rights of women if, in some circumstances, aborginal governments chose to override those rights on native lands.[74]

Moreover, many of the major charter groups—for example, women, linguistic minorities, and aborginals—are themselves divided internally over constitutional questions, often along the very sorts of old-style linguistic and territorial lines that, as emerging groups, they were supposed to have crosscut and superseded.

During the Meech lake debate, women's groups divided along linguistic and territorial lines over the distinct-society clause: those outside Quebec feared that the clause would have enabled the Quebec government to override the rights of women in order to preserve Quebec's distinct society; the Federations des Femmes du Quebec insisted the clause was integral to the protection of their own identity, which they thought of as embracing not just gender but language. Linguistic minority groups also were seriously divided over the distinct-society clause. The francophone minority outside Quebec largely supported it, and the anglophone minority inside Quebec opposed it.[75] Aboriginal groups, as well, are unlikely to be able to surmount certain territorial and language-based cleavages—especially when it comes to constitutional questions.[76] Notwithstanding the charter,

72. F. L. Morton, "Group Rights versus Individual Rights in the Charter: The Special Case of Natives and the Quebecois," in Neil Nevitte and Allan Kornberg, eds., *Minorities and the Canadian State* (Oakville, Ont.: Mosaic Press, 1985), p. 83. See also Evelyn Kallen, "The Meech Lake Accord: Entrenching a Pecking Order of Minority Rights," in Behiels, ed., *The Meech Lake Primer*, pp. 349–69.

73. *Senate Debates*, November 18, 1987, p. 2202.

74. Morton, "Group Rights versus Individual Rights," p. 75; and Williams, "Changing Nature," p. 126.

75. Within the francophone linguistic minority there is additional fragmentation along federal-style territorial lines. On constitutional as well as political questions, francophones outside Quebec think of themselves variously as Franco-Ontarians, Franco-Manitobans, and so on, more than they think of themselves as French Canadians. The francophone minority has not cut across federal divisions so much as it has been "provincialized." See Alan Cairns and Cynthia Williams, "Constitutionalism, Citizenship, and Society in Canada: An Overview," in Cairns and Williams, eds., *Constitutionalism, Citizenship, and Society*, p. 21.

76. See Douglas Sanders, "An Uncertain Path: The Aboriginal Constitutional Conferences," in Joseph M. Weiler and Robin M. Elliot, eds., *Litigating the Values of a Nation:*

the centrifugalist forces of federalism—language and territory—will thus die hard in Canada.

The Charter and the Other Three Ideologies

Various aspects of the charter show points of both resonance and conflict with the other three English-Canadian ideologies discussed above. Although Reform ideology is consistent with charter provisions regarding individual rights (the Reform would like to add a charter section on property rights), it is implacably opposed to the charter's constitutionalization of the group-implicated (hyphenated) citizen—the multicultural-Canadian, the linguistic minority–Canadian, and so on. Although the social-democratic strand in Canadian nationalism predisposes it toward certain charter sections (particularly those concerning affirmative action), its anti-American strand sits uneasily with the heightened role the charter accords to the judiciary, which is seen by some as an American-style innovation in the functioning of the Canadian state.[77]

Despite Trudeau's central role in establishing the charter, his thought—and more exactly, his views of the federal state and the cosmopolitan citizen—lead to mixed conclusions with respect to the two types of rights embodied in the charter, group and individual. As a devotee of the strong federal state, Trudeau supported the charter's group rights provisions, viewing them as a way to counteract the divisive force of language and territory in Canada, strengthen the ties between Canadians and federal institutions, and forge a national culture of citizens' rights that would command powerful group support.[78] As a proponent of cosmopolitan individualism, however, Trudeau has always been lukewarm toward the

---

The Canadian Charter of Rights and Freedoms (Toronto: Carswell, 1986), p. 74; and Peter M. Leslie, "Canada as a Bicommunal Polity," in Clare F. Beckton and A. Wayne MacKay, eds., *Recurring Issues in Canadian Federalism* (University of Toronto Press, 1986), p. 128.

77. Charles Taylor, "Shared and Divergent Values," in Watts and Brown, eds., *Options for a New Canada*, p. 72; and Seymour Martin Lipset, *Continental Divide: The Values and Institutions of the United States and Canada* (Toronto: C. D. Howe Institute, 1989), p. 116.

78. See Katherine E. Swinton, "Competing Visions of Constitutionalism: Of Federalism and Rights," in Swinton and Rogerson, eds., *Competing Constitutional Visions*, p. 281; Peter W. Hogg, "Federalism Fights the Charter of Rights," in Shugarman and Whitaker, eds., *Federalism and Political Community*, pp. 249–50; Peter H. Russell, "The Political Purposes of the Canadian Charter of Rights and Freedoms," *Canadian Bar Review*, vol. 61 (March 1983), pp. 30–54; and Laforest, "Interpreting the Political Heritage of André Laurendeau," p. 104.

idea of group rights as embodied in the charter. "Only the individual is the possessor of rights," Trudeau has declared. A "collectivity can exercise only those rights it has received by delegation from its members."[79] Conversely, Trudeau's conception of the cosmopolitan citizen is supportive of the charter's individual rights provisions, while his philosophy of the strong federal state is less so. One thinks here of the Trudeau who, in the name of individual choice, reformed Canada's divorce laws in 1967 with the ringing declaration that "there's no place for the state in the nation's bedrooms," but who, in response to a 1970 outbreak of separatist violence in Quebec, ran roughshod over individual liberties in defense of what he perceived as the imperiled state.[80] Trudeau's twofold capacity to uphold the rights of the individual as a free agent in almost metaphysical terms, *and* to denounce as "bleeding hearts" those who defended individual rights when the integrity of the federal state was threatened, reflects the mutually conflicting influences of his cosmopolitanism and federalism. Taken together, they highlight the ambivalence his thought shows toward the charter's conception of individual rights.

In both its uneasiness with the idea of group rights and its recognition of their nation-building potential, in its dedication to individual rights and its concern that they not impede the prerogatives of federal-state authority, Trudeau's thought incarnates the ambivalence with which a certain strand of English-Canadian political culture viewed the charter.

The Charter and Quebec Nationalism

If the relationships between the charter and the various English-Canadian ideologies show points of both resonance and conflict, the

79. Trudeau, "Values of a Just Society," p. 364. Trudeau's cosmopolitanism sits uneasily not only with the group rights provisions of the charter, but also with the multiculturalism policy—also introduced by his government—that the provisions build upon. One scholar has described that policy as the attempt to reinforce the "legitimate ancestral cultures which are the legacy of every Canadian," yet Trudeau continues to extol the idea of "human personalities [that] transcend . . . ancestral traditions, being vassals neither to their race, nor to their religion, nor to . . . their collective history." See Morton Weinfeld, "Myth and Reality in the Canadian Mosaic: 'Affective Ethnicity,'" *Canadian Ethnic Studies*, vol. 13, no. 3 (1981), p. 94; and Trudeau, "Values of a Just Society," pp. 363–64.

80. See Colombo, ed., *Colombo's Canadian Quotations*, p. 595; Abraham Rotstein, ed., *Power Corrupted: The October Crisis and the Repression of Quebec* (Toronto: New Press, 1971); and Donald Jamieson, "Overkill," *Saturday Night*, April 1, 1988, pp. 26, 29. These positions were echoed in Trudeau's foreign policy pronouncements. In 1971 he had the opportunity to criticize the Soviet government for enforcing its laws against Ukrainain dissidents but refused. "Anyone who breaks the law to assert his nationalism," he said at

relationship between the charter and Quebec nationalism shows a much clearer mutual hostility. It is a convention of Canadian constitutional scholarship that the charter has contributed—and will continue contributing—to a centralization of power in the federal judiciary.[81] Thus the charter implies developments in the federal state that conflict with Quebec nationalism's goal of increasing the powers of the province.[82] The charter now has a "negative image in Quebec," an image that has been "sustained by the fact that up until 1989 Quebec had had more statutes struck down [on charter grounds] than any other province, and these had tended to be major statutes dealing with language and education." As for "Quebec political and scholarly analysis," it is "replete with negative references to the homogenizing, universalizing thrust of the Charter."[83]

Quebec nationalists additionally view the charter's entrenchment of the group-affiliated citizen—its elevation to constitutional status of multicultural groups, gender groups, and so on—as a threat to Quebec's special status.[84] Indeed, these very groups were among the most vehement opponents of the Meech Lake Accord, objecting to it on the grounds that the distinct-society clause would have depreciated their own constitutional standing. French Quebecers, charter groups urged, should not be given any constitutional provision, such as the distinct-society clause, that would accord them special or superior constitutional status; rather, they should take their place alongside all other group-affiliated citizens. Consequently, the charter's entrenchment of the group-affiliated citizen has "had the negative side effect of antagonizing Francophone Quebecers," who see it as depreciating their stature as a "founding people."[85]

---

the time, "doesn't get much sympathy from me." Quoted in Andy Stark, "Pierre Trudeau's 15 Years of Failure," *Wall Street Journal*, April 12, 1983, p. 34.

81. Henri Brun, "The Canadian Charter of Rights and Freedoms as an Instrument of Social Development," in Clare F. Beckton and A. Wayne MacKay, research coordinators, *The Courts and the Charter* (University of Toronto Press, 1985), p. 8.

82. Allan Blakeney, "Remember the Tanks in Montreal," *Globe and Mail* (Toronto), July 8, 1991, p. A21.

83. Cairns, *Disruptions*, p. 24; and Cairns, "Constitutional Change and the Three Equalities," p. 87.

84. Cairns, *Disruptions*, p. 119. See also Taylor, "Shared and Divergent Values," pp. 59, 71; and T. C. Christopher, "The 1982 Canadian Charter of Rights and Freedoms and Multiculturalism," *Canadian Review of Studies in Nationalism*, vol. 14 (Fall 1987), p. 339.

85. Cairns, *Disruptions*, p. 119.

Conclusion

Four powerful ideologies of state and citizen are prominent in English Canada today. All are home-grown products, indigenous to Canadian soil, the fruits of singular confluences of minds and events that could never have appeared elsewhere. Although some exhibit greater mutual affinity than do others, they all display important points of bilateral conflict. Certainly they would suffice, in and of themselves, to create significant cleavages within any state. Their formidable resistance to a fifth ideology, Quebec nationalism, simply makes matters worse.

Trudeau propounded a strong federal state with an eye to global integration. The Reform movement has been devoted to constructing a strong federal state with an eye to regional integration. Canadian nationalists dream of building a social-democratic state. And the charter implies a "universalizing" and "centralizing" state. Although their views of the state differ, all four ideologies are at one in their opposition to any significant devolution of federal powers. And devolution is one key aspiration of Quebec nationalism.

The four ideologies also present different views of the citizen. I have discussed Trudeau's cosmopolitan Canadian, Canadian nationalism's identity-less Canadian, the Reform's unhyphenated Canadian, and the charter's group-affiliated Canadian. Each of these conceptions works, respectively, to transcend, thwart, deny, or diminish the distinctiveness of Quebecers within Canada. And, of course, distinct constitutional status is the other key aspiration of Quebec nationalism.

Such a balance of ideological forces—English-Canadian against Quebec nationalist—is untenable over the long run. Either these various forces must show some give (perhaps through a resurgence of the Canadian tradition of pragmatic compromise), or else the entity currently known as Canada must do so.

Northrop Frye once made an interesting observation about the differences between Canada and the United States. For the purposes of Americans who are trying to understand Canada's current predicament, Frye's observation is particularly evocative. It serves as an appropriate coda— as much as a conclusion—for the preceding discussion.

The United States, Frye noted, was born in a war of independence against a European power and came to maturity with a civil war fought decades later. Canada, by contrast, was born in a civil war between two

European powers and has been fighting a war of independence against the United States ever since.[86]

This is an obviously suggestive observation, and one of the many things it suggests is the following: A country that *first* wins a war of independence and *then* fights a civil war goes through two processes of self-definition—in the first instance, by separating itself from an external power, and in the second, by putting an end to an internal contradiction. By contrast, a country that is *born* in a civil war and *then* fights a continuing war of independence thereafter may run a greater risk of becoming a congenital schizophrenic and a perpetual adolescent.[87] Or, at least, perhaps that is the central distinction between the two countries that Northrop Frye was trying to suggest—in his reticent, diffident, Canadian way.

86. Northrop Frye, *Divisions on a Ground: Essays on Canadian Culture* (Toronto: Anansi, 1982), p. 65.

87. "Schizophrenic" and "adolescent" seem to be among the metaphors of choice for literary figures engaged in the task of describing Canada. See, for example, Margaret Atwood, *The Journals of Susanna Moodie: Poems by Margaret Atwood* (Toronto: Oxford University Press, 1970), p. 62; and Earle Birney, "Canada: Case History: 1945," in *The Collected Poems of Earle Birney*, vol. 1 (Toronto: McClelland and Stewart, 1975), p. 125.

KEITH G. BANTING

If Quebec Separates: Restructuring Northern North America

A house divided against itself cannot stand.
—Abraham Lincoln, 1858

MUCH OF CANADIAN history can be interpreted as an effort to prove that Lincoln was wrong, and that a country composed of distinctive and often conflicting cultures can stand and even flourish. The tension between French- and English-speaking communities has constituted a core element of Canadian politics for over two centuries. Indeed, in a report to the British government on the political struggles of the late 1830s in what was then called Lower Canada, Lord Durham observed that he "found two nations warring in the bosom of a single state."[1] The subsequent establishment of a federal state in 1867 was an attempt, in part, to find a political framework in which two cultures could coexist peacefully.

That historic accommodation now faces its severest challenge. In the aftermath of the rejection of the Meech Lake Accord, support within Quebec for independence and the creation of a separate Quebec state reached record levels, and the provincial legislature adopted a statute requiring a referendum on sovereignty to be held during 1992. The intensity of that opinion has softened since then, but it would be premature to conclude that the threat has passed. The tortuous process of constitutional debate and negotiations on which the country is now launched is replete

I would like to thank Daniel Bonin, Alan Cairns, Stéphane Dion, and Robert Young for helpful comments on an earlier version of this essay. In light of the rapidly evolving nature of the Canadian constitutional crisis, it is worth recording that this paper was completed in early October 1991.
1. *Report on the Affairs of British North America from the Earl of Durham* (1839) in T. P. O'Neill, ed., *British Parliamentary Papers* (Shannon, Ireland: Irish University Press, 1968), p. 8.

with opportunities for renewed conflict and recrimination, and the balance within Quebec could still tip toward separation.

There are three broad possibilities for the future of Canada. The first, which might be labeled the "rosy scenario," would see Canadians agreeing on a grand package of constitutional reforms that meet the expectations of all the major players in the current struggle. Under this scenario, a political accommodation among the contending forces would produce significant reforms in the country's political institutions and processes and would legitimate a new set of fundamental principles that would govern future conflicts. Quebec's reservations about Canada would be resolved, the provincial government would endorse the country's constitution (as amended), and public support for an independent state would fade away. Other provinces and the aboriginal population would also achieve their constitutional aspirations. The country could then put a generation of constitutional conflict behind it and move on. For reasons explained in part by Andrew Stark's essay, this seems unlikely. The constitutional agenda is immense; the positions of important groups in the process are not only mutually incompatible but are also held with increasing rigidity; and the amending formula for the constitution is formidable, requiring for some provisions the agreement of the federal government and all of the provincial governments. All of this suggests that such a grand accommodation is probably beyond the country's reach.

Early reaction to the wide-ranging constitutional proposals released by the federal government in September 1991 confirms this view.[2] The most comforting response has been that of the premier of Quebec, who declared that although the proposals are insufficient, they do constitute a useful starting point for negotiations. Nationalist elements in his party are much more critical, however, and the Parti Québécois has rejected the package completely. Aspects of the federal proposals designed to reduce interprovincial barriers to trade have been widely attacked in the province, and three separate public opinion polls have pronounced the Quebec public dissatisfied.[3] Reactions elsewhere are no more encouraging. The leadership of the Assembly of First Nations, which represents Indian groups across the country, has denounced the proposals as an insult, and many commentators from the West also consider that the

2. For the federal government's proposals, see Government of Canada, *Shaping Canada's Future Together* (Ottawa: Minister of Supply and Services, 1991).

3. For a survey of the Quebec reaction, see Norman Delisle, "Bilan des propositions fédérales: les Québécois sont insatisfaits," *Le Devoir*, September 30, 1991.

package falls short of their aspirations. These are hardly harbingers of the rosy scenario.

The second scenario might be labeled the "mushy middle." According to this scenario, the country would fail to master the full constitutional agenda, but federal and provincial governments would agree to a modest set of changes and commit themselves to continuing rounds of negotiations over a list of remaining items. Such an outcome would be extremely contentious in Quebec, with the Parti Québécois and other nationalist forces insisting that independence is the only alternative. Artful political maneuvering by the beleaguered federalist forces in the Quebec government might postpone a final, irrevocable decision, however, on the argument that it is better to give federalism another "last chance." For example, the premier might be able to amend the referendum legislation to authorize a vote on federalist reform proposals instead; or he might defer a decision by calling a provincial election and winning a mandate to continue negotiations. Under this scenario, the past becomes the future. Constitutional controversy is further cemented into the national agenda; *indépendantiste* sentiment continues to ebb and flow within Quebec; and the separation of the province remains a specter that haunts Canadian politics. While this outcome avoids an immediate rupture, it does hold its own sweet horrors.

The third scenario is an independent Quebec. Failure to agree on core issues, together with bitterness generated by the negotiating process, would undercut the federalist forces in the province of Quebec. Either the current provincial Liberal government of Robert Bourassa would lead the province toward independence, or the Parti Québécois would win the next election and initiate the process. As a result, a new state would be born, and the political restructuring of northern North America would be under way in earnest.

Assigning a probability to these three scenarios—or any others that might be devised—is inevitably hazardous. Nevertheless, the real prospects for Canada are probably to be found between the second and third options. Agreement on reforms sufficiently dramatic to resolve the constitutional agenda and lay to rest the specter of Quebec separation seems beyond reach. The real issue, then, is whether Quebec will separate in the near future or whether separation will simply remain a recurring component of the Canadian agenda.

From either point of view, it is important to reflect on the consequences of separation and the creation of an independent state of Quebec. This essay explores the implications of a decision by Quebec to do so. The first section examines the political issues and problems that would confront the successor states in the northern half of the continent. The second section then turns more briefly to the implications for the United States.

The Politics of the Successor States

The division of Canada and the emergence of a number of successor states would have pervasive implications, both international and domestic, for the inhabitants of northern North America. The international role that Canadians now have as a single country would decline dramatically. Canada is currently a middle-level power, with considerably greater economic and political standing than the average member of the United Nations. It is, for example, a member of the G7, which the *Economist* magazine recently observed "has replaced the superpower summit as the most influential meeting-place in the world."[4] Successor states would be much smaller countries, with considerably less influence in world councils. As a separate state, Quebec's symbolic role on the world stage would increase over its status as a province, but it would still be a decidedly marginal participant in world politics.

The big issues that would dominate the politics of successor states would lie closer to home, however. The division of the country would require major adjustments on the part of both Quebec and Canada, and its ripple effects would invade virtually every area of public policy. The political prospects facing an independent Quebec and Canada differ in important ways, and it is useful therefore to examine them separately.[5]

Quebec

Independence would launch Quebec on uncharted waters, with dangerous reefs lurking just below the surface. In the early years, however, Quebec would start with three important political advantages. First, the

4. "The World Order Changeth," *Economist*, June 22, 1991, p. 13.
5. Nomenclature is becoming complex in this area. Recent debates have spawned an exotic array of names for the Canada that would remain after the separation of Quebec, including "Rest-of-Canada" or ROC, "Canada-without-Quebec" or CWQ, and "Canada-outside-of-Quebec" or COQ. All of these seem unnecessarily cumbersome and unduly apologetic about the political entity they describe. This essay simply uses the term "Canada." Where necessary, the text makes clear whether the term refers to the current Canada, including Quebec, or a future Canada without it.

establishment of a sovereign state would constitute a national affirmation for the Québécois people. There would be anxieties, to be sure. A referendum campaign on independence would be divisive; the "yes" vote would probably not exceed 60 percent; and significant minorities such as anglophones and natives would be bitterly opposed. Nevertheless, a decision to separate would reflect considerable self-confidence on the part of the Québécois, and in many ways the central psychological framework of that historic society would remain intact. Second, the Québécois have been devoting considerable thought to independence for over a generation. The new state would therefore begin with a reasonable sense of where it wants to go, at least in broad outline. Third, Quebec would start with a coherent set of political institutions. Shifting to the formal status of a republic would not necessarily involve an immediate restructuring of the political institutions and political parties that already guide the destiny of the province. In time, Quebec might opt for a presidential system of government; and with the achievement of sovereignty, the major issue dividing the two major parties would fade, leaving room for new forms of political alignment in the future. Nevertheless, Quebec would have the luxury of designing new political institutions in its own time. Enthusiasm, strategy, and institutions do not themselves guarantee success in such adventures. They do represent important advantages, however, and—as will be discussed below—all three of these advantages would be denied to Canada after a split.

The principal objectives of the *indépendantiste* movement are clear. First, Quebec would become a sovereign state with the same boundaries as the current province. Suggestions that the boundaries of the new state would be subject to negotiation would be resisted strongly. Second, the new state would adopt a foreign policy carefully designed to reassure its major neighbors, including the United States. Quebec would undoubtedly have close links with France and with French-speaking nations around the world, but the main outlines of its foreign policy would be decidedly North American. Membership in NATO and joint bodies such as NORAD and the International Joint Commission would set the general international orientation of the new state.[6] Third, Quebec would seek to minimize the costs of sovereignty by maintaining close economic links with both Canada and the United States. The Parti Québécois proposes that Quebec retain the Canadian dollar as legal tender, accept its share

6. In its early days, the Parti Québécois favoured a neutralist foreign policy, but in 1979 it decided that an independent Quebec should remain a member of NATO and NORAD.

of the Canadian national debt, and maintain close trading relationships with Canada, especially Ontario.

Separatists also wish to retain the free trade agreement with the United States. Quebec has few of the reservations about the agreement that seriously divide English-speaking Canadians. The distinctive language and culture of Quebec provide greater confidence that closer economic integration will not lead to cultural assimilation, as many other Canadians fear. During the 1988 election campaign, fought almost exclusively over the trade proposal, Quebec's support was essential to the reelection of the Conservative government and the implementation of the agreement. And in the current context, the agreement, with its promise of access to the large U.S. market, represents a bedrock of Quebecers' confidence in the economic feasibility of a separate Quebec state. In effect, closer economic integration with the United States has lowered the perceived costs of the political disintegration of the current Canadian federation.

Thus the *indépendantiste* strategy is to minimize the economic and international disruptions inherent in political sovereignty. The success of this strategy, however, would depend heavily on the reactions of others. A new Quebec state would require the agreement or at least the acquiescence of the minorities within the province and of the countries that surround it. This will not come easily, as can be seen in two issues: the boundaries of the new state and its economic relationships.

The boundaries of an independent Quebec would be subject to challenge from outside and inside. Already some English-Canadian commentators have argued that Quebec should be allowed to take only the territory that it held when it entered the federation in 1867 or, in other versions, that it held before the extension of its borders to incorporate northernmost Quebec in 1912.[7] Within the province, there could be what Maureen Covell calls "a spiral of claims to self-determination."[8] English-speaking regions in the South and West of the province might attempt to invoke a parallel right of self-determination and remain part of Canada, making impassioned appeals for support to their Canadian compatriots.[9]

7. See David Jay Bercuson and Barry Cooper, *Deconfederation: Canada without Quebec* (Toronto: Key Porter, 1991), pp. 148–57.

8. Maureen Covell, "Thinking About the Rest of Canada: Options for Canada without Quebec," Occasional Paper 6 (York University Centre for Public Law and Public Policy, 1991), p. 28.

9. Naturally, the issue of boundaries is discussed primarily by opponents of separation. See, for example, the brief presented by the leader of the federal Liberal party, Jean Chrétien, to the Commission on the Political and Constitutional Future of Quebec,

The critical challenge, however, would come from the aboriginal population. In August 1991, Cree leaders served notice before the United Nations
Panel on Indigenous Populations that in the event of Quebec separation,
natives would assert their claim to the northern part of Quebec—territory
the size of France—and would choose whether to remain part of Canada
or to become a sovereign nation in their own right.[10] Given the intensity
of opinion among the anglophone and native minorities, it is possible to
imagine Quebec dotted with barricades and "no-go" areas during the
transition to independence.

Such developments hold considerable potential for violence. Americans
familiar with the politics of secession in their own country or elsewhere
in the world are often amazed by Canadians' apparent assumption that
the use of military force to preserve the union is not an option. There will
be no Yugoslavian tragedy here. Nevertheless, the escalation of tension
before a split would undoubtedly generate more debate about the role of
the military, and battles over boundaries could lead to confusion and
localized violence. The protracted standoff between heavily armed natives
and the Canadian army at Oka, Quebec, in the summer of 1990, and the
related shooting of a police officer, stand as stark reminders of the dangers
inherent in conflicting claims to sovereignty.

The economic prospects of an independent Quebec would also depend
heavily on the reaction of others. No issue has received greater debate
than the economics of independence. There is reasonable agreement that
in an open international trading regime, small states are not necessarily
at a disadvantage. Indeed, there appears to be no correlation, either
positive or negative, between the size of a nation and its level of economic

December 17, 1990, p. 28. The press has also picked up the question; see, for example,
Norman Delisle, "Un Québec souverain pourrait perdre un tiers de son territoire," *Le
Droit*, December 7, 1990; Stephan Bureau, "Les frontiers d'un Québec independant font
la manchette aux États-Unis," *La Presse*, June 8, 1991; and Christopher Young, "A
Potential Dispute over Quebec's North," *Toronto Star*, June 10, 1991.

10. André Picard, "Crees Vow to Seize Land if Quebec Separates," *Globe and Mail*
(Toronto), July 31, 1991. The constitutional debate has become embroiled in a bitter
dispute between the Cree and environmentalists on one side and the Quebec government
on the other over the Great Whale hydroelectric project in northern Quebec. Power from
this project would be exported to the United States, especially the state of New York. For
arguments between the premier of the province and Cree leaders, see Rheál Séguin, "Hydro
Delay Angers Bourassa," *Globe and Mail* (Toronto), August 5, 1991; André Picard, "Great
Whale Will Fail Like Meech, Chief Says," *Globe and Mail*, August 7, 1991; and Picard,
"Mercredi Chides Bourassa," *Globe and Mail*, August 8, 1991.

well-being.[11] In the specific case of Quebec, however, there is substantial debate about the economic costs of the *transition* to independence. The lack of theoretical and empirical knowledge about such transitions maximizes the uncertainty and therefore the range of predictions made by economists. With little in the way of hard comparative data to discipline the imagination, predictions tend to correlate highly with the political orientation of the analysts.[12] Projections prepared for a commission on Quebec's political future, established by the provincial government after the defeat of the Meech Lake Accord, suggested that the transition costs would be minimal.[13] This analysis has come in for considerable criticism, however, and the real debate among economists is whether the costs would be manageable, with some answering in the affirmative and others insisting that the costs to both Quebec and Canada would be very high indeed.[14]

Much of the uncertainty about transition costs centers on the political reaction of others to a newly independent Quebec. All analysts agree that the more acrimonious the breakup and the greater the political instability within Quebec, the greater the negative effects on investment. The relationships between a sovereign Quebec and its neighbors, Canada and the United States, would also be critical. The leaders of the Parti Québécois assume that the United States would quickly extend the free trade agreement to Quebec, an issue that is discussed more thoroughly below. Separatist leaders also assume that economic necessity would force Can-

11. See John Helliwell and Alan Chung, "Are Bigger Countries Better Off?" in Douglas D. Purvis, Robin W. Boadway, and Thomas J. Courchene, eds., *Economic Dimensions of Constitutional Change: The Eighth John Deutsch Roundtable on Economic Policy*, vol. 1 (Kingston: Queen's University, John Deutsch Institute for the Study of Economic Policy, 1991), pp. 345–70.

12. In the words of a leading Quebec economist, "the correlation between political beliefs and economic appraisal is probably close to 100 percent." Pierre Fortin, "The Threat of Quebec Sovereignty: Meaning, Likelihood and Economic Consequences," in Purvis and others, eds., *Economic Dimensions of Constitutional Change*, vol. 2, p. 337.

13. Commission on the Political and Constitutional Future of Quebec, *Eléments d'analyse économique pertinents à la révision du statut politique et constitutionnel du Québec*, Document de travail 1 (Quebec City, 1991).

14. For example, contrast the analysis by Fortin, "Threat of Quebec Sovereignty," with that of Richard Harris and Douglas Purvis, "Some Economic Aspects of Political Restructuring," in Purvis and others, eds., *Economic Dimensions of Constitutional Change*, vol. 1, pp. 189–211. See also Thomas J. Courchene, *In Praise of Renewed Federalism* (Toronto: C. D. Howe Institute, 1991); André Raynauld, "Les enjeux économiques de la souveraineté: Mémoire soumis au C.P.Q." (Montreal: Conseil du Patronat du Québec, 1990); and the briefs presented to the Commission on the Political and Constitutional Future of Quebec.

ada and Quebec to establish a new set of linkages with a minimum of fuss. They assume that Quebec's continued use of the Canadian dollar would be acceptable, the division of the national debt and assets would be largely an accounting exercise, and the maintenance of close trading relationships would not pose serious problems. Others assume even more elaborate economic linkages, involving supranational institutions along the model of the European Community.

These assumptions are probably overly sanguine about the reaction of Canada, however, for two reasons. First, the separation of Quebec would probably trigger a wave of resentment throughout the rest of the country, and the level of economic magnanimity that Canada would bring to the table would be less than zero. In that climate, the scope for bitter conflict over the division of the debt and assets, the use of the currency, and trade relations is immense and would undoubtedly increase the transition costs for both parties to the dispute.

The second reason that Quebecers are too sanguine is that they do not fully appreciate the political turmoil that separation would create in Canada. The Canadian political structure would be thrown into crisis. The country would have to establish a new internal equilibrium, and the outcome of that effort would be unpredictable. To fully understand this dynamic, it is time to turn to the other side of the constitutional table.

Canada

The rest of Canada would be deprived of the three advantages with which Quebec would begin. First, there would be little celebration in the truncated Canadian federation. Admittedly, a few voices are already insisting that Canada would be better off without Quebec, and their number would undoubtedly swell if separation seemed imminent.[15] Nevertheless, Canada would undergo collective psychological disorientation. The historic conception of a nation stretching unbroken from sea to sea, incorporating different languages and cultures in a tolerant and peaceful society, would be shattered. In its wake would be a bifurcated country and a difficult debate about its direction. Second, Canada has not devoted a generation to debating its future without Quebec. In part because the possibility of Quebec's separation was often discounted, and

15. See Bercuson and Cooper, *Deconfederation*. In addition, the Reform party is emerging as an instrument of psychological adjustment to living without Quebec.

in part because of a desire to avoid self-fulfilling prophesies, Canada has not engaged in a collective reflection about how to proceed without Quebec. It would therefore enter into the transition phase at a considerable disadvantage. Third, and most critically, Canada would lack stable political institutions through which to develop a conception of its future.

The lack of stable political institutions would present two sets of problems, one transitional and one more fundamental. The transitional problem is best illustrated by asking who would speak for Canada in the aftermath of Quebec's decision to leave. Who would develop the country's basic strategy and negotiate on its behalf with Quebec? The current government could not do so. The prime minister, many of his cabinet colleagues, and a major proportion of their backbench supporters are from Quebec. The leader of the opposition and many of his closest colleagues are also from Quebec. Neither could negotiate the terms of separation. A major restructuring of the party system would be inevitable, but the changes would be neither simple nor rapid. A multiparty coalition government composed of leading members of Parliament from provinces other than Quebec might emerge as a temporary solution, but such a government would be weak and probably short-lived. Little of substance could be accomplished until a national election created a new government. Even holding such an election would not be simple, however. If Quebec were to simply announce its intention to leave, as opposed to making a unilateral declaration of independence, would Quebec elect members to the new Parliament? Under existing law, the province could not be excluded. But what role would Quebec MPs play? This could become an important issue if the new government had the support of only a small majority or a minority among the MPs from the other provinces.

Moreover, during this confusing period, the federal Parliament would face potent competition as the legitimate representative of Canada. One source of opposition would be the premiers of the remaining nine provinces, who would undoubtedly claim to speak for the country. They would represent the stable component of the political system. Backed in the main by majority governments at the provincial level and faced with a weakened federal counterpart, they would demand a powerful role—perhaps the dominant role–in the redesign of Canada and negotiations with Quebec.[16]

16. The premiers would start with considerable popular support in this area. In April 1991, the CBC/*Globe and Mail* poll asked Canadians, "Who do you think would do the best job representing the concerns of people like you in handling constitutional matters— the Prime Minister of Canada or the premier of your province?" In their responses, 59.5

History, however, suggests that premiers would have considerable difficulty in rising above the interests of their immediate constituencies to develop a pan-Canadian conception of the country. A nation dominated by premiers would be an awkward political animal, slow to make decisions and plagued by internal tensions.

Others would also claim to speak for the nation. The public credibility of established political leaders in constitutional matters was badly damaged by the Meech Lake debacle and would be further compromised by the splintering of the country. A wide range of social and economic interests would insist on being involved in the redesign of Canada, and the demands for some form of constituent assembly, or constitutional convention, already strong, would be strengthened. Once again, Canadians would fight not only over substantive issues of constitutional choice, but also over the process through which its collective future should be shaped. A period of political instability would be inevitable.

Underlying these transitional problems would be a more fundamental question, however. Could Canada continue as a single state? Or would the departure of Quebec initiate further fragmentation? Would Canada's collapse be complete? On this point there is considerable disagreement.

The optimistic view holds that a strong sense of Canadian identity and patriotism would sustain the country through turbulent periods. The wellsprings of this sense of national solidarity are admittedly difficult to identify. In part, it flows from a common history that has created a humane and prosperous society. In part, it flows from the 1982 Charter of Rights and Freedoms, a statement of values around which Canadians outside of Quebec seem to be rallying. And in part, national solidarity reflects a sense of distinctiveness from the American giant to the south. Differences that Canadians value include a greater commitment to collective as opposed to individual responsibility for human needs, manifest in social programs such as health care; lower levels of violence; more secure cities; and more stringent controls on the sale of firearms. Individually, these differences may seem small, but cumulatively they represent a distinctiveness cherished by Canadians. For optimists, these public senti-

---

percent chose the premier of their province, 21.3 percent chose the prime minister, and the balance were unsure or rejected both. Interestingly, the proportions did not differ between Quebec and the rest of the country. Even given the unpopularity of the current prime minister, the preference for premiers is striking. Canadian Facts, *Report: CBC/Globe and Mail Public Opinion Poll*, vol. 1, April 4–15, 1991 (Toronto, 1991).

ments represent a social cement strong enough to hold the new Canada together.[17] Indeed, the separation of Quebec might lead Canadians to accentuate those features of national life that distinguish them from the United States, a dynamic that could be accompanied by a revival of anti-Americanism.

The pessimistic view holds that the sense of Canadian identity is too slender a reed on which to build a stable country. Pessimists are convinced that the departure of Quebec would unleash deep divisions among the regions remaining within Canada and that no stable equilibrium would emerge. The argument here resembles that advanced by Mancur Olson, that changing the boundaries of a country disrupts the distributional coalitions that have emerged over time.[18] Olson's examples focus on the expansion of a country, but his logic applies to splintering as well. Quebec, as a large province in the current federation, represents an essential component in coalitions that have built up over time and that sustain the existing distribution of economic and political power. Without Quebec, those coalitions would break down, creating a set of deep interregional conflicts in Canada. This can be seen in two areas: interregional redistribution and the balance between the West and Ontario.

As a poorer province, Quebec has supported the substantial interregional redistribution that is characteristic of the current federation. That redistribution is made explicit in the system of equalization grants, which are unconditional grants paid by the federal government to the governments of poorer provinces to enable them to provide public services comparable to the national average without above-average tax efforts. In addition, significant interregional redistribution is implicit in the design of major national programs, such as unemployment insurance and economic development grants. After Quebec's departure, however, Canada would be dominated by the rich provinces of Ontario, British Columbia, and Alberta, whose residents are the net contributors to these interregional flows. These three provinces would represent over two-thirds of the population. In such a Canada, the pessimists argue, interregional redistribution would wither, seriously undermining the economy of poorer areas, especially the four Atlantic provinces. Cut off physically and cast adrift eco-

17. For an argument that English Canada has developed a considerably stronger sense of social cohesiveness, see Kenneth McRoberts, *English Canada and Quebec: Avoiding the Issue* (York University, Robarts Centre for Canadian Studies, 1991).

18. Mancur Olson, *The Rise and Decline of Nations: Economic Growth, Stagflation, and Social Rigidities* (Yale University Press, 1982).

nomically, this region would have less incentive to remain part of Canada and more incentive to think about alternatives.

The same logic can be applied to relations between Ontario and the West. Quebec has been a buffer between these regions, although its alliances have shifted from issue to issue. For example, Quebec has been an ally of the West in resisting a more centralized federation, which Ontario might have wished. However, Quebec's interests have been much closer to those of Ontario in resisting the West's demand for greater control over national institutions through such reforms as an elected Senate with equal representation from each province. Deprived of the counterbalance of Quebec, the showdown between the West and Ontario would be dramatic. Ontario would have about half the population of the new country and would be hard-pressed to agree that the tiny province of Prince Edward Island should have equal weight in a reformed Senate. Representation by population in the central government could not be abandoned so completely. Given a long history of conflicts between the resource-based provinces of the West and the manufacturing heartland of Ontario, however, the West would be adamantly opposed to the domination of a strong central government by the legions of Ontario voters.

Pessimists assume that any initial popular preference to remain a united country would erode steadily under such regional strains. The affluent westernmost provinces of British Columbia and Alberta would join the Atlantic region in thinking about alternatives beyond a single Canada. This would be especially the case if the economic costs of change proved large for both Quebec and Canada and northern North America generally looked less and less enticing to the world's footloose investors.

The pessimistic scenarios have different end points. Some see the emergence of a number of small successor states from the wreckage. The possibility that some parts of the country would seek to join the United States is a common prediction, however. After all, the north-south economic linkages have grown steadily at least since World War II and have been recently reinforced by the free trade agreement. Over time, with no compelling political vision to offset economic drift, a reorientation southward might begin. Indeed, during the final days of the debate over the Meech Lake Accord, the premier of Nova Scotia warned that if Quebec separated and the country fragmented, the Atlantic provinces would have no choice but to join the United States.[19] The comments provoked a

19. Premier John Buchanan's actual words were: "What are we going to do? Form our own country? That's absurd. Stay as a fractured part of Canada? A good possibility,

TABLE 1. Public Opinion in Canada about Quebec Separation, 1990

Percent

Question and response	Atlantic provinces[a]	Ontario	Prairie provinces[b]	British Columbia	All provinces except Quebec	Quebec	Total
Perceived effect on status of rest of Canada[c]							
Continue as an independent country	80.6	74.0	76.1	86.5	77.2	67.0	74.5
Become part of the United States	10.8	17.6	14.3	8.6	14.6	19.9	16.0
Don't know/not sure	8.6	8.1	9.6	5.4	8.1	13.2	9.3
Refused to answer	0	0.3	0	0	0.2	0	0.1
Personal preference for English Canada[d]							
Continue as an independent country	95.7	94.5	89.7	95.1	93.6	78.7	89.7
Become part of the United States	2.2	2.9	5.5	3.8	3.6	9.3	5.1
Don't know/not sure	2.2	2.2	5.1	1.1	2.7	11.5	5.0
Refused to answer	0	0.3	0	0	0.2	0.7	0.3

SOURCE: Canadian Facts, *Report: CBC/Globe and Mail Public Opinion Poll*, vol. 1, June 26–July 4, 1990 (Toronto, 1990), pp. 92, 93.

a. New Brunswick, Newfoundland, Novia Scotia, and Prince Edward Island.

b. Alberta, Manitoba, and Saskatchewan.

c. Question was: "If Quebec were to separate from the rest of Canada, do you think the rest of Canada would continue as an independent country or would it become part of the United States?"

d. Question was: "If Quebec were to separate, would you personally want to see Canada try to keep going as an independent country or would you want to see it become part of the United States?"

ground swell of angry indignation, but the issue remains below the surface of the debate.

In assessing the plausibility of the optimistic and pessimistic scenarios, it is important to underscore the initial strength of public opinion concerning Canada without Quebec. Table 1 reports the results of a poll that plumbed Canadians' views during the immediate aftermath of the death of the Meech Lake Accord. The results are clear. Although a small minority of Canadians outside of Quebec admit some doubt as to whether their country could survive, their desire to remain Canadian is overwhelming. Joining the United States was simply not a public option, at least in the emotional period of July 1990.

Such public sentiments do not guarantee the long-term viability of Canada, of course. Pessimists believe that over time the strains imposed by protracted regional conflict, economic problems, and the physical separation of the Atlantic provinces would erode those noble sentiments and leave the country at risk. This view was reflected by Peter Leslie: "I acknowledge that at present, sentiment in the [rest of Canada] favors sticking together as a federation, if Quebec were to secede. But the obstacles to creating a new form of union would be formidable and, in the end, the incentive slight."[20] Similarly, Thomas Courchene worries that "the march of events on the economic front might be such to overwhelm the values that bind Canadians in [the rest of Canada] together. It really does not matter how [Canadian] governments or citizens *feel* about designing a Canada without Quebec. What matters is getting the *economics* on side."[21]

The deep well of public commitment suggests that the persistence of Canada after the departure of Quebec is the most likely prospect, at least in the short term. The warnings of the pessimists clearly demonstrate that nothing is assured, however, and that complete collapse would follow if the country could not surmount the economic and political tensions generated by the departure of Quebec. A future with more than two successor states in northern North America is therefore not impossible, which would raise interesting questions for the government and people of the United States.

---

but that's all. Or be part of the United States? There's no choice." "Buchanan Raises Spectre of Joining United States," *Globe and Mail* (Toronto) April 19, 1990.

20. Peter M. Leslie, "Options for the Future of Canada: The Good, the Bad, and the Fantastic," in Ronald L. Watts and Douglas M. Brown, eds., *Options for a New Canada* (University of Toronto Press, 1991), p. 134.

21. Courchene, *In Praise of Renewed Federalism*, p. 75.

Implications for the United States

The United States inevitably has an interest in the configuration of northern North America. Admittedly, the intensity of that interest has declined with the easing of the cold war, which has reduced the military significance of political instability on the northern flank. In effect, the passing of the bipolar world has opened up greater geopolitical space for internal discord within the members of the old alliances, and the American government can be expected to take a more relaxed attitude now than it held at the height of its military anxiety. Nevertheless, the politics of Canadian discord do catch the eye of the eagle.

During the early years of their movement, Quebec separatists often speculated about the attitude of the United States toward the emergence of an independent Quebec on its northern border. Given the size of the anglophone and immigrant communities in Quebec, leaders of the Parti Québécois have always known that a victory in a referendum on sovereignty would be a narrow one and that explicit U.S. opposition might doom their efforts. They have hoped that Americans would feel a deep empathy between their own revolutionary beginnings and the struggle of the Québécois for independence. But in the words of Eugene Rostow, a former senior official in the U.S. State Department, Americans tend to identify "the Quebec separatist movement not with Thomas Jefferson, but with Jefferson Davis."[22] The Civil War still casts a shadow across the collective American imagination, and the idea of separation or secession tends to be associated "with regression, tragedy and political myopia."[23] This basic instinct is reinforced by the close economic and political relations that have emerged between the United States and Canada since World War II. Despite occasional frictions between the two countries, Canada stands as an ally in international politics and a major trading partner. As Joseph Jockel argues, although "the breakup of Canada would

22. Quoted in Jean-François Lisée, *In the Eye of the Eagle* (Toronto: Harper Collins, 1990), p. 6. This study provides a detailed examination of American attitudes toward Quebec nationalism and the prospects of an independent Quebec from the 1960s until the referendum in 1980. It draws heavily on U.S. government documents, many obtained through the Freedom of Information Act, and on interviews with former American officials.

23. Lisée, *In the Eye of the Eagle*, p. 7. When René Lévesque associated Quebec sovereignty with the Declaration of Independence during a 1976 speech to the Economic Club of New York, the reaction of his Wall Street audience was anything but sympathetic. Ibid., pp. 127–28.

pose no fundamental challenge to the U.S.," the United States also has little to gain from such an outcome.[24]

The predominant American view was captured in an internal study of Quebec separation prepared by the State Department after the election of the Parti Québécois in 1976. The lengthy document concluded by stating a clear preference for a united Canada:

> This is clearly in our national interest, considering the importance of Canada to U.S. interests in defense, trade, investments, environmental questions, and world affairs. . . . We see a possibility that either an independent Quebec or the remaining Canada would become more anti-U.S. than is the case for Canada today. Quebec because of a shift in focus in defending its cultural identity against American rather than English Canadian encroachments, Canada without Quebec because of an increased need to emphasize a non-American identity, having lost its bi-cultural peculiarity. . . . We have serious doubts about whether the rest of Canada could stay united if Quebec separated, and see the alternatives of a smaller and weaker Canada or several mini-states to the North as less desirable than the present situation.[25]

The official position of the U.S. government over the last twenty years has been a two-track policy. On the first track, American officials repeatedly insist that the issue is for Canadians to resolve; on the second track, they make clear that the United States supports a united Canada. After the election of the Parti Québécois in 1976, U.S. officials privately briefed major U.S. newspapers and columnists on the undesirability of Quebec sovereignty. President Carter stated that the United States regarded Canadian stability as "an integral part of our lives," that he preferred the federal option, and that—of course—the decision was for the Canadian people to make. While Secretary of State Cyrus Vance was more strictly neutral in comments just before the referendum on Quebec sovereignty in 1980, the American preference was clear.[26] The basic pattern has not changed in the current round. President Bush restated the two-track

24. Joseph Jockel, "If Canada Breaks Up: Implications for U.S. Policy," *Canadian-American Public Policy*, no. 7 (September 1991), pp. 1–44, quote on p. 6.

25. Department of State, "The Quebec Situation: Outlook and Implications" (secret), August 1977, reprinted in Lisée, *In the Eye of the Eagle*, pp. 283–302, quote on p. 301.

26. Lisée, *In the Eye of the Eagle*, pp. 118–19, 152–53, 232–33, quote on p. 152.

position in March 1991. Although indicating that he did not want to interfere with domestic Canadian politics, he commented on "how much we value a united Canada. . . . We are very, very happy with a united Canada."[27]

As the Canadian struggle heats up again, other interests may attempt to move the United States to stronger forms of intervention. The most politically salient question would be whether the free trade agreement, which was originally negotiated with the government of Canada, would be extended to a sovereign Quebec. As noted earlier, the trade agreement is important to the economic confidence of separatists. The media or commercial interests on either side of the border might therefore attempt to prod the administration or key members of Congress into making statements about the status of the agreement in the event of Quebec's separation. Any answer to the question would be seen as an intervention in the Canadian debate. A positive answer that the agreement would be extended to Quebec would be interpreted as a sign of American acceptance of an independent Quebec; it would strengthen the separatist cause and would be criticized by federalist forces in Canada. Conversely, a negative answer, or even a statement that automatic extension cannot be assumed, would damage the separatist cause and elicit pained responses from its leaders.

Larger issues would impose themselves if Quebec did, in fact, separate. Their scope would depend, however, on whether the optimists or pessimists were correct about the future of Canada without Quebec. If the optimistic view prevailed and two stable successor states emerged, then the task would largely be limited to refurbishing international agreements, such as NATO and NORAD, the International Joint Commission, and the trade agreement. The Bush administration would most likely propose the extension of the trade agreement to Quebec. After all, it is engaged in a campaign to create a free trade region throughout the entire Western hemisphere, incorporating economies at very different stages of development, and there seems no real reason to exclude Quebec. The outcome would not be automatic, however. Extension would require congressional approval, which would undoubtedly stimulate efforts to reopen the agreement by U.S. commercial interests who remain aggrieved by some of its provisions. Similar pressures would exist in the new Canada, where the agreement remains much more controversial than in Quebec. The result might be a general renegotiation in which Canada and Quebec

---

27. Ross Howard, "U.S. President Praises a 'United Canada' during Brief Ottawa Visit," *Globe and Mail* (Toronto), March 14, 1991.

would be divided and in a weaker bargaining position. Moreover, Quebec would find itself more tightly constrained by a renewed trade agreement. The existing agreement does little to limit the operations of provincial and state governments, but, as a fully fledged state, Quebec would face the full rigors of a North American trade regime.[28] Given the tradition of economic intervention in the province, there would undoubtedly be a tension between Quebec nationalism and free trade, as understood in the United States, with conflict centering on the role of subsidies and foreign investment in economic policy.[29]

If the pessimists are correct and Canada does collapse after the departure of Quebec, the United States would face more complex issues. Such an outcome would undermine the economic prospects of northern North America and stimulate higher levels of immigration to the United States, initially from the most vulnerable regions such as Atlantic Canada, but later from other regions as well. Pressures would grow on the United States to act as an arbiter among the factions; and in the event of a complete collapse, the United States might find itself having to respond to applications for statehood from some provinces.

Americans have not begun to think seriously about the implications of such applications.[30] The natural resources of the western provinces might be tempting. Given the free trade agreement and the evolution of the General Agreement on Tariffs and Trade, however, the United States already has relatively unrestricted access to Canadian resources, and Canada's domestic market is largely open to American products. In addition, there would be political barriers to statehood. The first is the small population of several of the provinces, especially in Atlantic Canada. Members of the U.S. Senate would be reluctant to dilute their power by 18 percent if all of the remaining nine provinces applied for statehood in their own right. Some combinations would undoubtedly be a precondition, especially in Atlantic Canada and possibly in the West as well. There might also be concern about governmental forms. Would the new states be allowed to retain their existing political structure, or would they have to adopt the separation of powers? Although there is nothing in the U.S.

---

28. Courchene, *In Praise of Renewed Federalism*, pp. 30–34.
29. Jockel, "If Canada Breaks Up," pp. 24–28.
30. American opinion has probably not moved beyond the view recorded in the 1977 State Department document, "The Quebec Situation": "The possibility that one or several Canadian provinces would seek to join the U.S. raises prospects that we have not contemplated. They could be negative or positive, but probably difficult to resolve." Quoted in Lisée, *In the Eye of the Eagle*, p. 301.

Constitution that bars parliamentary institutions at the state level, there might be resistance in Congress to such systems. More important, however, would be the implications for the partisan balance in Congress of the greater strength of the political left in Canada, as represented by the left wing of the Liberal party and the social-democratic New Democratic party. Republicans have been reluctant to approve statehood for the District of Columbia because of the certainty that it would elect two more Democratic senators. Although Canadian provinces would be more competitive than the district, the possibility of electing a number of senators who defined themselves as socialists would presumably give conservative forces in the United States considerable pause.

Canadian nationalists, conditioned by memories of Manifest Destiny and "54–40 or fight," have long suspected the American eagle of predatory instincts whenever it circled North. They might get a surprise if the issue of statehood were put to the test.

Conclusion

The decade of the 1990s has witnessed sweeping political changes that would have seemed impossible a few years ago. In Eastern Europe, political institutions have collapsed with astounding speed, and resurgent nationalism is undermining the Soviet Union. In Western Europe, a quieter process of integration is transforming the economic and political contours of the continent and pointing to the birth of a new kind of governmental system. Clearly the permanence of political structures and national boundaries cannot be taken for granted in the contemporary era.

Is the Canadian constitutional crisis a sign that this wave of dramatic political restructuring is about to reach the shores of North America? The scope and speed of political change elsewhere suggests that one should not be complacent about the future of the Canadian federation. The emergence of a sovereign Quebec on the international stage is a distinct possibility, and such a step could unleash a much wider economic and political restructuring of northern North America. Nevertheless, it is important to keep these possibilities in perspective. Although the constitutional negotiations on which the country is launched are unlikely to resolve fully the deeply rooted divisions that threaten the country, more modest changes might forestall the separation of Quebec. And even if Quebec does become independent, the collapse of the rest of Canada seems unlikely, at least in the short and medium term. Sewing extra stars on Old Glory at this stage would be decidedly premature.

Index

179